SURVIVING THE ODDS

SURVIVING THE ODDS
D-Day to V-E Day
with the Fourth Division
in Europe

Jack Capell

Regina Books

Claremont, California

Book design: Mark Morrall Dodge
Cover design: Mary Stoddard

LIBRARY OF CONGRESS NUMBER: 2007923345

ISBN 1-930053-49-5
   978-1-930053-49-6

Regina Books
Post Office Box 280
Claremont, California 91711
Tel: (909) 624-8466 / Fax (909) 626-1345

Manufactured in the United States of America

DEDICATED TO MY BELOVED WIFE,
SYLVIA

1926-2003

CONTENTS

ILLUSTRATIONS

MAPS

Foreword

Jack Capell's account focuses on his experiences from D-Day (June 6, 1944) when he landed on Utah beach to VE-Day (May 8, 1945) when he learned that the war in Europe was over. He spent the first months in France as a wireman—laying and repairing wire between command centers and outposts—and then was assigned to other duties, but whatever his particular job he remained a frontline rifleman. He never portrays himself to be other than a typical soldier, which he indeed was, but Capell was also an unusual one in that he survived 300 days of combat which included some of the hardest fought battles in the European campaign.

He places his memoir in a larger context by basing it on material taken from the published history of his regiment (the Eighth) and his division (the Fourth) so that the reader has a sense of the whole campaign as well was his part in it. He refreshed his excellent memory with a number of conversations with comrades so that he could check his version with theirs. The result is a story that is both compelling and authentic prompting a well known military historian to comment: "I am sure that Capell's book will be of great interest not only to World War II buffs, but to professional historians as well." That endorsement is high praise, but I believe that it is well merited.

After the battle of the beaches, his division helped clear the Cotentin peninsula. By that time rifle companies that numbered 190 men on the morning of June 6, 1944 often had no more than 30 men left who had landed three weeks before. Without any rest, the Fourth Division was ordered to help clear the Germans out of the hedgerows. After weeks in the hedgerows, the American army finally broke though into open country in the last days of July. After the breakout the American forces moved rapidly across France in pursuit of the fleeing Germans.

It seemed that the end of the war might be near, but it was not to be. The shattered German armies rallied at the frontier. Fighting was intense and losses heavy. There was no harder battle than that of Huertgen Forest where Capell's division lost 5,000 men in just three weeks. Shortly after the Fourth Division was pulled out of the Huertgen Forest and sent to a "quiet" sector of the line, only to find it was soon in the thick of the Battle of the Bulge. After crossing the Rhine and heading south into Bavaria, the Fourth was present at the liberation of the infamous Concentration Camp at Dachau.

On VE-Day (May 8, 1945), Capell was one of a handful of men in his division who had been on the line from the beginning to the end. This fact alone gives a special authority of his account. He had seen it all and then some. His division suffered more total casualties then any of the other 62 American divisions which fought in North Africa and Europe, a total of over 30,000—more than twice it original strength.

I have said Capell was almost continuously in or near the frontline, but that is not strictly true. On December 14, 1944 he was selected with seven other men to spend 48 hours in a rest camp. There he had the his first real shower in five months, slept on a cot with sheets and a pillow, and had hot food—a rare treat after K-rations. He was, Capell wrote, in "paradise," but not for long. After only one day in the camp he and his comrades were called back to the front to help stop the German breakthrough in what became known as the Battle of the Bulge. Capell relates the incident matter-of-factly. Whatever disappointment he felt he knew that orders were orders.

Capell was never decorated although on a least two occasions he certainly acted above and beyond the call of duty. He accepted the decision of his superior not to put him in for a medal, although many years later he did ask his captain why he did not receive a decoration for one particular act of derring-do. The captain explained his reason. Capell thought it over and decided that the captain probably made the right decision. S.L.A. Marshall in his well-known study of combat soldiers in the Second World War, entitled *Men Against Fire*, wrote that wars were won not by heroes but by men who do their duty conscientiously day in and day out. It is those men who are the real heroes. He claimed that the highest honor one can bestow on a frontline fighter is simply, "He was a good soldier." Capell, surely merited that accolade.

As the ranks of World War II veterans of inexorably thin year by year we can be grateful that men like the author have given us a chance to, at least vicariously, share their experiences. I can only say that Capell was indeed a member of "the Greatest Generation."

Jon Bridgman
Department of History
University of Washington

PREFACE

A number of very good books have been written about World War II in Europe many of which are listed in the bibliography. Among the best is *The Battle of Normandy* by the British author Robin Neillands, who has written a number of very fine books about World War II in Europe. Stephen Ambrose, an American author and historian, also has written several books about the infantry battles in Europe. The generals' point of view is represented in Omar Bradley's book, *A Soldiers Story*. Ernie Pyle, although a war correspondent himself, spent enough time with the front-line GIs to tell their stories very eloquently. There are some excellent battle accounts written by rifle company infantry officers, but few, if any, written by the guys who did most of the hand-to-hand fighting. These men were the private and private first class soldiers.

This book is by a GI who held the ranks of Private and Private First Class, which were the ranks that had the worst living conditions, rarely ate a cooked meal, received the lowest pay and did most of the dying. The narration that follows is an account of my experiences as a wireman in Normandy, and later while on various other assignments. Although primarily a rifleman, I served in a company of specialists rather than in a regular rifle company.

Accuracy is of prime importance to me in presenting this account, however I have taken liberty to withhold revealing one individual's name out of consideration for his family members. Also in reproducing direct quotations I have eliminated some profanities and obscenities that were not important to the meaning of the quotations. Indeed, foul language was commonly heard in combat but I knew a surprising number of men who never used it no matter how horrible the conditions.

The motivation to write a book about my own personal experience during World War II would never have occurred without the encouragement and assistance of my wife, Sylvia. My ongoing paralysis from Lou Gehrig's disease left me helpless to gather the material necessary to support and verify my personal recollections. This project began in the late 1980's to verify and expand on my earlier recollections. We were ordered not to keep diaries or photographs taken in combat. It was unwise to be carrying anything of that nature in the event of one's capture. Therefore the account that follows is from memory aided by and supplemented by official records, conversations with other survivors, letters written at the time, and both unofficial and official U.S. Army histories of the 4th Division and its 8th Infantry Regiment. Copies of the 4th Division's and 8th Infantry Regiment's lists of command post locations with dates were of great assistance to me, especially when used with extremely detailed maps.

As suggested by my wife the following includes my own impressions and feelings at the time, wherever I felt it appropriate. There may be those who will be offended, however, as Lloyd Gilmour, the great hockey referee often said, "I called it the way I saw it."

Jack Capell
March, 2007

ACKNOWLEDGMENTS

On the 40th anniversary of D-Day, June 6, 1984, after attending several functions honoring veterans who landed on the Normandy coast that notable day in 1944, my interest in recollecting events of World War II was stimulated. For some years after World War II I had no desire to relive the horror. The impact of traumatic occurrences from that period now were no longer a problem to me. I began to realize what an important piece of history I had been a part of and knew it needed to be preserved. Paralysis of my arms and legs, however, seemed to rule out the prospect of my recording any of my experiences in writing.

Mrs. Vaneta Hicks, however, encouraged me to preserve accounts of my experiences. She volunteered to type whatever narration I put on tape recordings. It was a generous offer which I felt I should not refuse. A friend, Robert E. Lynott, with whom I worked in the government weather office also took quite an interest in my story and offered his services in typing and editing. My wife Sylvia assisted me in gathering material in many different ways, and then with my son John's help, particularly in obtaining detailed maps and other material, and with son Tom' s assistance in obtaining a copyright, I was able to complete an abbreviated version of this book in 1990.

With my wife Sylvia's encouragement I resumed serious work on an expanded and revised version of the book in the summer of 2001. I had since collected more complete facts and learned more of the incidents in which I was involved after talking to survivors who were still living. Most helpful was the resumption of my acquaintanceship and the development of a close friendship with Frank Glaze of Clearwater, Florida. During World War II his title was Capt. Francis W. Glaze, Commander of Headquarters and Headquarters Company, 8th Infantry Regiment, 4th Infantry Division. I was directly under his command. We have exchanged reminiscences and verified the accuracy of our memories regarding certain incidents. Thus I was able to expand and accurately update the account I wrote in 1990.

In the meantime, son John set up a voice activated system on my computer so that I could use it and compose text, which is the system I have used to write this book. After converting my spoken words into text it was necessary to carefully edit the printed words. Those who helped me with the job of editing included Layla Anderson, an international business student and psychologist; Holly Wendell, a dietitian and nutritionist; Erin Fujii, a business and finance graduate; and Nathan Obregon, a psychologist and theologian. The hand-drawn sketches are by Ron Weil. The general assistant on the book was Miraluna Su.

INTRODUCTION

The date for the invasion (D-Day), which was to begin the long-awaited attack on the western defenses of German-occupied Europe, was finally set for June 6, 1944. Allied forces would attempt to break through Hitler's "Atlantic Wall" on Bay of the Seine beaches along France's Normandy coast that were across the English Channel, south from the English coast. Code names assigned to the beaches were Utah, Omaha, Gold, Sword, and Juno. Utah and Omaha were assigned to American forces, the others to British and Canadian.

General Dwight Eisenhower headed the Supreme Headquarters Allied Expeditionary Force (SHAEF) and American ground forces were divided into VII Corps (General J. Lawton Collins) and V Corps (General Leonard T. Gerow) both under the command of General Omar Bradley of the U.S. First Army. The 4th Division, of VII Corps, would land on Utah Beach. V Corps was to land on Omaha Beach led by the 1st Division followed by the 28th Division. Inland from Utah Beach the 82nd and 101st Airborne Divisions were to be landed by parachutes and gliders. The 4th Division attack was to be spearheaded by its 8th Infantry Regiment, followed by the 22nd and 12th Infantry Regiments also of the 4th Division. Each regiment had three battalions, each of which had four rifle companies. In addition, each regiment and battalion had headquarters companies and support companies, i.e. cannon, antitank, supply, and a medical detachment. The 36 rifle companies of the 4th Division, when at full strength, would total about 6500 men.

Headquarters and Headquarters Companies of the 8th, 12th, and 22nd Infantry Regiments were basically composed of trained combat riflemen assigned to specialized duties. In each company were Message Center, Intelligence and Reconnaissance, Orderly, and Wire and Radio Sections, all of which served the entire Regiment. I was assigned to a Wire Section.

Wire Sections laid telephone wire where needed, but mainly from Regimental Headquarters to its three Battalions. New wire was laid whenever a battalion or regimental headquarters moved, then it had to be maintained. Wire was laid on the ground, through bushes, or on sides of hedgerows; but rarely was it put overhead lest wiremen be in view of the enemy. When a line was severed, a crew was immediately sent to find and repair the break. Wire crews were comprised of three or four men who usually worked a considerable distance from their company, so in the event of an enemy ambush they could not expect help.

Enemy patrols would sometimes cut the wire and wait to ambush men searching for the break. Occasionally a vehicle would cause a break, but most breaks occurred where there was heavy fighting. Artillery shell fragments were the main cause. The method of finding a break was for members of the crew to spread at intervals along the line, and each pull on the wire to check that it was secure. If the line was loose, the break was soon located. Splicing the broken ends together repaired the wire.

During active combat the Wire Section to which I was assigned was busy around the clock and often a wireman would spend many hours servicing lines without more than an hour or two of unbroken sleep. At night and with no light wiremen could communicate only by voice, thus risk revealing their locations to nearby enemy patrols or snipers. In the nearly eleven months of combat between D-Day and VE-Day (Victory in Europe Day, May 8, 1945) the chance of a wireman surviving the entire period was about one in five. However, the chance of a rifleman in a rifle company in the 4th Division surviving unscathed was virtually nil.

According to figures published by the Army Service of Supply, in 1946 there were more than 65 American Divisions that fought in Europe between D-Day (June 6, 1944), and VE-Day (May 8, 1945). The Division I fought with, the 4th Infantry Division, had the greatest number of dead and wounded of all the American Divisions that fought in World War II. Each unit was rated from 1 to 65, according to their numbers of casualties, and of these, the 4th Infantry Division was at the top of the list, with well over 30,000 casualties. In the book, The 4th Infantry Division, published in 1946, the total 4th Division casualties in Europe from D-Day to VE-Day were listed as 34,309 (note, this is an upward revision of the SOS tabulation). The Division at full strength numbered somewhat less than 15,000 men.

The company I was in, Regimental Headquarters Company, had as many men killed or wounded (total casualties) from D-Day to VE-Day as landed on Utah beach on D-Day. Since there was no system of rotating men between the battlefront and the rear echelons, the men who entered battle initially on D-Day or came in later as replacements for casualties, remained in battle until killed or so seriously wounded they were unable to continue to fight. Replacements were fed in almost continually, but rarely fast enough to keep pace with the casualties. The Rifle Companies of our Regiment had the highest number of casualties, with the casualty rates being lower in some of the more specialized areas in the support companies.

Not only was life expectancy short in rifle companies, but living conditions in combat were dreadful. Often companies would be involved in battles that lasted around the clock for several days. Every move required a new foxhole for each man—if he had time to dig one. There was little protection from weather and often, when a man did get a chance to rest, he would be lying in mud or in winter, snow and ice. In combat, food consisted of condensed rations.

Some men got cooked food on a regular basis, others went for months having nothing but hard biscuits, a condensed bar of dried fruit or chocolate, and a small can of chopped pork or cheese. When feasible, one battalion would be held in reserve while men got rest and possibly hot food prepared in kitchen trucks. Some soldiers got regular days off and periodic furloughs, others never did. Some slept on cots with blankets and pillows, and others slept on snow or ice with no more than two blankets. Others still slept in mud with no shelter unless they had time to rig something up that would supply protection not just from the weather but also from enemy shells or shell fragments. Some infantrymen lived outdoors day and night and stood sentry duty in temperatures of 10 to 20 degrees below zero Fahrenheit, and were not issued overcoats. Some slept on air mattresses and sleeping bags with pillows. However, for an enlisted infantry rifleman in combat, a regular sleeping bag was never issued. The Army eventually did issue two blankets with their edges sewn together. However, such things as air mattresses and sleeping bags would be far too much of an additional load for a rifleman to carry.

For an enlisted infantryman in combat, a shower or a bath could be expected no more than once a month, and only then would he be issued laundered clothing. Some members of the armed forces never looked at a hostile enemy face to face. Some never saw the people they killed. Some men lived through traumatic experiences that haunted them for the rest of their lives. Others lived lives in the Service not much different from what they did in civilian life. Some men slept warm at night while others were afraid to fall asleep for fear of freezing to death. Nearly all suffered from homesickness, but the less fortunate also from such mental illnesses as "battle fatigue", as it was known in WWII, or "shell shock", as it was known in WWI. While some men never knew the overpowering stink of the battlefield, others lived with it.

Chapter I

GRADUATION TIME

Congratulations! It's time to graduate
from family home, to a world with hate,
but love is strong, and hate is weak,
So face the world with love to seek.

Capell '03 in memory of high school graduation and entry to war, 1941

In Hamilton, Ontario at the intersection of Main and Ottawa streets in the summer of 1923, was an attractive corner drugstore. A large sign over the recessed corner entrance identified the business as "THOS. CAPELL / Druggist", and in signs over the display windows were the words, "CAPELL'S DRUGS" with smaller signs reading "pharmacist - optometrist". Looking at the building, to the left was a modest-sized white house occupied by Thomas and Mabel Capell and their newly born son John Carver Capell. Much a part of the family was one-year-old Barney, a happy, energetic Border Collie.

In a little more than three and a half years, the family was aboard a Canadian Pacific Railway car headed for Vancouver, British Columbia, where my father, Thomas Capell, had just taken a position with Owl Drug Company. After a year and a half more, the family moved again and settled in Seattle, Washington, where my father Thomas or "Tom" started with Bartell Drug Company. Young John Carver Capell, who became better known as Jack Capell (which was myself), was happy growing up in West Seattle with wonderful Lincoln Park and beaches nearby. My pal, Barney, joined us after his quarantine period expired and he was eligible to immigrate to the United States. I inherited my father's interest of playing ice hockey and boxing. With American sports, such as baseball and basketball, which were not as popular in Canada at that time, I had to start from the beginning.

Capell Drugs, Hamilton, Ontario

My father did very well during the first of the Depression years, but about seven years later, disaster struck the family when my mother contracted a very serious form of cancer. A prominent doctor in Seattle was experimenting with a new treatment using radium and, although very expensive, my father made sure she got the treatment. There was no health insurance available to us and the Company had no plan, so we were soon in debt. However, all we really cared about was that my mother survived. When my mother took ill my parents had begun the required schooling to get their U.S. citizenship. After she got better they were required to go through all the schooling again, and by that time I had just graduated from high school and turned 18 years of age.

My father had been told my citizenship would be automatic if my parents were citizens before I was 21, but now with war looming, immigration laws were changing and the critical age for me now was 18, and I was too late. The government notified me I was an alien and was restricted in many ways. For one, I was not allowed on the Seattle waterfront, which is where my job took me nearly every day. I immediately registered and was able to get a special waterfront pass, but I could not enlist in the Merchant Marine, the Navy, Marines, or even the Army. However, I was required to register for the draft. I had never thought of doing anything but going to sea during the war, especially in the Merchant Marine. Now that seemed to be out of the question. I applied for citizenship, but doubted I could get it before I was drafted. I was told that I could apply for the Navy once I was drafted.

It wasn't long before I got a notice to report for my physical examination and classification for the draft. I was classified 1A, which meant I would be the first classification to be called. At the time I was working as a boat handler, boat repairer, and bait fisherman for West Seattle Boathouse, and although I enjoyed the work the pay was low. I soon had a good job as a short haul truck driver for Blake, Moffitt and Towne Paper Company. The work was very physical but I enjoyed it thoroughly, and the Company itself was superb. At the beginning of April 1943, came my greetings from the government that I had been called for the draft. When I reported to the draft board, I remembered the promise that I would be able to choose my branch of service. When I selected the Coast Guard, it was no surprise to learn their quota was filled, so I opted for the Navy. When I was informed their quota was also filled, I was extremely disappointed. I was warned not to protest and told there was absolutely nothing I could do about it. The Marine Corps sounded interesting, but it was the same story with them. Had I not been so naive, I might have realized that an alien with no political power and who was healthy and able, would be picked to be an infantry rifleman. Nobody volunteered for that job, and they needed men. I had no choice but to be inducted into the Army. I was sworn in and given a week to finalize my affairs before reporting to Fort Lewis, Washington.

My parents drove me to Fort Lewis. I felt no man had ever had better parents, and how I would miss my dog. I knew it would be a very sad parting. My father's health was failing from years of hard work and he was aging. I was leaving my happy home to stinking, smoke-filled barracks, which was my introduction to Army life. It was filled with sounds of coughing and hacking, and the air was further polluted with foul language. The cots were two tiers and pushed quite close together. Oh, to be home again! The day was consumed by getting Army clothing and numerous immunization shots. The following day we were given IQ tests, and tests for mechanical and radio aptitude. I did very well, especially on the first two. We started the day at 6 in the morning by spending half an hour picking up cigarette butts around the barracks. The rest of the time we did training, first by doing close-order drill and learning to take orders, next learning about poison gas, and then about surviving under fire. In the gas training, we went into gas chambers pumped full of tear gas both with and without gas masks. We came out gasping, choking, and miserable but it was a valuable and vivid lesson. Next was a machine gun firing range where we were to crawl facedown under live machine gun rounds. We were told that to rise up would mean certain death. They were clearing us by just a few inches, which was made apparent by the periodic tracer bullets. It was frightening and some men became so unnerved they were considered unsuitable for an infantry combat role and were weeded out. Finally, after about ten days, our time at Fort Lewis was at an end. It was none too soon for me, and now I was ready to take my chances on another Army camp.

We boarded a troop train in Fort Lewis, and then headed south. A few hours later we were rolling into Portland, up the Willamette Valley to Eugene, and into the Cascade Mountains and south. It was extremely scenic and most interesting when looking out the window to see our old steam locomotive winding through the curves along the mountainside, spewing out dirty black smoke and cinders. With some of the windows open the cinders blew in our eyes, hair, mouth, and even inside our shirts. Nevertheless it was a beautiful sight. Finally we rolled down slope into a huge valley. This was Northern California and it was very hot and certainly not like the climate to which I was accustomed. I had not been south of the northwest tip of Oregon before. The land was becoming more barren and dry every mile. We were eventually about half way between San Francisco and Los Angeles. Here was Camp Roberts, our next home, a few miles from San Miguel and a little further from Paso Robles. The camp, now used by the California Army National Guard, is no longer a desert, for much of the area is now fertile irrigated farmland. The wind blew continually and sand was always in the air. The ground was mostly sand with scattered sagebrush and desert shrubs. There were a few areas of brown desert grass growing in the arroyos, or dry riverbeds, that streaked in from the mountains. Not a drop of rain fell while we were there. Clouds appeared over the mountains to the west, and disappeared before reaching us. However, the barracks were much better at Camp Roberts with a little more room between the cots, and better ventilation. We also had a shower room.

Jack in uniform for basic training at Camp Roberts, California

At Camp Roberts we were to get serious infantry rifleman training. We would learn to fight with rifles, bayonets, grenades, other light weapons, as well as our hands. In short, we would be well-trained killers, a sobering thought. When that would be completed I could consider myself fully graduated from my home life with my family to that of a fully trained killer. First, we learned our rifles thoroughly, how to take them apart and to clean them. Bayonet training was done with dummies. In hand to hand combats, we learned to kill with our hands. Forced marches with each man carrying up to 80 pounds with his full field pack and equipment were done frequently. Obstacle courses were a challenge but enjoyable because I was in top athletic shape. We trained with hand grenades, dynamite and TNT. We learned a light machine gun and trained to fire a rifle grenade. The culmination of our training was a practice battle incorporating all we had learned. We were to capture an enemy stronghold on a hilltop. Fortunately, I was selected to lead a squad in the attack. I was to brief the men on what each of them was to do. I reviewed with them the hand signals we were to use and then ordered them forward. Each man followed the signals and did exactly as he was told. At my order they all fired at once and the stronghold surrendered. The Camp Commander as well as the Company Commander observed the exercise and were both elated. The Camp Commander ordered the Company Commander to send me to Officer Candidate School in Fort Benning, Georgia immediately following my training at Camp Roberts, California. This was the break I needed. I would have preferred becoming an air cadet, but this would at least get me into Officer Training. I was a little concerned that my citizenship papers were not through yet, but there was still plenty of time before my Camp Roberts time was up. Because I was so sure I would get my citizenship papers in time, I thought it better not to mention it.

For the remainder of my infantry training, the Company Commander was especially tough on me. I thought he hated me but then I realized he was doing it for my own good to make it easier for me in Officer Candidate School (OCS). He taught me a lesson that saved my life on at least one later occasion. He taught me that if I was suddenly surprised by shots from the front to leap to one side or the other and roll and, if running toward the enemy, zigzag sharply. I made these moves instinctively after that.

Because of my high grade in mechanical aptitude, I continued at Camp Roberts for another month to take motor mechanic training. I needed this break to squeeze a little more time to get my naturalization papers. In the meantime, the extra month of training was useful as we learned to drive and make minor repairs on various Army vehicles. Every chance I had I visited Camp Headquarters to check on my papers and I got the same old story "They'll be here any day, you'll just have to wait." I couldn't wait any longer, I knew I must tell the Company Commander, however, he had already discovered my problem when he put in the application for OCS. He was furious. He listened to my story though and began to see why I did what I did, and was sympathetic. He said he would send me to Fort Benning and enroll me in the Motor Mechanic School and while there, if my papers came through, he would transfer me to OCS.

I went east on a troop train with a layover at New Orleans. There I met 18-year-old Sally Pacheco from Roswell, New Mexico who was headed for a girl's school near Miami, Florida. She had a train layover there and we had a wonderful day together. She was a beautiful girl and I felt I was in love with her, and although we corresponded throughout the war I was never able to see her again.

I entered the school in Fort Benning. Even after nearly three months, my citizenship papers still had not come through, and my training course in the school was completed. I was immediately put into the replacement pool and assigned to the 4th Infantry Division with the rank of private. However, I had done well in school and the officer in charge of the Motor School called me into his office and asked me if I would like to stay on at the school as an instructor. He gave me the option of turning down the offer, but hoped I would agree to stay. It was the only one of two times in the Army I was given a choice on anything, and I didn't make a good choice on this one. I liked the school very much, but I did not like the part of the country it was in. Racism was at its height then and this part of the south was a terrible place to be. I did not like the food at Fort Benning, which was mostly deep-fried, and I never got accustomed to hominy at nearly every meal. But underneath it all was the unbelievable feeling that I would miss the big upcoming invasion of Europe. It was the biggest mistake of my life and my parents were devastated when they heard I had turned down the chance to be an instructor. I was to report to Fort Meade, Maryland to prepare for going over seas.

Since I declined the offer to stay at Fort Benning, I was released to the 8th Infantry Regiment of the 4th Infantry Division as a replacement for a man by the name of George Cash. I found out from some men returning to the 8th Infantry from hospitalization that Cash was still hospitalized after a training accident. I was told by these men that a 4th Division convoy of landing craft was hit by a hurricane off the coast of Florida. Cash later rejoined our company in France some time after the D-Day landing on June 6th, 1944. It is not surprising that I did not realize Cash had returned as a replacement because we were getting so many replacements for the killed and wounded after we got into combat and I did not know many of the men that joined our company by that time.

When my time at Fort Benning was completed in December 1943, I was to report to Fort Meade, Maryland. I was given nine days to make the trip, which normally would take about three days by train. The extra days I was given were called a "delay en route". It was designed to give me a few days at home before going overseas. I lived in Seattle and I would never be able to go that far in that length of time on the crowded trains. I was determined to go home anyway for a day or two. I boarded the train at Columbus, Georgia and there was not much room left even on the floors of the cars, so I laid my blanket down on the all-steel vestibule between the cars. In Kentucky there was a train wreck blocking the track ahead of us. It was very cold and the heating system in the cars was shutting down. The passengers climbed off the train and built huge bonfires outside for warmth. The engine ran out of water and the entire train was frozen. After more than twenty-four hours, the track ahead was cleared but we were unable to move. A steam engine came down from the north with water and pumped steam into our engine and through the train. At last, now more than two days late we headed for Chicago. I pondered my options and knew I was determined to go home regardless of what the Army might do. If I stayed home for two days and then headed back, there was really nothing they could or would do. I was already a buck private and could not be busted, and they would not lock me up because I was needed overseas. That was the one advantage of being a private.

After all that training I had, including a month of extra motor school in California and three months in Georgia, where I did well,

I still had no more rank than on the first day I was in the Army. I was still a buck private and would stay that way for more than nine months. I was still being paid just $50 a month. My friends who were in the Navy tell me that they got an automatic promotion as soon as they finished their basic training.

I finally rolled into Seattle on the train and phoned my parents from the station. My father met me in his 1932 Chevrolet with my mother and my dog Prince. It was a joyous reunion and I loved every minute of it. My parents and I took a quick trip to Vancouver, British Columbia then back to Seattle in time for me to prepare to leave. I never regretted taking time to see my parents then for it was the last time I would see my father before he died 14 months later.

Jack with his father Thomas

Difficult as it was to leave home again I realized I had no choice and headed back feeling somewhat renewed. Traveling through Montana, our train stopped in a small town near a girl's college. There was a large group of them waiting to board the train to go home for the holidays. I watched them for about 30 minutes while they waited to board. This gave me a chance to study each one of them to see how they interacted with their classmates and, by their expressions, something about their personalities. Happily, the one I thought prettiest of all best had these qualifications. They were boarding the car I was on although there were only a couple of seats left and they quickly filled. I had but to stand up in front of the girl

Jack with his mother Mabel and dog Prince

I liked and offer my seat. That gave me the opportunity to stand by her and become acquainted. She was getting off at Minneapolis and since I had a few hours before I could get a train going east from there we decided to spend that time together. We had a wonderful time and kept corresponding throughout the war. She was from Hibbing, Minnesota and was a surprisingly intelligent girl with a great appreciation for classical music and literature.

I arrived at Fort Meade and was shoved into a barracks with other replacements for the 4th Division. This was undoubtedly the worst barracks I had ever been in. The double-decked cots were jammed close together, the cigarette smoke was thick and the coughing and hacking were miserable. Fortunately, I was shipped out to Camp Kilmer, New Jersey the following day and joined a smaller group of replacements for the 4th Division. We each had our own cot and there was room between them. We were given frequent passes out of camp. We were not far from New York City and that was where I went whenever possible. One of my first stops was the Stage Door Canteen, which was operated for servicemen by theater people. Margaret "Topsy" Bradford was one of the regular hostesses there and she and I had a great time together. She was a pretty blond who worked in an office in New York and also did some theater performing. She arranged for me to do a guest spot with a famous big band called Shep Field's Ripplin' Rhythm because I had done some professional singing before going into the Army. We had some fantastic evenings at the Canteen but she was not allowed to date a man she had met at the Canteen. After I left New York we also corresponded regularly throughout the war.

After a few days and about the middle of January 1944 we loaded on trucks headed for the New York waterfront. We were about to go "over there".

Chapter 2

THE YANKS ARE COMING

We'll be over, we're coming over,
And we won't come home until it's over over there!
"Over There", George M. Cohan, 1917

At the dock we arrived next to a large ocean liner, where we unloaded from the truck. On the starboard bow printed in bold letters was the name "Mauritania II". I felt a surge of excitement when I saw that name because it had been familiar to me. It had been familiar to me as a famous Atlantic liner ever since I was a child. However, the original ship of that name had been scrapped, and this was the second ship to carry on the tradition. The keel was laid in 1931, but because of the Depression years, she was not completed as a passenger liner until 1935. She had only a couple of years of service in the luxury passenger trade before wartime priorities had her converted to a troop carrier. There was certainly no luxury left on the decks to which we were confined

With our duffel bags over our shoulders, we were directed up the gangplank, and from there down two ladders, which took us one level below the lowest passenger deck. The man behind me was directed to another compartment, which meant I was the last man in that group. As I went down the ladder, I saw that every hammock was taken, and below them were tables covered with bodies, as was nearly every square inch of deck space. There was just one bit of deck space left, and that was under the latrine. This consisted of boards ten inches wide with their bottom edges set against each other, forming a trough. Seawater was being pumped through this trough continually. I knew that the moment we got out to sea, that water would be slopping over the deck below, and I was not about to sleep there.

The man next to me said, "You can't sleep there!"

"No, and I'm not going to!" I responded emphatically.

"I'll go talk to someone."

"Who are you going to talk to? They have guards at the top of the ladder to keep us in, and nobody seems to be in charge. But don't worry, I already have an idea."

"By the way, my name is Redfield, Gene Redfield. Although my real name is Clifford E. Redfield, from Omaha. Assigned to Headquarters Company, 8th Infantry Regiment as a Replacement."

"Well, I'll be damned! So am I. Capell is my name. Call me Jack, but my real name is John C. Capell. We'll be seeing lots of each other I'm sure, but right now I've got to work on getting out of here."

There was just one little dim light in the compartment, and that was right next to the guards, so I could see them easily, but they would not likely see me. They were both sitting at the head of the ladder, and I was sure they would soon get drowsy. I pulled a blanket out of my duffel bag and was ready to go. I told Gene what I had in mind and asked if I could leave my duffel bag next to him and hoped it might deflect some of the splash from the latrine. My plan worked perfectly and I brushed by the guards so fast they didn't know which way I went. Now I just had to find a place to sleep in the almost completely blacked-out ship. The ship was kept as dark as possible to avoid being seen by German submarines.

I found a ladder that would take me up one deck, and already being

British ship Mauritania II while in passenger service before being converted to a troop ship

in the bow (front) area of the ship, I searched toward the forepeak. A structure had been built along the starboard side almost to the forepeak. That left just enough room to squeeze by, and there was a nice little area for me to sleep. Once at sea I bounced around plenty, being right there in the peak of the ship, but I was happy. I also knew that if we hit an iceberg I would be the first at the scene of the accident.

I came out after daylight and went down to the compartment where my duffel bag was. As I expected, the guards were no longer there and men were leaving the compartment with their mess kits so I knew there must be a chow line somewhere. I found Redfield and together we got our mess kits and joined the line, which was two decks up. After about one hour we got one big scoop of oatmeal porridge and a canteen cup full of coffee. There was nothing to go with the oatmeal such as toast, sugar, bread or milk. We both wanted more oatmeal, but since it would take another hour to go through the line again, we were afraid they would quit serving before we ever made it. There was no noon meal so this had to last us until late afternoon.

The line was about the same for the next meal, which consisted of a piece of bread with watered-down hamburger poured over it and a canteen cup full of coffee. Since neither Redfield nor I were seasick, we were miserably hungry, and the only way to supplement the rations was to buy biscuits from the British canteen. This turned out to be the structure next to where I was sleeping. If the Americans were paying the British to feed us then somebody was making money, because the canteen did a booming business.

During the daylight hours, unless the weather was particularly stormy, we were ordered to stay out on the weather deck, or in other words, the unsheltered deck areas. The ship was so crowded that we stood almost shoulder to shoulder. There was one entertainment celebrity aboard who was going across to entertain troops in England. He was the well-known actor James Cagney, best known for his gangster roles, but at the time very popular because of his portrayal of George M. Cohan on Broadway and in film, and his singing of "Yankee Doodle Dandy." He walked among the men singing it over and over at their request.

After dark everyone was ordered to be in their assigned compartments, although a little time was allowed for men to buy food at the canteen. Nobody was allowed on deck after dark. We speculated that it was for fear of someone lighting a cigarette that might be seen by an enemy submarine or torpedo boat. Since I was stowed away, I could get out on deck whenever I wanted if I was careful not to be seen. Since I was a non-smoker, there was no cigarette problem with me. Because of the submarine threat, we steered a zigzag course, which meant changing course about once every seven minutes or so. We saw no submarines or enemy craft of any type during the crossing, nor did we see any German aircraft. Nevertheless there were several anti-aircraft guns set up and manned by the Navy all of the time.

Looking for a place to get away from the crowd, I picked a spot on a specially built boat deck to which I could climb. It was really just a ledge that was built out from the side of the hull to accommodate more lifeboats when the ship was converted to a troop ship. I found a spot between lifeboats where I had a good view of the ocean and was fairly well protected from the wind. I took a little paperbound book with me and found the spot quite enjoyable. I invited Redfield to join me and we spent the majority of our days at sea that way, even though we were in an area that was "off limits" to troops. Those days at sea were the most enjoyable I had while I was in the Army at least until after the war in Europe ended. Coming back from overseas over a year and a half later, however, was like a pleasure cruise. It was an American troop ship that had individual cots with mattresses and three meals every day of good food. We didn't even have submarines to worry about.

Somehow the word got around that we were following a much more northerly course than usual, and being midwinter there was no particular threat from icebergs breaking loose from the Arctic ice pack. We were thought to be safer from submarines by staying well to the north. The coast of Iceland might have been visible but I could not be sure because of a haze on the northern horizon. It was shortly after that a severe storm began to reach us. The swells kept getting larger and soon after the wind and seas increased rapidly. It was amazing to see such a large ship diving and plunging at the mercy of swells that rose higher than the height of the ship. The entire stern of the vessel rose out the sea when the bow plunged, and the propellers shuddered in the air. Everyone had been cleared off deck, but I managed to keep hidden. I did not want anything to keep me from experiencing the full power of that storm. I had never before been at sea in a storm of that magnitude. As a person who has made a career of being a professional meteorologist, I can say with some authority that the wind in that storm exceeded the criteria of hurricane velocity.

The worst of the storm passed but the seas and swell remained heavy when we reached the north coast of Ireland. Our course gradually became more southeasterly and then southerly as we entered the Irish Channel. We were soon at our destination, which turned out to be Liverpool, England. It was very interesting to enter the harbor that I had seen only in photographs. The Liverpool docks looked just as I expected. After landing we did not disembark immediately for some reason, but I was fascinated by watching the Liverpool longshoremen beginning to unload the ship. The stevedores and the crane operator had one royal verbal battle with a fine selection of salty Liverpool waterfront verbiage the entire time I watched.

Finally we began to unload on 2½ ton GMC trucks which took us to the British Army camp a few miles east of the city. As we passed through Liverpool I noticed the pall of coal smoke that lay over the city. The buildings all appeared very old and each one had its own tall chimney gushing black smoke. There was no chance to see much more of the city as we moved directly to the camp where we spent the next two days. The food was much the same as on the troop ship except they added a noon meal. There was a soccer field and because we really had nothing to do, I thoroughly enjoyed it. Soccer was not played much in the U.S. at that time, and this was a rare opportunity for me. After dark on the second day at that camp we were taken to a train station and loaded on a train, destination unknown.

After our short stay at the camp near Liverpool we were loaded onto a train heading south. Since most of the trip was at night I could not tell where were going but eventually we arrived at a camp a mile away from Honiton in the county of Devon. The nearest larger town was Exeter, 14 miles along the railroad to the west. The Fourth Infantry Division had arrived in the area a few days before. The Headquarters Company of the 8th Regiment of the Division included the Wire Section, to which I was assigned, the I & R Section (Intelligence & Reconnaissance) and the Radio Section. We were in an old English camp, which probably predated WWI. The Wire Section barracks housed about 25 men, each with a canvas cot. There were no showers, and all men shared a single bathtub. We were all trained riflemen, but specialized in our particular jobs. The wiremen learned to lay telephone wire along the ground or through bushes to other elements of the Regiment, and to immediately find and repair breaks in the lines. The breaks were caused mainly by enemy shelling, or from explosions by grenades or mines. Sometimes an enemy patrol would discover the telephone lines, cut them, and wait to ambush the crew that came to repair them. This was a constant danger the wiremen had to face because of the extreme importance of keeping the field telephone lines in operation. The telephone was our basic means of communication.

The Wire Section trained under simulated battle conditions. Entire regiments were involved in numerous practice combat exercises. Many of these were simulated beach invasions from small boats known as 'Landing Crafts'. Some areas of the English coast were evacuated of civilians for this reason. The closer we got to D-Day, the more realistic these practices became, and began to involve the Air Force and the Navy. Live ammunition was now being used, resulting in increased accidents and fatalities of our own men. In one practice, we were attacking a concrete bunker such as the Germans used for housing guns. A 60-mm mortar crew was about 10 yards to my right; suddenly the mortar blew up and all 3 men were dead. It was either a result of faulty ammunition, or the mortar man who dropped the shell into the base, failed to pull his hand away soon enough after he dropped the shell, and striking his hand was enough to explode the shell. This was just one example of how men died during training while using live ammunition. A number of men died when the Navy fired on a beach we were attacking because the Army and Navy did not properly coordinate the time that the firing was supposed to stop.

OPERATION TIGER: THE BIGGEST TRAINING COVER-UP

Operation Tiger was the code name for the biggest and most complete D-Day rehearsal. We moved to the marshalling area on the 22nd of April 1944, and then began loading on various types of landing craft. I boarded an LCT (Landing Craft Tank), which carried both personnel and vehicles. I had thoroughly waterproofed my jeep by using putty over all openings, namely vents. The carburetor and distributor were also waterproofed but nothing was done to the exhaust pipe because pressure from the exhaust was expected to keep the water out. A hose was extended upward from the carburetor intake and mounted on a long stick secured to the side of the jeep. We put to sea in a driving rainstorm and, although the Navy men had enclosed quarters, we were locked out on the weather deck. My jeep was near the stern and the following wind blew diesel fumes over me, which made me feel nauseous. A Navy man pushed a container of hot coffee out to us and I promptly filled my canteen cup and drank it, even though it tasted sickly sweet. I realized that a container of sugar must have accidentally been spilled into it and that's why the Navy men were so generous. I soon began puking and retching from the diesel fumes and sweet coffee. The rain saturated my clothes and the wind felt as though it was directly from the Arctic. Finally, we approached the beach where we were to land, even though I felt almost too weak to stand up. I was signaled to drive the jeep through the shallow water and onto the beach after the landing craft gate had been opened. The waterproofing had held and we made it onto the beach. Now we were to move inland to obtain our objective and, amazingly, I began almost immediately to feel better. I had a classic case of carbon monoxide poisoning from the diesel fumes and as soon as I got away from the fumes and back into fresh air, I felt much better and was soon back to normal.

The exercise we were participating in was much larger than I had expected. Units of engineers, tanks, and artillery were attached to the 4th Infantry Division temporarily. By the time we landed on the beach at Slapton Sands on Lyme Bay, the last of the troops in the exercise had just left Plymouth Harbor. We came in on smaller landing craft, but the support troops and rear echelons were on Navy landing ships known as LSTs. These were large, ocean-going ships of about 4,500 tons with gates in the bow, which opened to unload men and equipment into shallow water near the beach. They were in a straight-line convoy of ships spaced about 400 yards apart. They were to be protected by a British corvette and destroyer. Also there were minesweepers to protect the convoy from enemy mines.

The Germans had U-Boats (submarines) and E-Boats patrolling the same waters. The E-Boats carried torpedoes and mines and could travel as fast as 40 knots; thus the convoy was traveling through extremely dangerous waters, even with a corvette and destroyer to protect it. However, the destroyer never arrived. It was involved in a minor collision when leaving port and was called back. Our convoy did not receive a replacement destroyer.

Unknown to those of us who were already on shore and proceeding inland, one of the LST's was suddenly attacked by a German E-Boat. Then more E-Boats moved in and sunk two more LST's. There was heavy loss of life on the American crafts, and those aboard who were not killed by the torpedoes were thrown into the water where most of them drowned. The E-Boats continued their attack, and several other LST's were hit and badly damaged but not sunk. The Germans were now between the American vessels so the British corvette, which was now the only real protection, was unable to fire a single shot at the attackers without hitting Americans.

The total loss of life is unknown to this day. The 4th Division figures initially showed the loss of military personnel to be 749. One British researcher believes the total loss was about 1,000 men.

About 10% of the casualties were Navy crewmen of the LSTs. One of the reasons for the heavy loss among the American soldiers was that they were issued inflatable life belts without training as to how to use them. Because of a soldier's equipment it was difficult to wear the lifebelt much above the waist. The navy men were trained to wear flotation devises high on the body to keep them upright in the water. When the lifebelt is too low on the body, the man becomes unstable and tends to go facedown in the water, especially if he wears a steel helmet and equipment above the waist.

The attack at sea was not known to those of us moving inland from the beach because it occurred at about 1:30 AM - at least 8 hours after we landed. If we heard the sounds of the explosions we would have attributed them to the fact that live ammunition was being used by our own troops as part of the exercise.

For good reasons, the disaster was kept as secret as possible by the US and British armed services. It was probably the biggest cover-up of the war. One of the reasons for the cover-up was that it would have been bad for the morale of the 4th Division men who were about to make the initial attack on D-Day. It could have been damaging to our confidence to realize we had lost about 1,000 men even before the attack began. There was also great concern that had the Germans known the convoy was as big as it was, they might have anticipated the D-Day attack would come from the Southwest coast of England and most likely would be toward Normandy. Part of the reason for secrecy, in my opinion, was simply to avoid embarrassment by the American and British armed forces for allowing such a thing to happen.

The survivors of the attack were sworn and threatened to secrecy, and immediately transferred individually to units in other parts of England hoping their stories would not be believed if they did talk. However, a few British farmers who had not been evacuated noticed the huge number of bodies being carried away and buried in mass graves. Their suspicions were further aroused in later years when a British fishing vessel snagged its net on a sunken American tank in Lyme Bay. Ken Small of Slapton Sands was determined to find the truth and gleaned information from witnesses who saw the bodies, from fishermen, and British and US Government records. US Government officials made every effort to refuse him information at first. Years later he began arriving at the truth. He published his book *The Forgotten Dead* in 1988, and was instrumental in preserving the American tank as a memorial. It now stands on Slapton Sands in remembrance of the 4th Division men, Navy and other Army men who lost their lives in Operation Tiger. Also in 1985, Edwin P. Hoyt told the story in *The Invasion Before Normandy* (The Secret Battle of Slapton Sands).

- - -

In contrast to the horror of Slapton Sands, an earlier practice by our Regiment on the North coast of Devon at Barnstaple Bay left me with pleasant memories. We boarded small landing craft, commonly called "Higgin's Boats" (officially LCVP) which were used mostly for personnel but could carry one or two jeeps. The weather was pleasant and I enjoyed the few days at sea on the Bristol Channel. After the practice we stayed near Barnstaple one Sunday. With no particular duties assigned to me, I took the opportunity to stroll through the countryside. I slipped out of camp late in the morning and followed a narrow, winding road up the nearby hillside. The fields were green, flowers around the cottages were in bloom, the sea below was a brilliant blue, and the springtime sun was warm. It was undoubtedly the most pleasant day I had spent in England. My enjoyment was enhanced upon encountering two young women in British Naval Auxiliary uniforms. We spent the rest of the afternoon together.

Devon was interesting, but we had little chance to get out of camp legally. Being a jeep driver though, I was often dispatched to drive officers to other parts of southern England. One place I enjoyed going to was Seaton on the south coast, but I could not wander around the town because whenever we were on dispatch we were required to wait by the jeep until the officer was finished with his business. Occasionally I was assigned to drive for the MPs (Military Police), which mainly involved breaking up drunken brawls or any other disturbances in the nearby towns. Besides the Americans who were training for the D-dDay invasion, there were English, Scottish, and Ulster Irishmen. They were all stationed in various nearby camps, which did not make for a peaceful social atmosphere when booze was involved.

The fact that I was a driver for the wire crew resulted in me being a member of the motor pool whenever the wire crew was not doing special training. That meant that I could be dispatched to drive officers at any time, which I enjoyed doing because it enabled me to get out and see the countryside. I had one embarrassing incident when I was dispatched to our company commander, Francis Glaze. I was adjusting the parking brake on my jeep when the sergeant in charge of dispatches gave me the assignment, which he said was to be done immediately. I said, "I tightened the adjustment to the service manual specifications but I need to road test the jeep before I would ever take it out on dispatch." The sergeant said "Don't you trust the specifications?"

"No. On a jeep that's run as much as this one has, the brake sometimes has to have extra clearance. I'll drive it and see if it gets hot and if it doesn't, I'll know the adjustment is ok."

"This time, we'll trust the manual. Take the jeep out right now."

"No!"

The sergeant took my feeler gauge and checked the adjustment himself and said, "There is plenty of clearance, so get going."

I picked up Capt. Glaze and after about 8 miles, I began to smell the brake. Capt. Glaze also smelled it immediately and said, "What's that?" I stopped the jeep and said, "Sir, I think we have a problem with the brake. Please wait and I'll loosen the adjustment, and then it should be fine." I grabbed the tools, which I had left handy in the back of the jeep and we then proceeded on our trip with no more trouble, although the smell of burning lingered for a while. Glaze said, "How did that happen?" I tried to briefly explain without laying all the blame on the Sergeant. I felt very embarrassed about the whole situation.

Horace Sisk rushed over to me when I was in the noon chow line and said, "We have a dispatch and you're the driver. Let's get our chow and then we'll go."

"What's this all about?" I said. "How come I'm taking you instead of an officer?"

He said, "This dispatch is made out to me with you as driver. This is a reward that Major George Mabry gave me for spending many hours helping him with a report. He told me to take an afternoon off and deliver some papers to a city official at Seaton and take your time. He said, "You and Capell could spend a little time looking over the resort areas on the south coast of England."

We had a most enjoyable time touring one of the nicest spots on the south Devon coast. We left in time to get back for evening chow and passed through the town of Honiton. There, Horace saw a man from our regiment he knew and the guy called to him. We stopped and he came over and asked for a ride back to camp. He was drunk and we knew this would cause trouble for everybody when the MPs at the main gate checked us, since Horace was not even an officer, and yet the dispatch was made out to him. Horace said, "We can take you back to the camp but not through the main gate."

I said, "You know where the hole in the fence is, don't you?" And he nodded his head that he did.

"Well, that's where we'll let you off."

We got to where the hole was and stopped the jeep and told him, "This is it. You get outta here and walk through the hole." Usually, men could get into the camp that way, but occasionally they would get confronted by our I & R men who would rough them up. The leader and some other men liked to use that as a method of training for hand to hand fighting. I said, "You won't have any trouble if you keep your eyes open."

He said, "No, I want through the main gate."

I said, "Get outta this jeep right now. We told you what we were gonna do." He didn't move.

"Get out or I'll throw you out." He responded with an obscene name and I became furious. I leaped out and ran around to get him where he was sitting on the other side of the jeep, behind Sisk. Sisk jumped out and grabbed my arms and stood in front of me. Finally, the guy got out and headed for the hole in the fence but I was still very, very angry.

Sisk told me about this guy's history and I found out he once was an officer who got into some kind of trouble through drinking and was busted to a private. A few weeks later, Sisk told me that he was restored to the rank of an officer, specifically, a 2nd Lieutenant. Shortly afterward, I was given a dispatch to take him out on a mission of some sort. I ran over to the Company Headquarters building, where I thought I would find Sisk and told him. Both Sisk and I agreed, the best thing, and only thing I could do was to act like I'd never seen him before. I drove the jeep to pick him up and not a word was said between us, except to tell me exactly where I was to take him. A most uncomfortable silence continued throughout the entire trip.

- - -

When I got a pass, which was usually for just a few hours, I went to Exeter (about 14 miles away) because there was a train that ran directly there. I had very little social life, but did meet Sally, who, though not from the upper class, was clever and fun. Later I met a beautiful well-dressed girl, Barbara, a higher-class girl in a very class-conscious society. Barbara and I met on several occasions in the park but she would never invite me to her home. I realized it would be unacceptable for her to bring home an enlisted man rather than an officer.

Barbara and I ran face-to-face into Sally on the street and I expected a scene. Instead Sally started to walk by as though she had never seen me before. I couldn't help but look back, and got a wink and a smile. I was impressed and grateful. On a previous occasion, Sally came to my rescue when I slipped out of camp without a pass and went to Exeter. After I met Sally on the street, we saw two MPs coming down the block. Sally knew I did not have a pass and that I was about to be picked up, sent back to camp and restricted. She immediately engaged the MPs into conversation and kept them entertained while I slipped off into an alley. She then walked away from the MPs and went to find me. It's no wonder I had warm feelings toward Sally, but we never communicated once I left England.

- - -

We were about through with our training by mid-May and word got around that we were to be visited by some top brass-some of the head planners of the invasion. Whenever dignitaries came to inspect us, there was not only extraordinary cleaning and polishing, but a lot of standing around and waiting. We even polished jeeps of road dirt that had accumulated just minutes before. Since I was considered a part of the motor pool and was often sent out on dispatch with the jeep, I asked if I could go out on assignment. The sergeant said "I know what you mean. I'll make sure that you get out of camp during the big day." I had mixed feelings because I was curious as to who was coming, and have ever since regretted that I did not stay and witness this bit of history. They were coming to visit the 8th Infantry Regiment because we were the ones that would be making the initial assault at Utah Beach on D-Day. It was an honor for us to be singled out at such a historic moment. Those who came included General Eisenhower, the Supreme Allied Commander of the European Theatre of Operations; General Montgomery, the Commander of the British Forces; General Bradley; General George Patton; Raymond O. Barton; the 4th Division Commander; Brigadier General Theodore (Teddy) Roosevelt Jr. (son of the former president of the United States); Air Marshall Sir Arthur Tedder; and Sir Winston Churchill himself. Afterward, I was astounded to learn that all of them had met with our Regiment at the same time. It was an extremely important historic moment and I had inadvertently, but nevertheless deliberately, missed it.

Late in May we began moving toward a marshalling area to prepare an attack on a beach in Normandy. First, we were moved out of Honiton to near Taunton, where a convoy was to form. We were assigned a captain from another unit of our division to direct the Wire Section in the convoy. We did not know him and he did not know us, but obviously he soon regretted he had ever met us. The feeling in the Wire Section was that no matter what we did there was no way they could punish us. To be arrested and put in the stockade would have been most welcome to some of our men who had no desire to enter combat. Most of us, however, were dedicated to enter battle no matter what it entailed but we weren't anxious to let the captain know that. He got unwelcome remarks whenever he gave a command and must have been completely frustrated. However, after giving him a bad time we did as we were ordered.

We drove to the marshalling area in a convoy of army vehicles, encountering one air raid on the way. The captain ordered everybody out of the vehicles and we went up in the bushes. When the air raid was over, the captain spent a frustrating half-hour convincing the guys to go back. We had no intention of deserting, but enjoyed teasing him. The marshalling area was set up with 20-man tents and was completely surrounded by barbed wire. The Captain managed to get the men assembled in front of him while he issued the order, "No man under any circumstances is to leave this camp until you are ordered to." He said we would be attacking the French coast in a few days, and we would stay put until it was time to load the landing craft. The gate was partially open and when he finished his speech, about two-thirds of us headed for that gate, brushing past the Captain who stood there in a daze. There was a small town nearby where we spent the evening getting our last good fill of stout, the only type of beer available at the time. At dawn we all came back, as we had planned. One man, who did not go out of the camp with us, was sound asleep in his cot when we came back. We picked him up, cot-and-all, and carried him out to where the Captain would call assembly in the morning. He stayed sound asleep, or at least pretended to, and was there to greet the Captain.

We spent the next day at the marshalling area camp and then early the following morning, we joined in a convoy of 4th Division vehicles, to head to the coast in order to board the landing craft. We were not told what port we were to leave from, so we didn't know exactly where the convoy was heading. There were about 14,000 men of the 4th Division in the convoy and the jeep I was driving, accompanied by Horace Sisk, was about halfway back in the line of vehicles. The convoy moved very slowly as it converged into the narrow roads leading to the coast. Because of the danger of air raids, we remained spaced out and as a result; the only vehicle I could see in the convoy was the one directly in front of me. I moved when it moved.

In early afternoon, we stopped in front of an English cottage where there were three girls about 18 to 20 years old, sitting on the lawn. I felt it my duty to get acquainted, so I went up to talk to them, telling Horace to yell for me if things started to move. The girls and I started to play tag, and pretty soon we were up in the woods behind the cottage. Suddenly Horace arrived saying, "The convoy moved, but I couldn't find you." I ran back to the convoy but it was too late. With nearly half the convoy following me, I hurriedly drove as fast as I dared in order to catch sight of the vehicle that had been ahead of me and yet not too fast for the rest of the convoy that was following. The MP at the road crossing indicated which way he thought our convoy went by recalling the 4th division marks on the vehicle bumpers. It was evening before we found the 4th Division vehicle that had been ahead of us. The horrible thought had come to me that if I had taken the wrong road, I would have gotten half the division lost, but I was lucky. Fortunately, nobody behind me knew the difference.

The town we arrived in was Dartmouth, a seaport in the county of Devon, on the south coast of England. Dartmouth is situated at the mouth of the Dart River, hence its name. It was late at night on June 1st, 1944 and with the roads so jammed, it took several hours to go from the edge of town to where the ships were loading.

Chapter 3

STORMING THE WALL

Into the jaws of Death, Into the mouth of Hell...

Alfred Lord Tennyson

We boarded a type of vessel called a landing ship, larger than the landing craft we had used before in beach invasions. It had gates in the bow that swung outward and a ramp that dropped to unload soldiers and vehicles. I didn't know at the time but we were to be transported across the English Channel and when about eleven miles from the beach, we were to transfer to smaller landing craft. Among the last of the supplies loaded were cases marked "Blood Plasma." With that aboard we knew we would be in combat within a few days. While in training we practiced numerous landings on the coast of England but never before had plasma been loaded. We were still not given the exact date of the invasion. At daylight the ship was secured for sea and cast off. As we passed through the harbor, other landing craft were still loading. I marveled at the beauty of the bay and the surrounding hills. The horrors that lay ahead were not yet evident, but the signs of the impending battle were all around. More landing craft and combat ships, some towing barrage balloons, were putting to sea, which was becoming rougher as the rain began. A swift British destroyer passed nearby, knifing through the waves. Our landing craft wallowed in the roughening seaway. The south coast of England was nearly out of sight, leaving me with memories of the more than four months of training.

Later various officers briefed us. We were to land on the coast of Normandy in France at five A.M. on June 5th. We were to be the first troops to hit the beach. Beyond the head of the beach we were to look for a road to fight our way inland. The road served as a dike over low-lying fields behind a nearby dam. The fields could be flooded to a depth of three feet. We were shown a detailed map, which displayed the type of terrain and the location of the German fortifications. Once inland, we would link with units of paratroopers and glider troops somewhere between the beach and Ste. Mere Eglise. An officer in our Regimental Interrogation Unit came to the microphone. The unit he headed was made up of mostly German-Jewish refugees. He explained that the German troops that were members of the SS (Schutzstaffel) were not to be taken prisoner but killed immediately. They could be identified by their uniforms, which displayed an eagle on the upper left sleeve. Regular German soldiers wore it over the right breast. He said the SS men could not be trusted and may be carrying suicide bombs.

In spite of the rough sea, wind, and rain we were confined to the weather deck. We had only K-rations, which is a box of condensed food about the size of a 1-lb. block of margarine. We envied the Navy sailors who stayed in their dry quarters and had hot food. On June 4th, the unsettled weather and rough sea continued and another briefing came over the microphone. The invasion would not take place as planned, but because of weather would be postponed one day to June 6th.

We were moving toward an assembly area where there were many ships and craft of different types, some British, some American, and some Canadian. The naval vessels included destroyers, torpedo boats, and even battleships. The assembly area was about 11 miles off the Normandy coast opposite what I later came to know as Utah Beach.

Late on June 5th, we were ordered to prepare to move to smaller landing craft. The sea was still rough and I wondered how we would be able to transfer the vehicles. An LCT began to move in stern-first toward the bow of the ship that we were on. The gates on the bow of our ship were opened and the ramp dropped to meet the stern of the LCT. The two vessels were rising and falling out of phase with each other. For brief moments the ramp on our landing ship would line up with the LCT.

I was ordered to bring my jeep toward the bow and wait for a signal from a navy man, at which time I was to drive from one vessel to the other. We made the transfer without apparent mishap although the jeep bounced hard when it dropped on the deck of the LCT. I was worried that some of the waterproofing had jarred loose.

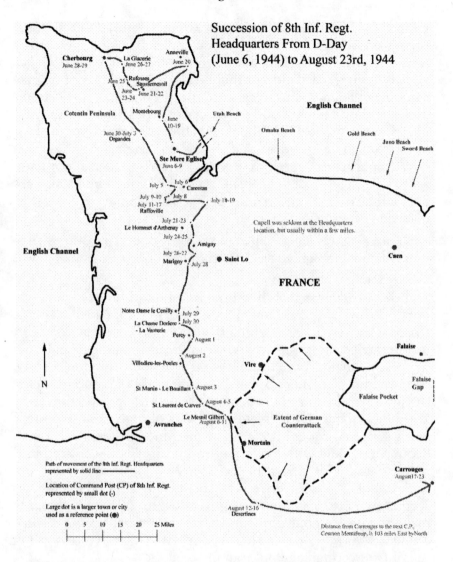

Succession of 8th Inf. Regt.
Headquarters From D-Day
(June 6, 1944) to August 23rd, 1944

Once on board the LCT, I realized we would be landing with some of the first troops to reach the beach. According to plan, the first men were on LCVPs, followed closely by some of the LCTs.

Off to the starboard were the Islands of St. Marcouf. Nearby the American battleship Nevada was firing on German gun positions on the shore. Coastal guns were firing on the battleship. The shells were landing in the water but we saw no hits on the Nevada, in fact, some of the shells were landing closer to us than to them. Fear was mounting in all of us although few would admit it. At this point, there were some rare cases of men completely losing their nerve. Most men who were overcome by the thought of the invasion had already been weeded out but there still were a number of cases of suicide and feigned illnesses. I encountered one man in a dejected mood on the craft who had been determined not to go. He was with me when we broke out of the marshalling area camp and told me of his plan to "get so dosed up with VD (Venereal disease)" that they would never take him. I was so surprised to see him and I asked what happened to his plan. He said, "I got dosed up all right but all they did was give me shots of penicillin in my ass, and they made me go anyway."

Horace Sisk was a big help to me, in spite of his size. Too small to be a rifleman, he served as clerk in the company I was in. He was as brave a man as I knew.

The sky had cleared early on the morning of June 6th, and was now filled with aircraft towing gliders. They contained airborne troops who were to land behind the beach. Farther west, transport planes carried paratroopers who were already landing inland from the beach. Obviously we were less than an hour from the landing, and fear and excitement began to mount. I tried to concentrate on the job I was to do rather than to focus on the prospect of being killed or wounded. My greatest fear was of high explosive shells and I gave less thought to rifle or machine gun fire. Some men became quiet and withdrawn but most of us became boisterous. I remembered brief visions of seeing myself blown apart with my arms and legs separated from my body. Our envy of the Navy's seemingly-better conditions was a catalyst for some of the men to make an attack on one of the navy storerooms and carry off some canned goods that we could load in our few vehicles. I took a gallon can of fruit cocktail and put it in my jeep.

The approach to the beach was heavily mined and an LCT close to our port side was blown up. Our craft struck some of the wreckage and may have been the reason the skipper of our LCT opened the gate and ordered us out in deeper water than we had ever experienced in training. Some of our vehicles may have made it, but I was a so concerned about the one I was driving I didn't pay attention to the others. As my jeep went into the water I was relieved that it ran for a few seconds, then suddenly the engine began to miss and soon quit. Two men were in the jeep with me.

LCVP's, Higgins Boats, carried many of the soldiers onto the beach on June 6. Not all of them made as good a landing as this one

One was Sisk, and the other, Sergeant Baer, who was a member of the interrogation team of the 8th Infantry Regiment.

Neither Sisk nor Baer could swim and they immediately inflated life belts, which were unstable. They were in danger of drowning. I didn't inflate mine because I was a strong swimmer and helped Sisk and Baer get a hold on the jeep. With enemy bullets sweeping the water surface and randomly picking off men struggling for survival, I swam for shore and took off my heavy ammunition belt, shirt, pants and shoes, and swam back to the jeep. I first assisted Baer to get to the beach. On the way in, he struck a dead man floating in the surf, which totally unnerved him. After reaching the sand he bolted for the head of the beach, and we didn't see him again for two days. I then got Sisk in, and once on the sand Sisk, ignoring the enemy bullets, asked me, "How do you think we should try to get the jeep in?" I was immensely pleased that he offered to help even though we were under heavy fire. I spotted an amphibious vehicle coming toward us, which was designated by the Army as a DUKW and commonly referred to as a "Duck."

These vehicles were on a chassis about the size of a 2½ ton truck. This one was being used to carry wounded men off the beach and onto landing ships, which were set up as hospitals. I told the driver I had a sunken jeep that I wanted to bring in and asked if he could help. He courageously agreed and was extremely cooperative. He said he had a rope I might be able to tie to my jeep's bumper. The duck driver hitched the other end of the rope to the end of his winch cable and, after winching in the cable, he dragged the jeep into shallow water. From there we had him tow it to the edge of the dry sand. We sincerely thanked the duck driver for his courageous assistance while under heavy fire from the Germans. This generous act of heroism impressed me deeply, and yet I never even asked his name or what unit he belonged to. There certainly was a wide array of degrees of courage and cowardice alike displayed on that one historic day.

Fully aware that it might take us more than an hour to drain the engine parts of water before we could get the jeep running, I asked Sisk if he was willing to help. Sisk said, "Sure I'm willing, because I think we should do it. This wire jeep could be very valuable to the company." The German artillery seemed to increase and we had one strafing by an enemy fighter plane, a Messerschmitt 109. The jeep being in the center of the sand was a prime target for the Messerschmitt, and the rounds it fired came so close they threw sand in my face but neither of us was hurt. We tried to make light of the situation by joking about his bad aim.

Medics were assembling more and more wounded and loading them onto DUKWs. Many of the wounded had stepped on anti-personnel mines that were concentrated along the head of the beach. They often maimed a man without killing him. His toes were usually blown off, and since the mines fired projectiles at the body, they were aptly called "castrators." Clearing the jeep of salt water was more of a problem than anticipated. It was necessary to disassemble and dry most electrical and carburetion parts, and remove and dry the oil pan. After we put everything back together we got oil from a DUKW driver and started the engine by pushing the jeep, but it stopped within a few seconds. I discovered that the gas tank was filled with salt water even though it had appeared to be thoroughly waterproofed. With saltwater once again in the engine, we had to go through more cleaning procedure as well as completely drain the gas tank. After getting more oil and gasoline we were able to start the engine and drive it to the head of the beach.

After frantic hours of repair work on the jeep, we finally escaped from our deadly exposure.

While the jeep was in the water, nearly everything on board had been washed away, including our rations. Sisk had secured both his pack and mine to the jeep. The only food left was a gallon can of fruit cocktail from the Navy stores. Every man on shore was on limited rations so we decided not to ask for food. All that we had was fruit cocktail for D-Day and the following day. The fruit cocktail was much too sweet, and I have not wanted to taste it since. Our rifles and ammunition were easily replaced by those left by the wounded. We were ready to move inland and search for the Company and I was eager to start. Sisk wasn't so sure, since the sun was already going down. He said, "We landed in the wrong place, you know, and we have no idea where we are."

Utah Beach late on D-Day. A destroyed German gun position is at right

I said, "Yeah, I know." Nothing was matching with what we were told.

One of the medics heard our discussion about moving inland and said, "You'd be crazy to start out now. You're not going to find your Company in the dark."

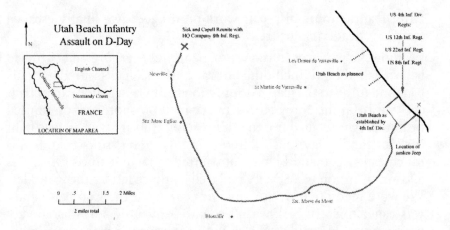

Utah Beach Infantry Assault on D-Day

Then Sisk said, "I don't fancy tiptoeing through the minefields, besides there are a lot more Germans than there are of us, and they sure would enjoy killing us."

"OK. So we dig in by the seawall here until daybreak," I said.

I didn't find out the reason for the error in landing until after the war. The Navy had landed us in the wrong place. We were about 1 km southeast of our planned landing area. Apparently the navy boats that were to mark the landing place had drifted to the southeast with the tidal current and this was not properly accounted for. Obviously the junior officers in the first wave of landings were uncertain as to what to do. Some wanted to move along the beach to the planned landing spot, others felt that this was too dangerous. Fortunately, Brigadier General Theodore Roosevelt Jr. was our Assistant Division Commander. He had made a special request to Supreme Allied Headquarters to be allowed to land with the first troops. Reluctantly the Supreme Headquarters granted his request, but it was against normal policy to allow a general to be in such a dangerous position. Roosevelt made an immediate decision, "We start the war from here"—and this saved what might have been a disastrous move along the beach under heavy German fire.

At first light we were up and ready to go. Suddenly an American fighter plane appeared over German territory to the east and was desperately trying to reach the beach before crashing. The pilot bailed out safely and some cheers went up from us. The plane went down in the water. A burst of machine gun fire from about 50 feet north of us put his body into writhing agony before it went limp.

Utah Beach obstacles and dead soldier 1 day after D-Day. Note the inflatable life belt around the soldier's waist

The American pilot hit the ground near the water and already the medics were running to him. The companions near the man on the machine gun immediately grabbed the shooter and pounded him to the ground. They were from a unit of American Engineers who had landed the night before. I was to see this type of irrational behavior happen all too often later in combat and never pretended to understand.

As a defensive measure, the Germans had flooded the fields' inland from the beach, the water being up to 3 feet deep; they had opened a valve at a navigation lock on the Merderet River system. There were several causeways crossing the inundated area and one was just to the north of us. About 75 feet away from where we were at the head of the beach, medics were assembling wounded to be taken back to England. Since the medics continued to stream in with more wounded, I knew our best bet to find the Company was to ask a wounded man from our Regiment. Following his advice, we took a nearby causeway to the town of Ste. Mere Eglise, which had been captured late on D-Day. Here the 8th Infantry Regiment linked up with paratroopers who had landed during the night prior to our beach landings. The German artillery fire seemed a little less intense than on D-Day, but the weird and eerily terrifying sound of the Nebelwerfers (rocket launchers), commonly called screaming meemies, continued. They made huge explosions, but were not nearly as dangerous as the German 88mm guns, which fired at a velocity about three times as fast as the speed of sound. The 88mm guns were used for antiaircraft and antitank fire and for destroying ground positions. They also were mounted on the

German Nebelwerfer

German Tiger tanks, and were so well balanced that they could be aimed almost as easily as a rifle. A more effective gun had never been developed by any nation.

The American glider troops started coming in during the night but most of them were crashing. After we passed over the flooded fields there were many of them all around us. A number of the glider troops were too seriously injured to fight and a number of them were killed just from the crash landing. One glider pilot came charging toward me, seething with anger and anxious to vent his fury. Pushing a map in front of me he said, "Look! Does that look like an empty field to you?" I had not seen a map of the area before and couldn't see what he was showing me with him waving it around, but I sympathized with him.

I said, "Is that your glider crashed against those trees?"

"Yeah, now I've got a plane full of wounded and some dead."

About that time another glider crashed between trees as a jeep it had been carrying came flying out through the nose of the aircraft. Sisk and I wondered whether glider troops were of much use when so few of them landed safely. However, I realized later that because so many of them were off-course and landing all over the place, it served to confuse the Germans as to where the enemy was coming from. The paratroopers also were a huge factor in confusing the Germans.

In Ste. Mere Eglise there was not only an enormous number of German bodies, but also of American infantrymen and paratroopers. Some were terribly mangled. Everywhere we looked were scenes of horror. At one point, I had to drive the jeep over bodies in order to get further down the road. There appeared to be many redheaded Germans, but this was only because their heads were mashed from being run over. Arms and legs lay on the ground, separated from the bodies they had shortly before been attached to. My brief vision of my limbless body earlier on the landing craft flashed through my mind again.

Once on the road out of Ste. Mere Eglise we met wounded men who had just left our Regiment, and within minutes we were at our Company Headquarters. The Wire Section was relieved to get one more jeep because they were extremely busy with wire breakages in the heavy fighting. Sisk was assigned to assist the Regimental Commander Col. Van Fleet. I was assigned to drive a three-man wire crew. We worked far into the night and into the next day without sleep.

At the beach, Sisk and I had thoroughly repaired the jeep, except for the starter. Whenever we left the jeep to work on a wire break, we had to leave the engine running if we needed a quick get-away. If the engine stopped, the jeep would have to be pushed before it would start. A couple of times, after being surrounded by Germans, we found it very hard to keep track of their movements through the bushes with the noise from the engine. The men in the wire crew considered this intolerable, and refused to use that jeep anymore without a starter, so it was abandoned. The thought was devastating when I considered all of the hours Sisk and I spent on it in such great danger.

- - -

On the 40th Anniversary of D-Day a television station interviewed certain men who had survived the landing and were living in or near Portland, Oregon. I was one and another was Heinz Hylla, who was one of the Germans attempting to defend against our advance. He was with the German 6th Parachute Regt. After we met, we became very good friends. He told me of how we were being shot down like clay pigeons, but for every man shot down there would be another to take his place. He recognized the insignia of our division and had been defending the ground upon which our regiment had been advancing. He said he and his comrades were astounded at our determination and courage, especially when we were not fighting for our own homeland. Later, Heinz was shot through the mouth and taken prisoner. After the war he came to the U.S. to settle in Portland.

He told me that while he was in Germany, coming of age, and about to be drafted, he joined the German Air Force. The Germans had lost so many airplanes in the Battle of Britain that they had more fliers than airplanes and transferred units of Air Force (Luftwaffe) into other divisions such as the parachute division he was in. He came to hate Hitler but felt it was his duty to fight for his German homeland. He passionately hated Nazis through the rest of his life.

- - -

At this point we were learning much about combat and how better to survive. Those of us who survived until later battles realized why an experienced man had a much better chance of surviving than a new replacement. One must learn to take cover when necessary and carry on duties with a minimum of risk. A man frightened or confused is a danger not only to himself but also to his comrades. One combat-wise general, however, believed that experienced troops were sometimes too cautious and lacked the element of recklessness helpful in waging an aggressive battle.

The Division command also had not prepared soon enough to prevent some of the hazards concocted by the Germans. One trick was to stretch piano wire at neck level across a narrow roadway from one tree to another. When in combat, windshields were kept down and covered to avoid reflection, there was nothing to protect from an unseen wire decapitating one or all of the jeep's occupants. Shortly after landing in France, Division Ordnance people took the jeeps back one by one to weld angle irons up from the front bumpers. The top of the iron would be about six feet from the ground and above the driver's head. A notch was cut in the upper side of the iron, which served to snag a wire stretched across a roadway.

One thing I learned the hard way was that I could not operate safely during long periods of little or no sleep. While still in the vicinity of Ste. Mere Eglise, my wire crew was called out one night in near-total darkness to find a break. I had gone a couple of days with almost no sleep. I found the trouble spot and used our prearranged signal to notify the others. I could promptly take care of the problem. I cut the ragged ends of the wires to keep bare wires from touching. I scraped back old insulation and spliced each wire and began individually winding friction tape around the wires to keep them from shorting. Suddenly I was overwhelmed by a feeling of dizziness and felt as though I were briefly dozing off. I finished wrapping the tape around as I tried to shake the cobwebs out of my head. I was just completely exhausted from lack of sleep. I signaled that I was finished and we all went back to the jeep and headed back toward the company. I had an eerie feeling that I had taped bare wires together. I couldn't believe I had actually done it, so I passed off the thought. Once back at the Company, a communications man yelled at us to go back, "The wire is still out!" It had briefly been restored for a few seconds before it went out again. A horrible thought came back to me that I did tape bare wires together. When we got to the same area we'd been before I said, "I saw where a shell had hit close to the wire a little further on from where I found the break, so I'm gonna' check it." I ran to the place where I'd repaired the wire, and sure enough, to my absolute horror I found that I had stupidly done what I feared. I pretended I'd found a new break. I was then fully aware of what a lack of sleep could do.

Another near-fatal encounter due to sleep deprivation occurred a couple of nights later when we came in late from a wire line. It seemed the German shelling was less intense and that there was a good chance I could get at least one or two hours of sleep before being called out again. Since I was at a point of nervous exhaustion, and needed something to settle me down before I could sleep. I went to where some brandy was hidden and took a good swig from one of the bottles. I went back to my hole and collapsed into sleep. It couldn't have been more than 20 minutes later that I was called out of my hole to repair another break. The brandy and lack of sleep sent my head into a swirl, but somehow I managed to drive the jeep to where the crew thought the break might be. We all got out and scouted the line. Now the German artillery seemed especially heavy, and there was machine gun fire coming from directions my brain could not detect. I felt absolutely helpless and was more frightened than I had been since entering combat. Fortunately, the other crewmembers found the wire break and soon we went back to the Company. I swore I would never ever again drink alcohol in combat. At times I bent my rule a bit but remained very cautious when I did indulge.

By June 9th, three days after D-Day, we had advanced about six miles inland from the beach and were near the little town of Fresville and about 2 miles N of Ste. Mere Eglise. We advanced slightly by the 10th and were almost 2 miles south of the larger town of Montebourg. The Germans continued to put up much heavier resistance in our area than they had on D-Day itself. Small-arms fire from rifles and machine guns intensified from nearby German strongholds. They also continued their bombardment with artillery and mortar shells. There were occasional Luftwaffe (German Air Force) attacks, but not nearly as intense as we had expected.

A jeep was hit just as I was returning to our Company. There was no sound of the shell coming in until after it struck, as was typical of an 88mm shell. The three men in the jeep were killed instantly and an officer nearby was grievously wounded. I immediately recognized one of the dead as being Bill Obewchowsky, who had been a good friend while we trained in England. He was our unofficial Company barber, although assigned to the Wire Section. He cut hair for all of the enlisted men in the Company for which we paid him 25 cents. Another of the dead whom I knew well was Corporal Peter Horback from New Jersey. Horback's body lies at rest today at the American Military Cemetery in Normandy. The other two men who died were apparently buried there originally but their bodies have been removed at the request of their families.

When the jeep was hit, our Communications Officer, Captain Herbert Krauss, had been standing by the jeep holding a map to direct the Wire Crew to the location of the line that was out. He was alive but it appeared to me that at least half his face was blown off, besides the serious wounds to his body. I assumed he would die very shortly. Immediately, I was ordered to go to our unit's Aid Station a mile or so back, and to bring a medical officer up to treat Captain Krauss. I sped back along the dirt road, but as I neared a church steeple on the left, I felt bullets popping by my head and quickly realized there was a sniper in the church steeple. I tried to swerve the jeep and drive erratically to be less of a target, but more bullets hit the jeep and popped by my head. Somehow I managed to get by without being hit and I drove into the Aid Station. The medical officer had somehow learned of Captain Krauss' condition and was already at our Company. He apparently got by the steeple just before the sniper got into position. I was ordered back but knew of no other route than to go by the steeple again. However, I took a diversion across an open field, preferring to risk running over a minefield rather than come that close to the sniper again. I cut back to the main road within the sniper's range but again escaping his bullets. When I got to the Company, the medical officer had tended to Captain Krauss. Krauss was put in an ambulance and was on his way back to the medical facilities at Division Headquarters a few miles back where he could be shipped to a hospital in England.

It wasn't until February 1996, that I learned that Captain Krauss had survived. I was very pleased to learn from a letter I received from Frank Glaze that Krauss had survived and was living with his family in Pennsylvania and had been a hospital administrator. He had lost an eye, a kidney, one arm, and part of a leg. As I stared at the mangled wreckage of the jeep that was hit, I realized it was the one I had been assigned to for most of the time while we were in England. Shortly before the invasion, I was ordered to add a radio generator that operated off the engine power train so it could also be used as a radio jeep. I made the installation but since I had no training as a radioman, I was transferred to another wire jeep. I felt an even more poignant impact of it all when I saw evidence of repair jobs and areas of fresh paint that I had recently put on the fenders of my old jeep.

The medical officer was ready to go back to the Aid Station, and I started out with him but warned him that we would have to come within range of a sniper firing from a church steeple. I told him I would try to get off the main road as soon as I could but there would be the danger of mines. He told me to go ahead and do the best I could. As we approached the area of the sniper's fire, we saw a squad of Infantry coming up from the side of the road opposite the church steeple and the first man that reached the road was struck by the sniper and went down. The medic with me yelled, "Stop the jeep!" And as I did, he jumped out and ran for the man that was down. I followed close behind him. We pulled the wounded man over into the ditch and began to work on him as the sniper continued to fire but now he had more targets and they were firing back at him. The man we were assisting had a severe bullet wound through the upper arm and was bleeding profusely. I followed the medic's instructions as we slowed the bleeding and bound up his arm. This done, he said we would go back to the jeep and continue to the Aid Station, and the wounded man would be picked up immediately by medics from his company as soon as the sniper was taken care of. I took him back, once again going off the main road, and in the meantime complimented him on his dedication and bravery to assist a wounded man while under fire from a sniper. He said, "Well, that's my job and thanks for sticking close by me."

- - -

I headed back and this time stayed on the main road to see what the situation was, and to my surprise the Infantry squad had the sniper down in the area in front of the church steeple. I was astounded they hadn't killed him as was the usual procedure with

snipers and doubly so by the fact that he seemed to be wearing an SS uniform. I ran over to see what was going on and they told me the man did not speak German but only Russian. I hadn't realized that not all SS men were German and that a non-German would, under some circumstances, be willing to fight to the death. What saved this man's life was that two of our infantrymen had climbed up the steeple and surprised him to the extent that he dropped his rifle before he was shot. They chose not to kill him but to try to interrogate him. He seemed to be speaking rather freely in Russian, but only one or two of the men in our squad had an idea of what he was talking about.

This was not my first encounter with non-Germans fighting for the Germans. At times, many of the prisoners we took spoke little or no German but were fluent in Polish, and sometimes Russian. Most of these troops were not dedicated fighters and many would surrender rather easily. Why so many former enemies of the Germans had chosen to join the Nazi cause was a puzzle. I was later to learn that some SS units were composed completely of Poles, Russians, Finns and even some French and English. Divisions were formed for each of the nationalities under German officers but some, such as the French and English, were never actually activated. Their motivations were mostly a mystery to me but I understand some, particularly the Russians, were so anticommunist that they were willing to fight for the Nazi cause.

- - -

Late that afternoon, I was ordered to take cartons of K-Rations and ammunition to E-Company of 2nd Battalion, which was at the center of a heavy German counterattack. Our Company Commander, Francis W. (Frank) Glaze told me he was going to ride with me to check with the officers at 2nd Battalion Headquarters while I delivered the food and ammo. I let him off at the Battalion Headquarters and said I would be back shortly. When I arrived at E-Company I saw how bad the situation was. The German's were pouring heavy small arms and machinegun fire in at the Company along with mortars and some artillery. I unloaded the supplies and noticed the great number of wounded. A sergeant came to me and ordered me to take as many wounded as I could carry in the jeep to an Aid Station about a mile back. He said the medics could not keep up. I told him I was driving our Company Commander who was at

Battalion Headquarters and would have to inform him. I rushed to Battalion Headquarters and broke into an intense conversation he was having with a Battalion Company Commander. Perhaps I was too abrupt and I'm sure both of them thought I was being obtrusive. Men's lives were at stake on the decisions made by the Battalion Commander at this point. However, I was trying to convey that I would return to pick up Captain Glaze as soon as I could help with at least one load of wounded.

I took as many wounded back as I could and then hurried back to find Captain Glaze so he would know where I was. However, he had left the Battalion Headquarters, and so had the Battalion officers. It was getting dark, but I frantically searched the area for Captain Glaze. The E-Company men that remained were getting ready to head back and said, "You had better go too. You'd be crazy to stay here with the German's advancing." I stayed a while and searched for Glaze, but realized it was fruitless. My concern was that he was lying wounded somewhere. I hurried back to our Company to report that he was missing, but as soon as I arrived I saw him walking out to meet me. My first words were, "Thank God you're alive Captain. I've been looking for you."

He said, "Well I thought you'd left so I came back."

Again I said, "Thank God you're all right" and turned and walked back to where my foxhole had been dug. I felt terrible about the miscommunication that we apparently had at Battalion Headquarters, and hoped he didn't think I had deserted him. I also felt discouraged and concerned that the Germans were advancing on us and would be here some time during the night. I knew our Regiment had a "no retreat" and "fight to the death" order. I expected to be killed or captured by morning, but to my amazement and relief, they stopped their advance and the 2nd Battalion was soon able to regain their original position.

From the afternoon of the 10th through the 19th of June, we made almost no progress against the Germans. Our Company Headquarters remained about 2 miles southeast of the town of Montebourg during that entire period. The Germans were raging a formidable defensive battle to hold the town and turned back any and all of the intrusions we attempted. Since we stayed in one place for several days, I had a good chance to dig a deep and relatively comfortable foxhole. It was here that I passed my 21st birthday without celebration because I had simply not thought about it. I

occasionally wandered back from the enemy lines for brief periods during which I thought I would not be needed. On one occasion, I found a few French houses that had not been evacuated of civilians and saw a little girl playing in front of one. Lying scattered around were unexploded shells and hand grenades. I was concerned the girl might pick one up, so I went to the house to tell the mother. She saw me at the door, screamed, and ran away. Surprised by this action, I wondered why there was such a change in attitude from what we encountered with most of the French civilians. Then I heard a commotion at a house, a short distance away and saw some men in our Regiment wrestling a man to the ground. I quickly ran over there and discovered he had just killed a French woman. He had been drinking cider, which was plentifully available in huge vats on every farm around this apple-producing country. He decided in his drunken state that he wanted something stronger, such as brandy. He walked to a house and demanded the woman give him a bottle of brandy. Frightened, she slammed the door and he fired through the door with his rifle and killed her. Had I come on the scene a few seconds earlier, I was so angered I am sure I would have killed him immediately. Other men in his Company had him subdued and he was taken back a few hundred yards and chained to a tree until the MPs came to take him back to an MP compound. The thought that these French people had waited so long for us to liberate them, and then to have such a thing happen, sickened me.

Farmers with small plots of land mostly inhabited the region we were fighting in. Most of the plots were smaller than football fields and were surrounded by what were called hedges, but they are not like what we think of as hedges in this country or in England. The Germans used the hedgerows greatly to their advantage by digging holes at the base, from which they could fire upon advancing troops while remaining almost completely concealed. This hedgerow country was referred to as the bocage. Combat here was carried on by foot soldiers and mostly hand-to-hand. Casualties were extremely high. E-Company of our regiment had only twenty-six men left of the nearly 200 men who landed on D-Day, after only three weeks of fighting.

- - -

The weather from before D-Day through the first two weeks of June was mostly cloudy and dull with occasional sun breaks. One morning while in that same foxhole near Montebourg, the cloudiness began to break and suddenly huge areas of blue sky began to predominate. The white clouds were towering; glistening in the sunlight. The German shelling seemed less intense and being June, the rising sun was producing its summertime warmth. I began to feel better immediately and filled with hope that I might survive. It was a brief period of spiritual renewal for me as I gazed at the beauty that still could be seen in this world, and the feeling that not all was misery and horror. I was so intrigued by the sharp outline of the gleaming white clouds that I wanted to learn more about them. It was at that moment that I determined that if I did survive I would someday study what made such beautiful formations in the sky. I could not have foreseen that this vision and these dark days at war would influence my later life and be a major factor of my career choice.

- - -

Later that same day I was in my foxhole for a few minutes to pick up some rations, when the greatest explosion I had been close to thus far jolted me. It was just behind the next hedgerow, a huge mushroom of smoke, dust and debris was rising in the air above. A round iron gun mount, weighing hundreds of pounds was blown high in the air. It dropped down into the same field I was in. I ran to the opening in the hedgerow near the explosion, and looked upon an amazing sight. What was left of a frame of a 2½-ton truck was flattened against the ground and debris and shell casings were scattered throughout the field. Most horrible were the four bodies, two of them completely naked. The explosion had torn every visible piece of clothing from them, yet the bodies remained intact. Altogether, there were four men dead. The only survivor was a man who was in a complete state of shock. He was babbling incoherently and shaking all over. It appeared that the man in shock had been about 50 feet away from the explosion while the others were on or near the truck. I suspected that an ammunition truck had blown up as a result of a faulty shell being handled by one of the men doing the unloading. Many years later in a conversation with Francis I. Smith, Commander of Cannon Co. of the 8th Infantry Regiment, I learned that the truck had taken a direct hit from a German 88mm shell that exploded an entire load of 105mm shells being delivered.

Chapter 4

TARGET CHERBOURG

But the wicked shall be cut off from the earth,
and the transgressors shall be rooted out of it

Proverbs chap. 2, vs. 22

Our move to the northwest was the best advance we'd made in one day since we landed and it was encouraging until we realized that the Germans were dropping back to an even stronger defensive position. After our move all new command posts were set up and wire had to be laid to each one. The wire crews were working day and night again; however, we felt we were making some progress against the Germans. Furthermore, the weather improved with the heavy rain ending the day before, on June 20th. One morning our wire crew stopped in a field to eat some rations. As usual, we dispersed somewhat to avoid all being hit by the same artillery shell. I had trouble finding a spot where I could get away from the smell of death because the field was littered with dead soldiers. I picked a spot about 15 feet away from a body and sat on the ground. As I put my hand back for support, I took hold of fingers. I pulled away and looked but there was no body - just a hand! I looked at the body lying 15 feet away and saw both hands were attached, so where had this lone hand come from?

The most horrible aspect of infantry combat cannot be depicted in pictures or adequately described in words. It is the smell—the piercing, penetrating, ever present, sickening stench. The distinctive smell of human death seems most offensive of all. Perhaps the clothing makes it worse, or possibly it is entirely psychological. In addition, there was the odor emitted from dead cattle in nearly every farm field. They lay bloated like balloons, with legs sticking straight up. On one occasion, a gas alarm was issued in which we were ordered to put on our gas masks. Later, it was determined the gas was not from a German attack, but from the great numbers of dead humans and animals, particularly cattle. Some of the German artillery was horse-drawn and thus, many horses were killed on the battlefield. Many times, even when the fighting was still going on, French civilians would rush out with knives to cut up the dead horses for food. In less than a day, the horses would be reduced to skeletons.

One time, we overtook a German artillery unit and killed or captured all of the soldiers and turned the horses loose. The horses were frightened, many of them wounded and berserk with terror. They raced around the field in which we tried to dig our foxholes. One of them attacked me and since I refused to fire at a horse, I tried to fend him off by swinging my rifle butt at him, but he kept coming after me. This went on for at least 15 or 20 minutes with the horse after me every second. I finally was able to get to the back of my wire jeep and pull off a section of wire. At last, I got the wire around the horse's neck and eventually got the other end tied to a tree before I could get on with digging my hole in relative peace.

- - -

After returning to the company, we were told to standby and be ready to install another wire line. The communications officer said he would have to do some checking before giving us the exact location of the command post it was to go to. It was sunny and I was tired and so I flopped on my back on the ground expecting a few minutes rest. When I heard a jeep pull up close to where we were, I paid little attention and closed my eyes for a moment before I became aware of someone walking near me. I peeked at the jeep to see what was going on and saw "Rough Rider" painted just below the windshield so I knew it was General Theodore Roosevelt Jr. and he was standing right by me. It was too late for me to jump up to attention so I pretended to be asleep. "Teddy," as we called him, just stood there at my feet. Finally, I couldn't resist opening my eyes a bit, and when I did he laughed. Before I could think of any response, he kicked me in the foot and said, "Take it easy soldier. You need the rest." I smiled, and he turned around and walked away, smiling too. It was the last time I was to see Teddy Roosevelt Jr., for he was soon to die on July 12, 1944.

During the third week in June, after the breakout from the Montebourg area, we made several days of good progress northward

Brigadier General Roosevelt (Teddy Roosevelt Jr.), 4th Divisions assistant commander

on the Cotentin Peninsula. Most of the roads ran between hedgerows, and in one particular spot there was a disabled German tank blocking over half the roadway. The wire crew was in the jeep with me as we tried to squeeze by it. The vehicle directly behind me was a ¾ ton weapons carrier. Just after I squeezed by, he tried to follow my tire tracks. An instant later the vehicle was twisting end over end some 25 to 30 feet above the ground on a thick column of smoke and debris. We were sure there were no survivors, and when we saw men from behind running up to check, we continued on our way. Obviously the vehicle had run over a mine, and we had just run over that same mine but it did not detonate.

The close encounter with the mine was just another narrow escape such as those that had been happening on an almost daily basis. Sometimes it would be a bullet popping close to my head and sometimes a piece of shrapnel or shell fragment. On one occasion, something hit the back of my helmet, knocking it off, and leaving a sizeable dent. At times shell fragments buzzed with deadly force, missing by just a few inches. Being ahead of the combat engineers carrying mine detectors, we sometimes passed through minefields without even knowing it unless a vehicle or person was blown up. It happened enough times that I felt a Divine force was protecting me. I wondered how long it could go on that way. I knew there were other men who had died that were far more worthy of God's protection. Nevertheless, in a heavy artillery barrage, while lying face down in a shallow hole, I would be digging the ground with my fingers and praying.

Our first objective in Normandy was to establish a good beachhead, which was an absolute necessity if we were to survive. If we could not do this we could readily be pushed back to the sea and destroyed. Those first two weeks after the D-Day landing were critical and the fighting was desperately heavy, but we succeeded in establishing our needed foothold. We had paid a heavy price in dead and wounded, some of our rifle companies had lost ¾ of their men already. The Germans were tough fighters and still determined to drive us back into the sea. The end of the war was not in sight and each day brought more close encounters with death. How long could I go on being lucky? I dared not think about it.

We moved to about 8 miles southeast of Cherbourg and dug foxholes in a field next to an apple orchard. There was a hedgerow

a much more effective solution. He took a can of gasoline from a jeep and poured gasoline freely around and in his hole. He thought the fumes would be a good deterrent. He climbed in his hole and announced with great satisfaction that his idea worked. Then he lay back, relaxed and absentmindedly lit a cigarette. The whole area exploded in flames and we finally got the fire down and rescued Stine, who seemed more dead than alive when the medics took him away. (In 1997, when visiting with Frank Glaze, I learned that Stine did survive and returned to combat.) The Germans saw the flare-up and immediately concentrated their artillery fire upon us. We were under an intense barrage for much of the night and several men in our regiment were killed.

Captain Francis W. Glaze our company commander

My encounter with fire happened a couple of days later when we were less than 8 miles south of the city of Cherbourg. We had just returned from laying a new wire line when we decided to take a break and have some coffee. One of the men took a 5-gallon gas can off the back of the jeep and opened the lid. He was preparing to pour a little gasoline into the bottom of a small ration can to fuel a small fire that would heat up our coffee. At that time, a German shell struck a few feet away and everyone scrambled for safety. At that moment I saw the partially opened gas can begin to tip over onto the small fire, which the man had already started. Before everything burst into flames, I tried to right the can and close the lid, but in my haste, I slopped gasoline over much of my upper body. I was already kneeling down to avoid fragments from the exploding shell and in an instant, my whole upper body was on fire although I didn't yet realize it. I could see the flames leaping up from my hands and arms and therefore took a dive face down into nearby saturated soil and wet grass. I didn't feel the burning on my back immediately because a gasoline fire like that burns its vapors first before burning the skin underneath. I then rolled onto my back. The fire was out but I felt severe pain on my hands and on the back of my neck. Someone called for a medic who led me back to my hole and treated my wounds. He concluded that the wounds were 2nd degree and should start healing within a few days, I would have no permanent injury. He bandaged my hands and neck heavily and started to lead me back to the aid station but another much more severely wounded man was calling for help.

"Look, is there any way you can cut this bandage on my right hand so I can use my trigger finger?" I asked him.

"Sure, I'll just cut an opening for your finger."

"Maybe you better leave me alone and go take care of that guy. He really looks like he needs help".

The medic agreed and said I would be all right but said "I didn't get your name and serial number so your wound won't be registered." I said, "Ok. That's not important. That other guy needs your help right now." And I thought of Harry Kuhn who refused to register his wound because he thought the medics were too busy to fool around with paperwork. I realized much later, though, that I made a mistake not to have my wound registered because I was not awarded a Purple Heart Medal nor did I receive the benefits that went along with it. At that time, all I was interested in was surviving.

We were now less than 10 miles southeast of the city of Cherbourg. The Germans were yielding, though fighting hard for every foot of ground we were able to gain. Our casualties continued to mount. More and more of the men I had trained with were killed, wounded, or captured. No casualty lists were issued so I knew only of those I witnessed or heard about directly.

This photograph appears in the 8th Infantry Regiment section of the 4th Division history book published in 1945. It is captioned, "On July 19th, 32 D-Day men and officers remained in A Company

After 6 weeks of fighting after D-Day this photo illustrates the reduced number of men in A company 8th Infantry Regt. This was typical of most of our companies which started out with over 190 men in each

of the over 190 who landed on June 6th." A U.S. Army historical publication called Utah Beach to Cherbourg noted that some of the 8th Infantry Regiment Companies were reduced to fewer than 30 men in just the first 3 weeks. A steady flow of replacements were coming in to replace the casualties but were not sufficient to keep up with the number of dead and wounded. Few of these replacements had any previous battle experience and were more likely to quickly become casualties than were the veterans. Replacements were often killed or wounded on their first day and medics complained that the wounded men sometimes did not remember what company they were assigned to.

A group of 20 men was walking between hedgerows, with Colonel Steiner in the middle. He wore a white band down the back of his helmet as did many officers. A sniper in the field next to where I was spotted the insignia and shot him. The bullet went through his neck and killed him instantly. Steiner was the assistant commander of our regiment. He was a good officer and well respected.

We hoped that if the D-Day landings were successful and good beachheads were established, the German defenses inland would soon collapse. By now, however, we realized the Germans in many cases, would fight to the death. With death so close day after day, my thoughts were less on whether I would survive, but rather on how long it would be before I was either killed or wounded. Thus I began to realize why so many of our men were wishing for the "million-dollar wound". This meant a wound serious enough for a man to be taken to a hospital but not serious enough to kill or maim him. Self-inflicted wounds began to occur more frequently at this time. While still southeast of Cherbourg, my foxhole was close to where another man was dug-in. I did not recognize the man but assumed he was in our company as a replacement. I was eating my ration when I saw the man put his foot up on the edge of his hole, aim his rifle at it and blow his toes off. This was the most common type of self-inflicted wound at that time. However, the Army Command quickly took measures to discourage this activity by establishing special prison hospitals for the "self-inflicteds". I never saw one of them again so I don't know exactly what their ultimate fate was. We had great disdain for a man who attempted to escape from battle in this manner.

- - -

The first signs of weakening in the German forces were the greater numbers of Germans who allowed themselves to be taken prisoner. The number of prisoners we took increased each day until Cherbourg was captured. Gene Redfield told me our Regiment had taken a German general. His name was General Karl Wilhelm von Schlieben. Redfield and I hurried over to where he was being held and heard much of the interrogation. He refused to surrender his troops, which were in the area of Cherbourg and along the end of the Cotentin Peninsula. He declined to admit that his troops were completely surrounded. He may have known that Hitler had issued an automatic death sentence on any general who surrendered his troops. We had to move on and I did not ever find out what happened to him.

Finally on June 25th and 26th the 4th, 9th and 79th Infantry Divisions penetrated Cherbourg and continued to clear out small pockets of Germans, taking many of them prisoners. The Wire Section was not busy at the time and Gene Redfield and I took the opportunity to explore some of the city. Most of the city was on a hillside overlooking an almost land-locked harbor. There was a jetty extending out on the western edge and at the end was a bunker that had been built by the Germans. It was still firing and American artillery on the hill near us was firing at it. Gene and I stopped to watch the dueling artillery and heard a broadcast on a radio somewhere near by. The BBC announcer was describing exactly what we were watching. It was a news broadcast back to England and we were receiving it as it was being done. We watched the shots being fired and at the same time, heard the radio broadcaster's description of the action. He was somewhere on a nearby hill. The battle lasted for about an hour as the Germans held out to the last man. Not a single one survived.

Redfield and I then wandered near the top of the hill toward the east and came upon a curious-looking cave entrance. There was a German rifle propped across the 4-ft. high opening. It looked very suspicious and Redfield and I wanted to see what was inside but we felt there was a good chance the rifle was booby-trapped. We checked around for small wires and found none but very carefully stepped into the cave without touching the rifle. The small cave led off to the right and got bigger as we went along for about 20 feet. Suddenly it opened into a chamber with a thick concrete wall. Inside were shelves and tables covered with weather instruments and radio equipment. Next to this chamber was an even larger one with more equipment and with fold-down cots for the crew of men who manned the bunker. There were observation ports viewing the harbor and the Atlantic Ocean beyond. We were convinced it was a U-boat and E-boat (submarine and torpedo boat) control base. I saw two intriguing barometers, one French and one German. I stuffed them into my shirt. I had no idea I would ever get them home but wanted to examine them more thoroughly, so I hid them in the back of a truck. Surprisingly enough I later got them sent home, thanks to Gene Redfield, our Mail Orderly, and still have them today.

What really interested us was a huge safe in the larger room and next to it, a smaller one. As we expected, they were both locked. This type of discovery was supposed to be reported immediately for the Interrogation Section to examine. Redfield and I knew how important it was that any papers be carefully scrutinized for information that might help the Allied cause and did not intend to disturb anything of that sort. However, we thought if there was money to be taken, we would rather do it than give them first chance at it. Redfield, as Mail Orderly, was responsible for all money orders that went back to the States. Some of the officers, especially the Interrogation Team, had sent thousands of dollars back already which they obviously had gotten from Germans who had looted them from the French.

There was a workshop in one corner of a large room with a wide selection of tools from which we took some heavy chisels and 1 and 2 pound hammers. We went back to the safe and began chiseling around the main lock. We worked as hard and as fast as possible with one of us pounding on the chisel with the 2-pound hammer for a while then switching off with the other one and began to make some progress. It was a long, hard job and no doubt took more than an hour but finally, the lock broke loose and we pried the door open. What a disappointment! It was absolutely empty with the exception of one small semi-automatic pistol. The Germans must have cleaned it out when they left. Disgusted after all our hard work, we turned to the small safe which was rather quickly opened and, to our amazement, found it to be full of bundles of French money. We gathered them up as fast as possible and stuffed them in our clothes and rushed to get outside of the bunker, going back through the tunnel from which we had entered. We were no sooner outside than a squad of American Infantry approached. I ran over to the Officer in charge and said we had just discovered a German bunker overlooking the harbor. I suggested it be checked out immediately, following which, Redfield and I disappeared back into the bushes with our clothes bulging with money. I recovered the two barometers which I had set in some bushes when I saw the American soldiers approaching. Redfield counted out and divided the money, which was all in French francs. Obviously the Germans had stolen it.

I said to Gene, "Now that we have the money, what are we going to do with it if we can't send home any more money than our pay?"

"I think I can take care of it but it'll take a few months probably. I have friends back at the Division Mail Section who can get extra money through for us if we don't send an enormous amount at one time."

Redfield did as he said and all of the money was home within about 3 months. I calculated that once converted to American money, it amounted to almost 2 years of pay at the rate I was being paid at

Major George Mabry, later Lt. Colonel, of the 8th Infantry Regt., one of its most respected officers

the time. In American currency, that was about $1500 in cash for each of us. This was a tremendous help to me because I was very concerned about my family back at home with my father having been ill and unable to work for such a long time. My mother had been sick with cancer prior to that and was still unable to work even if she did not have my father to take care of. Bartell Drug offered no health insurance for the management employees and therefore refused to pay him when his illness proved fatal. The money we found was a God-send. I stored the barometers in a compartment under the front seat of one of the small trucks, Redfield got these sent home for me as well.

German position dug at base of hedgerow

Chapter 5

OUT OF THE BOCAGE

Made for orchards and grazing of cattle,
And never ever designed for battle.
Just bushes and grass over earth and stone,
But in war, each one a fortress alone.

Capell '03 in memory of the hedgerow fighting, Normandy, 1944

Ever since the landing on D-Day, we had been fighting in the type of country the French refer to as the bocage, which is what we called hedgerow country. It is a network of relatively small fields surrounded by earthen walls containing small amounts of rocks overgrown by vegetation which consisted of brush, grasses, and small trees. The height of the earthen part would be four to six feet high with the vegetation extending above. The rows were built up over the centuries as farmers cleared their fields. They were usually quite wide at the base and made an excellent place for the Germans to build their foxholes and gun emplacements. It was a tremendous deterrent to tanks, making it superb defensive country for the Germans but extremely difficult for advancing troops. Most of the Cotentin Peninsula was bocage country.

The last few pockets of resistance were cleared out in the northern Cotentin Peninsula shortly after the complete surrender of Cherbourg, so we went without resistance. The first town of any size we came to was Valognes, which was the most completely destroyed town I had so far seen, with the possible exception of Montebourg. The French people were paying a high price for their liberation. We continued south, passing about 5 miles west from where we fought after the capture of Ste. Mere Eglise and before the Battle of Montebourg. After passing through Orglandes, which is 17 miles from Cherbourg and 4 miles west of Ste. Mere Eglise, we stayed in a nearby field for the next three days. There we received replacements for our dead and wounded and had a short rest. We could hear guns in the distance but we were not directly in combat for the first time in over 3½ weeks.

Our kitchen truck set up and served hot meals. A General from Corps Headquarters arrived after we were all lined up in the field. He asked that all men that had landed on D-Day, and were still with us, step forward. There was just a minority of us who were still left, the rest having been killed or seriously wounded. He noticed the majority of us who survived were still buck privates, which was the same rank we held the first day we were in the Army. On the spot we were all promoted to private first class. The extra five dollars a month was important to me because of illness at home.

Nearly all the men in our company were from the Eastern States with Redfield and I being the only ones from west of the Mississippi. There was a small group who were die-hard "Rebels", which meant their allegiance was still to the Confederate army, which they refused to accept was ever defeated. Their one common bond was that they hated black-skinned people, whom they called "niggers" and they bragged about how they "kept them in their place." Most of the Rebels had little formal education and usually were from the poorer areas of Alabama, Georgia, and Mississippi along with other states of the Deep South. We had no problem working with these men either in training or in combat but in social situations, we were poles apart in our thinking. Most seemed to be well trained with rifles from their experience as hunters. Their principal recreational interests were drinking and fighting. The fighting, however, was confined to their own group and rarely involved "Yankees", which meant men from the Northeast or their northern sympathizers. Perhaps this feeling came about because they were outnumbered by the latter and wanted no really serious trouble.

While near Orglandes, eight of them took a vehicle and drove to the nearest town and got drunk. When they arrived back a few hours later, they were fighting. It was an amusing scene with seven of them in the back of the vehicle punching each other, and the driver sitting up front minding his own business. When they arrived in the field where the rest of us were, they poured out of the small truck and continued fighting. We found it rather entertaining and stood in a circle around the brawling to watch the rebels beat on each other. Suddenly, one of them came reeling out of the center of the melee and bumped into Thomas Crowley from Michigan. Crowley vigorously pushed the man named Richard Ritch back into the fight. Ritch immediately took offense at a Yankee laying hands on him and pulled a knife. Instantly, Ralph Atkins who was more or less, the leader of the rebels grabbed an M-1 Garand rifle by the barrel, swung it like a baseball bat, and caught Ritch right in the side of the face with the butt. Ritch went down like a fallen tree. The rest of the rebels stopped fighting and looked on in awe. Atkins knew that Ritch had violated their rule not to attack a Yankee. Shirtless, Ritch lay unconscious on the ground with blood streaming down the side of his face. The Rebels slowly left and went back to where they had dug their holes. Those of us watching realized that none of the Rebels were going to help Ritch, so not wanting to interfere in their business we also left him alone. My hole was about fifty yards away from where Ritch was lying. It was already getting dark by that time and had Ritch been felled by enemy action, any one of us would have rushed immediately to his aid, but this was strictly a matter of rebel business and Ritch continued to lie there. After dark I looked and saw Ritch by the light of the moon still lying there shirtless. I decided not to interfere.

When morning came and the kitchen truck had breakfast chow prepared, I walked over to fill my mess kit. On the way back to my hole, I saw a group of rebels sitting on the ground eating their chow, among them was Richard Ritch, this time with his shirt back on. He looked none the worse for wear but it was hard to tell because his face was already so messed up from previous fighting. I'm sure the rebels considered it a very successful night; they got drunk, they fought, and no one was killed.

Some of the rebels were assigned to the wire section and often I had one or more with me. We usually worked reasonably well together except for Richard Ritch. He made me quite angry with his cruelty to animals, and several times when he was riding in the back of the Jeep I was driving he used them for target practice. I told him what I thought of such senseless cruelty. I had already developed a dislike for him when in England he taunted me for being the youngest and one of the newest men in the company. One day in Normandy while out locating a break in a wire line, Ritch was sitting behind me in the Jeep. As we drove between some bushes a rifle exploded near my left ear. I immediately reacted, thinking it was a German hidden in the bush firing at us. I stepped hard on the accelerator to get out of there and the Jeep leaped forward. Ritch laughed, and I realized it was he who had fired the rifle. I began to fly into a rage when I heard him laughing, but I restrained myself when I considered that we were on a wire mission and that had to take priority. I told Ritch I would deal with him later.

Early the next morning I had just checked the gasoline level in the Jeep and decided to fill it before going out on another mission. I was using an American gas can, which was slow to use, and had just inserted the funnel and began pouring gas (the German ones were more efficient and did not require a separate funnel). Just then the call came for us to go out and find a wire break. I had to finish pouring enough gas in to take care of our needs and seal the can to prevent a fire. Ritch, who was over on the other side of the field, yelled, "Git off yer f--- ass, Capell!" I exploded into a sequence of profanities directed at Ritch and promised to "pound yer ass into the ground when we get back." Everyone in the wire section within earshot heard the exchange, which is exactly what I wanted. There were several remarks made toward Ritch to the effect that he had better be ready. I was hoping this would make him nervous and I think it did. It also helped me that I had a somewhat exaggerated reputation as a boxer, which I did nothing to discourage. The reputation started when I had a friendly boxing match with another fellow in our company. He was big at about 220 pounds and 6 feet, 6 inches tall. He was a bit slow and I had no trouble getting in punches, although I had absolutely no desire to hurt him. He didn't hesitate to tell everybody how good I was. That reputation kept me out of a lot of fights.

When we returned from the wire line and drove into the field where we were dug in, I was greatly relieved to see Ritch get out immediately and head for his hole. I knew I had to keep the bluff going so I jumped out of the Jeep and followed him to his hole. I kept yelling, "YA READY FOR IT!" and Ritch kept going and I knew the battle was won. I stood over him and told him he had better stay there for awhile because if he tried to get out now, I'd knock him right back in. Ritch never bothered me again and the other men that witnessed the display had new respect for me. The entire wire section soon heard about the incident and Ritch and I were never assigned to the same crew again.

Ritch was deathly afraid of anti-vehicular mines. When he was riding with me he was repeatedly harassing me about driving over a mine. He accused me of being careless and needlessly risking the lives of all of us. The uncanny outcome of Ritch's time with our company was prophetic. After he was put in a separate wire crew, he was riding with another driver checking a wire line when the Jeep hit a mine, the most fearful thing of all to him. I did not ever hear whether he was killed or just seriously wounded, but he was taken away by the medics and we never saw him again. None of my friends knew anything about him either. Much as I thought I hated him, I did feel bad about what happened.

A damaged German 88-mm gun. This scene was in Merigny, France

On July 6th we were on the move again and entered combat about seven miles south of Ste. Mere Eglise and a few miles west of Carentan. For the next ten days we remained between four and six miles from the town, working our way from southeast to southwest before moving closer to St. Lo. One day the wire section got very busy setting up lines to the new battalion command post positions as it did every time we moved. Our crew was getting very low on our supply of wire and we reported it to the Communications Officer.

He said the whole Regiment was short of wire and a new shipment would be arriving soon. He said, "Lay all the wire you have and then wait until we send a jeep up with more wire."

I thought there was no hope of getting wire before morning so I dug a foxhole next to a hedgerow and settled in for the night. The July sun rose in a cloudless sky the next morning and I thought this would be an excellent time to heat up some water. I poured it in my steel helmet to wash and shave. I took my shirt off and was about halfway through shaving when another wire crew in a jeep drove up and said we would have to get our own wire. A new supply had just arrived but they had no truck available to bring it to us. I was not happy about the timing because I wanted to finish my shave, and I probably delivered a few audible curses. One of the other men in our wire crew said, "Don't worry about it, Capell. We'll take the jeep back and get the wire. By the time we get back, you'll be all shaved and washed and we'll be able to look at you without getting sick."

I began my shave and felt the warm July sun on my back, when I suddenly became aware of engine noise somewhere behind the adjacent hedgerow. It was just as I feared, the sound of a German tank, which got louder as it came closer. I jumped up from shaving and quickly clambered up the hedgerow to peek over. I looked face-to-face at a Mark 4 German tank armed with a 75mm gun. I was looking right down the barrel as it approached me. We must have seen each other at precisely the same time, because as he fired I was jumping as fast as possible to my left. A cow that was grazing just behind me was instantly killed. I landed facedown on the ground and squarely on some fresh manure the cow had just left and then continued to scramble as fast as I possibly could to the edge of the field, keeping close behind the hedgerow. I heard the tank turning away from the direction I had gone and was getting farther away from me. After firing the first shot at me, he continued to fire five more rounds, leaving a row of six holes in the hedgerow, all of them in the opposite direction from which I made my escape.

I was bare from the waste up and almost completely covered on my front side with cow manure, my steel helmet filled with shaving water was right where I had left it. The other men in my wire crew arrived back with a load of wire to see me looking like a walking manure pile. In front was a freshly killed cow, and a hedgerow with six big holes blasted through it. I told them a German tank had come to visit but I chased it away. I said, "Now will you let me finish my shave?"

In the above incident, my instinctive leap to my left saved my life. Had I dropped straight down, I would certainly have been hit. I can thank the Captain in our training camp at Camp Roberts, California, for ingraining this move in my mind. He taught me never to drop straight down: that is the most natural place for the enemy to fire a second shot. Always dart directly to one side or the other, or if caught in the open, to run in sharp, short zigzag moves.

Goliath remote controlled bomb

We completed the wire line to 1st Battalion then returned to near Headquarters Company where the Wire Section was dug in. I chose to dig my hole behind the hedgerow next to the field with the rest of the Wire Section. In the morning I heard the noise of a strange sounding engine coming from over the hedgerow near me and to the left. I looked over to see a vehicle of a type I had never seen before, passing through the opening at the end of the field. It was a fully tracked vehicle, such as a tank, except there was no turret on top and the whole thing was about 3 ft. high. I had never seen or heard anything about a vehicle of this type. It was coming from the direction of the German position and going at the rate of about 15-mph. A dog was in the field and he failed to get out of the way and was run over. The miniature tank-looking vehicle proceeded on and went toward a nearby opening in the hedgerow to my right. I ran to the dog and found that he had a broken, or at least, a sprained leg. I picked him up and carried him back over the hedgerow and proceeded on with the intent of finding a French farmhouse. Meanwhile, I remained completely puzzled as to what type of vehicle ran over the dog. At first, I thought it might be a decoy of some sort. Little did I realize that it was a bomb. I kept walking back toward the rear with the dog until I found a French farmhouse. I burst in the door, encountering a farmer and his wife who were startled by the sight of a tough-looking, bearded G.I. with a rifle over his shoulder, carrying a dog. I laid the dog on the table and said, with my little knowledge of French, "Ecoutez, le chien le jambe est casse." They quickly agreed and with my fierce-looking appearance I was sure they would take care of him.

I asked everyone in the company that I encountered that day if they had ever seen anything like the little tank I described. None of them said they had. Some thought I was hallucinating but it wasn't until long after the war that I found a picture and description of the weapon, for that is what it was. It was indeed a bomb directed by radio control. Because of the numerous shell explosions I could not distinguish between which was from artillery and which could have been from a bomb. The Germans called it a Goliath. My good friend Heinz Hylla, whom I met 40 years after the war and who was in a parachute division that fought directly against us in Normandy, told me about the weapon in detail. He explained it was a very powerful bomb directed by radio from a controller who had a visual sight on its path. That explains why it was able to find the openings in the hedgerows. It must have been directed towards an American installation in the Division's rear area. These bombs were also used in Italy, but obviously had not been common in Normandy, as I could find no one else in our Company who had seen or even known about them.

The German Air Force (Luftwaffe) was not very active in the daytime, but occasionally fighter-bombers came over and strafed. One I clearly remember was while I was driving a jeep with the wire crew over a small hill when we came face to face with a fighter plane. It was a Messerschmitt-109 (ME-109) and before we could take any evasive action, he fired both his cannons at us but somehow missed and continued on. At night, however, the Luftwaffe became an absolute horror with an operation which we referred to as "Bedcheck Charlie". Usually there was only one type of aircraft that came over just after dark. We never saw the aircraft nor did we ever shoot one down that I am aware of. There was a peculiar throbbing noise to the engine as if it were a two-engine aircraft with the engines out of synchronization. It was most likely a twin engine German Heinkel fighter-bomber.

As he passed over us the first time, he dropped flares with small parachutes, which lit up the ground but were so bright they blinded us from seeing him. He then circled back and dropped clusters of small bombs directly on our foxholes. We were quite visible to him with the light from the flares. We quickly learned the only defense we had against him was to cover our foxholes with whatever wood or small tree trunks or anything else available. We then threw dirt on top to cover as much as we could. The anti-personnel bombs they dropped weighed between 10 and 15 lbs each and usually a covered hole was enough to explode the bomb. Hugh Jetton had his hole dug just a few feet from mine when it was struck directly by at least one of these bombs and although Hugh wasn't hearing very well for a while, he had no visible injury whatsoever. Our Company Commander, Capt. Francis W. Glaze, issued an order that all of us cover our holes securely. The night Jetton's hole was hit was a horrible one. Four Military Police from Division Headquarters were at the Company to pick up prisoners. They were in a weapons carrier, which had just arrived in our Company area when Bedcheck Charlie dropped a cluster of bombs. One dropped directly on the head of the driver, another fell on the lap of the man sitting next to the driver, and the other wounded both of the men in back. Several other men in our Company were wounded in that raid including our Warrant Officer, Mr. Powell.

That night we were in a field surrounded by hedgerows with a French farmhouse near one of them. When Bedcheck Charlie came over and dropped his bombs, one started a raging fire in the thatched roof of the farmhouse. Someone yelled to me from near the farmhouse to bring the jeep. When I got there, I found that next to the fire was the ¾ ton weapons carrier with the MPs. Once I arrived, the badly wounded men had been dragged away from the fire into some nearby bushes. Someone yelled for me to try to get the jeep winch cable pulled out and hooked onto the weapons carrier. By tightening the winch, they hoped to pull it away from the house in order to clear the roadway so that ambulances could get through to our wounded men. The hedgerow nearest the house was so close that another vehicle could not pass. The weapons carrier, being so close to the fire, was getting hot as a stove. I ran toward it to try to drive it forward away from the fire. Someone yelled, "DON'T GET IN! The driver is blown all over the front seat." Then I realized that he was blown over the front seat and jammed into the controls of the vehicle. It could only be operated by me standing on the outside to steer while someone towed it forward by winding in the winch cable. I yelled for someone to take up the winch cable and slowly we towed the bombed vehicle away from the fire.

We got the vehicle away from the intense heat just in time, for I could not have stayed near it any longer. I ran to the wounded men who had been pulled away, and found that one had a bomb land directly on his lap but he was still alive and conscious. Two others were less seriously wounded but the driver was dead, and, in fact, blown to pieces. The man who suffered the bomb explosion in his lap was grievously wounded with much of the lower part of his torso blown away. I admired the man's stoic and courageous demeanor. There was little hope that he could live, but he never uttered a word of complaint even though he was conscious and fully aware of what had happened to him.

There was a barn about 50 yards from the farmhouse and I remembered that was where we had herded about 40 German prisoners of war we had captured that afternoon. The MPs were coming up from Division Headquarters to begin taking these prisoners back when they were hit by the bombs. I went to the barn to see what the situation was. The scene was well lit from the fire. Bedcheck Charlie had dropped a cluster of bombs on the barn, which had penetrated the roof and fallen on the prisoners below. When I went inside, I saw that the bombs had wounded a number of the prisoners and many were in great pain. I then saw a medical officer standing by and doing nothing to help his fellow Germans.

"Why aren't you helping these men?"

He said, "Becuss I am vounded."

"Where?"

"In my arm."

I exploded with anger and shoved my rifle into his stomach and yelled, "You have one good arm and you had better start using it to help these men, or I'll kill you!" Needless to say he went right to work. I wondered if being an officer had anything to do with his reluctance to help the wounded who were all enlisted men. I was surprised by how well he spoke English.

I used my jeep to carry some of the wounded Germans back to where our wounded were assembled. One of them I told to sit in the jeep, but he refused and stood up facing backwards. I then realized why he didn't want to sit down when I saw where he was wounded. I laughed and he said, "Danke. Danke."

- - -

It was now the middle of July and after six weeks of fighting, we had still not broken out of the hedgerow country of Normandy. The Germans were yielding some ground but it was at great cost to us in dead and wounded. Our command posts moved a short distance every day or two and each move meant more wire lines had to be laid. Moving along with our command post at that time was the famous war correspondent Ernie Pyle. He associated freely with the enlisted men as well as the officers and was quite beloved by all because he told our story so well. His favorite company was ours and he spent much of his time with us. His book "Brave Men" is mostly about the men in our regiment. If we were not actively engaged in fighting he would sit and chat with small groups of us. We often made a small gasoline fire and heated coffee in our sooty canteen cups along with Ernie who carried a typewriter instead of a rifle and wore GI clothing except without a helmet, using his familiar stocking cap instead. One night Gene Redfield asked him for his autograph but Ernie didn't have any paper handy so he took a French 5 Frank note out of his pocket and signed that instead. Many years later Gene generously gave it to me.

- - -

We were about 5 miles south of Carentan, in the province of Manche, France, when the wire crew and I returned to Company

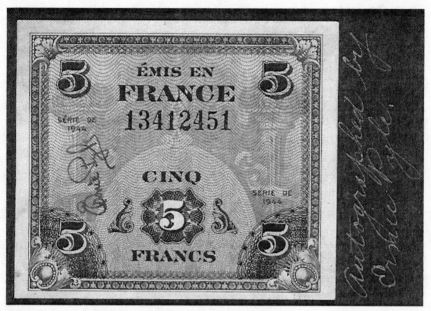

Small writing on this note is Ernie Pyle's autograph

Headquarters for the next assignment. There was a small group of switchboard men in an animated discussion and it soon became obvious to me that they were talking about some of our men being surrounded by Germans. I went over there immediately to see what the situation was and learned that our former switchboard location was surrounded and the men manning it were still there. If they were to be rescued, someone would have to rush past the Germans with a jeep, pick the men up and then try to escape. No one was willing to do this and they were being given up for lost.

I asked who was still back there and was told that Fred Braun was one of the three men trapped at the old switchboard location. Fred was one of my good friends and we had known each other since our training in England. I was still in the jeep when I instantly decided that I would be the one to make the rescue attempt. I knew exactly where the old switchboard was and the quickest way to get there. Darkness was coming on and that would be in my favor, so I made an instant decision to attempt to reach the trapped men. I yelled, "Tell them to hang tight, I'm on the way!"

The switchboard had been the one we were using in our previous location and whenever a move was made, another switchboard would be carried forward and wires run to it from the other units. When all the new lines were installed, then the old switchboard would be disconnected and brought forward for use on the next move.

Without lights, I raced back down the road, which I had traveled before. It led me to the wagon trail that passed by a farmhouse near the switchboard location. It had become dark enough that I could speed past the Germans without them being able to get off a good shot. I turned off the road onto the wagon trail, which went behind the farmhouse and then near the switchboard location, which was just on the other side of a hedgerow. A hole had been dug to help protect the switchboard men and I leaped out of the jeep over the hedgerow and into the hole. Amid the shouts of elation from the trapped men, I heard shots whizzing by my head.

They yelled at me to "Get down! The Germans are in the farmhouse and are firing at us from the second story window."

I said, "I just came from behind that farmhouse but apparently they didn't see me."

One of the men said "Well, we won't go by it on the way out."

I said, "Yes we will. That's the only way we can get out of this area. Get to the jeep now and we'll get outta here."

The sergeant in charge of the crew ordered the men to get the switchboard disconnected. Braun yelled back at him, "It's no good anyway - it's got bullet holes in it!"

I was worried that the Germans would move along behind the hedgerow on our right and attack us from there. They could easily move in close enough to lob one or more of their potato-masher grenades on us. I intently aimed my rifle at that part of the hedge with my finger on the trigger ready to squeeze it at the slightest movement. I yelled at the switchboard men who were trying to pick up some of the equipment, "RIGHT NOW! Get in that jeep right now. I can't hold these guys off if they come in."

They yelled back at me that they were heading for the jeep and ready to go. I ran back to the jeep, started the engine and jumped on the gas. It was very dark now and I tried to follow the wagon trail behind the house but about the time I reached the house, we slammed to a stop with a sharp jolt; WE WERE IN A SHELL HOLE. I floored the gas pedal but the wheels just spun. I yelled, "Everybody out and push. Fred, you lay on your face and push your hand on the accelerator!"

The jeep literally leaped out of the hole and we were on our way once again at full speed. The Germans had rushed to the back of the house and were raining bullets on us, but in the darkness failed to make a single hit. We had made our escape and yelled for joy. I was so elated I was quivering with excitement and considered that to be the greatest thrill I experienced in all of my time in combat. The other men swore their undying gratitude for what I had done and said they would make sure that I was given a medal for rescuing them.

- - -

In 1974, the American Federation of Television and Radio Artists sent me to a meeting in Hollywood, Florida as a representative of the Western Region. After the week-long meeting, my wife, Sylvia and sons, John and Tom, met me in Florida with the plan of traveling to New York on Amtrak and from there, into Ontario, Canada where I had many relatives. We stopped in Newark and Sylvia suggested that this would be a good chance for me to phone Fred Braun who lived on Lake Owassa in upstate New Jersey. Fred insisted we take a stopover in Newark and wait until he could drive down there and bring us back to his home. It was a lovely home in a beautiful location on the lake and Fred insisted that we stay a few days. Fred and his wife, Rose treated us with utmost hospitality while John

Fred Braun with wife Rose and four sons

and Tom played with Fred's children. Fred ran a company but did not go to his office the entire time we were there but rather devoted all of his time to entertaining us.

We had a wonderful time, and Sylvia expressed our feelings to Fred about how much gratitude we felt. Fred's response was: "Well after all, Jack saved my life!"

Sylvia had no idea what he was talking about and asked me, and though I had not thought about it in years it all suddenly came back to me. We reminisced about how he held the accelerator down with his hand while the Germans were shooting at us.

At the time, my Company Commander was Captain Francis W. Glaze. Now he is Frank Glaze, a valued friend. He paid a recent visit to me here in Seattle at which time we both learned about things that occurred during our time in battle which both of us did not know about. I asked him if he remembered the incident where I went back to rescue the men that were trapped in the old switchboard location. He said he did remember it. I told him the men I rescued had repeatedly asked me if I received the award that they had recommended, and if he knew anything about it. Did he know why I did not get it? Frank gave me a very honest answer. I did not get it because it was a "dumb" thing to do, according to him. My chance of succeeding in what I did was so small that it was not worth risking my own life. I was of value to the Company and had I not succeeded there would have been four men lost instead of just three. Furthermore, I did not have orders to undertake the mission and the odds were against me. I saw his point. We both agreed that sometimes considerations of humanity get in the way of good soldiering. I have since long pondered over the question of whether a good soldier can always be a humane one, or if a humane soldier can always be a good one.

Chapter 6

Armageddon & the
Falaise Carnage

...and, lo, there was a great earthquake;
and the sun became black as sackcloth...

Revelation ch.6 v.12

We moved to the area of resistance along the St. Lo to Perrier Highway. Here we were moving out of the bocage and the fields were open enough to be good tank terrain. It was difficult to lay field telephone wire where it would not be run over by tanks. In places where there might be tank traffic we had to dig the wires underground or stretch the wire overhead. To dig it underground would require spending too much time exposed to enemy fire, so our only option was to stretch it overhead. We were laying a particular wire along a paved roadway, which was lined with telephone poles. The poles were made of concrete and were square cornered. Little steps were cut up and down the pole on each side, which would make it easy to climb except that the Germans had wrapped them tightly with barbed wire. We decided that we would not have time to cut away the wire, which could tear away a man's skin if he slid down after being shot at or wounded. One of us would have to go up the poles in spite of the barbed wire. The nod went to me since I was youngest and most athletic. It was frightening but I started the climb and soon a bullet popped by my ear and then another and another. I pushed the telephone wire up and hooked it on the barbed wire and came down as quickly and gingerly as possible with the bullets flying close. I said, "I'm not doing that again!" To get the wire up on the next pole I asked the men to get about 50 yards away and pull. This would bring it up on the next pole and I could push it up further and hook it on with my rifle butt.

- - -

From July 10th to the 20th we were in various locations ranging from 4 to 6 miles southwest to southeast from Carentan. On the 17th of July Germans came pouring in with their arms up in surrender. The surrendering men all told the same story, "The war is over! Rommel is dead!" This most popular German general was in charge of the Normandy defenses and was known as a brilliant commander. The Allied air forces took advantage of this small break in German morale to drop leaflets urging Germans to surrender. Their leaflets were to be passes to safety. The truth was that Rommel's staff car was strafed by an American fighter plane and Rommel was severely wounded but not dead. The Germans fought to hold the line but were slowly yielding.

- - -

It wasn't until some time later that I learned of the situation that was occurring in Germany at the time. Germany was fighting the Russians on the eastern front, and losing ground on the western front, it became apparent to many of the high ranking German officers that Germany could not win. They knew Hitler would not negotiate a peace and so realized that he must be removed. Then the revolting officers could negotiate a peace with the allies on their own. This would save Germany from total destruction. The major conspiracy included in its leaders Colonel Count Klaus von Stauffenberg and General Ludwig Beck. Von Stauffenberg was to assassinate Hitler and Beck was to lead the new government.

On July 19th, when Hitler was at his Wolf's Lair headquarters near Rastenburg in northeastern Germany, the plot to kill him was executed. Von Stauffenberg planted a bomb in a briefcase next to Hitler under a table where Hitler was conducting a planning session. He then immediately left the room on the pretext that he had to make a phone call. Another officer bumped his foot against the briefcase and moved it beyond the end of the table behind the heavy table support. The bomb exploded but much of its force was deflected away from Hitler and although it killed several other officers Hitler escaped serious injury. Von Stauffenberg left the Wolf's Lair Compound and on his way he heard the explosion. He had an airplane waiting for him and flew back to Berlin thinking Hitler was killed. When he arrived in Berlin, however, he found that word of Hitler's survival had preceded him. Although the SS leadership was captured by the conspirators they were released when word came that Hitler was still alive. General Beck shot himself and the conspiracy fell apart. Von Stauffenberg was captured and killed. Altogether the Gestapo took 15 thousand suspects into custody and executed 5 thousand of them after a hasty trial.

Rommel did not have an active part in it but knew of the conspiracy and supported it, refusing to reveal what he knew of it to Hitler. His second in command, General Speidel, was actively involved and discussed it with Rommel. Speidel was not apprehended by the Gestapo. He took over Rommel's command in Normandy and therefore it was troops under his command that the 4th Division was fighting against when we broke out of Normandy. Speidel survived the war. The nucleus of the conspiracy had been mostly the Prussian military elite. Their extreme patriotism to Germany was greater than their loyalty to Hitler and they were determined not to allow Hitler to destroy their country.

Rommel was suspected of being in the conspiracy and was slated for death by Hitler. While recuperating at home from his injuries he was visited by two of Hitler's men who ordered him into their vehicle and forced him to take poison. This was, of course, by order of Hitler himself but nevertheless Hitler also ordered a hero's funeral and burial for Rommel. The German people could not be allowed to know that such a great military hero as Rommel could desire to remove Hitler. The anti-Hitler sentiment was still strong, however, and another conspiracy would have quickly developed had it not been for some unfortunate statements made by US President Franklin D. Roosevelt and soviet dictator Josef Stalin's determination to destroy Germany. Roosevelt said, "We shall accept nothing less than unconditional surrender," which is what the anti-Hitler forces were trying to avoid. This deflated the revolutionary effort and cost millions of lives as the war continued until Germany was destroyed and armistice signed in May of 1945.

- - -

By that time we were moving into a position five miles to the west from St. Lo and remained in that general area through July 24th. Here we were told we would be making an attack on the German position after a raid by heavy bombers. On the 24th we heard a giant rumbling sound off in the distance to the south-southeast. It was the sound of thousands of bomber planes, many of them heavies, approaching us from a distance. They passed to our east when bombs started falling, first about one thousand bombs from dive-bombers, and then thousands more as the heavies came over. I had never heard such a roar before. It was as though the whole world were exploding. Then after less than an hour the bombing stopped. The order came forward from the Regimental Command Post, "The attack is off, stay in your hole and hold your position!" I didn't know what had happened then but I found out later the planes were called back because some of the bombs had hit our own troops. That evening we were called together for a briefing on a new bombing and attack the next day. Our attack on the Germans would start promptly at 11 o'clock the next morning.

Early in the morning of July 25th I was in my hole on the crest of a hill looking down on the German position about a quarter-mile ahead. Some distance behind me was our Regimental Command Post in a stone thatched-roofed farmhouse. Suddenly an 88 shell passed just a few feet directly over my head. I spun around to see where the shell went and indeed it had hit the farmhouse. A faint area of dust and smoke welled up over the roof and I knew then that the building had been struck by an armor piercing shell or a dud. I knew the Colonel and other staff officers were in the building much of the time. I was particularly worried about Horace Sisk, who served as their clerk. I headed right back and Sisk saw me coming and headed out to show me his shoe, which had a section of the sole torn off. He said he was sitting with his legs crossed when the shell clipped the edge of his sole. It then ripped the leg off Capt. Mabry who was from another regiment and the brother of Major George Mabry of our Regiment. The shell pierced the stone wall in the center of the house, hit the opposite wall and dropped on the stomach of an officer who had been sleeping. The impact woke him and he promptly fainted when he saw the shell. Other officers rushed into the room and found him unconscious and yelled for a medic. Colonel Rodwell, who had been out of the building, returned at that time and seeing that the shell had hit the building rushed in to see Capt. Mabry with his leg severed and Sisk bending over him.

Rodwell yelled "What happened?"

"The shell came in that open window," responded Sisk. "It then crashed through the wall into the other room."

Rodwell rushed in to see what happened and saw the captain, unconscious with a 20 pound shell on his stomach, and commanded, "Get some water and throw it in his face!"

The captain came to, saw the shell and screamed, then babbled incoherently, obviously insane. Meanwhile Rodwell ordered a bomb disposal squad to get rid of the shell. Medics came in to take the captain back and we never saw him again.

Since we were to attack immediately after the bombing I thought this a good time to use the latrine. Of course there weren't any, so I did what I always did, which was to take my trenching shovel and dig a small hole. As I started I sensed a mighty roar coming from the distant south southeast much as I had heard the day before. Overhead the sky was filled with thousands of small strips of foil drifting downward. Known as "windows", these were dropped by high-flying aircraft and intended to interfere with German radar detection.

The great roar from thousands of bombers became louder and louder as they moved directly overhead. There were about 1000 dive-bombers leading followed by about 2000 heavy bombers. The dive-bombers were over their target about ¼ to ½ mile ahead of us, and each one went into its long steep screaming dive and released the bomb load. A wall of smoke rose up marking the target for the heavy bombers.

When the heavies came and released their thousand-pound bombs, an even thicker wall of smoke emerged and the shattering

American dive-bombers mark the target just ahead of us on the morning of July 25th

sound was as continuous as machine-gun fire. It became even more intense as the raid went on. The ground was shaking and shuddering, the noise was as though the Earth was exploding, and great black puffs of ack ack (anti-aircraft fire) from German 88s filled the sky. Here and there a heavy bomber twisted and plunged toward the Earth with smoke and flame bursting from its fuselage. Soon a parachute blossomed in its wake and then another and hopefully more. Another wave of bombers came over and dropped their bombs closer to us, dangerously close. Our attack would not start until the raid was over and that would give me a little time to take my trenching shovel and finish what I had started. I went a short distance from my hole, dug out three shovel fulls of dirt and lowered my pants. Then came a battering concussion, which knocked me flat. A bomb had exploded not more than 30 feet away and blasted me with dirt. I crawled back to my hole. The air was so filled with dirt and dust the visibility was zero. THE BOMBS WERE FALLING ON US!

I got to my hole while I could still find it. In the darkness of the smoke-filled air there came a vision. I WAS HALLUCINATING! A glaring terror-stricken countenance appeared before me. I had seen that face before. It was in Seattle when I stepped from my truck on Third Avenue near Union Street and I saw a man staring at me with a wild look. He walked toward me, stretching his arm out pointing his index finger directly at me. When he neared me he uttered in a quivering voice, "You will see ARMAGEDDON! YOU WILL SEE ARMAGEDDON!" I slowly turned and walked away while reflecting on the unusual experience. Now, here in Normandy so many months later, the scene was being played back to me in a most dramatic fashion.

Another bomb exploded nearby, and although I couldn't see anything, I sensed that it threw dirt over me and around my hole. Indeed, when the air cleared I saw that my hole was in the outer edge of a bomb crater. THEN ANOTHER EXPLOSION CLOSE BEHIND ME! The bombs continued to fall behind me as I heard the sound diminishing somewhat. The Regimental Headquarters must have been hit! WHAT HAD HAPPENED!?

I began to hear voices in the cloud of dirt "THE ATTACK IS OFF!" As soon as I could communicate with other men, I learned that our casualties were indeed heavy and we were too depleted to attack. Word reached us that the bombs that dropped at our Division

Headquarters had killed Gen. Leslie McNair. Also the bombs had dropped far enough back to kill an Associated Press photographer and two war correspondents. These men usually stayed well to the rear with the exception of remarkable men such as Ernie Pyle. Soon after getting the order that the attack was canceled we heard voices from the rear calling "THE ATTACK IS ON!" I grabbed my equipment and moved out, but of course, was puzzled by all that had happened.

- - -

I didn't learn of all that happened until nearly seven years later. In Ernie Pyle's book, *Brave Men*, I read his explanation of how the bomber crews were instructed to bomb the smoke line laid down by the dive bombers. Apparently, due to a missed or misused weather forecast, the smoke drifted over us, and the bomber crews, following instructions, bombed us. Max Strutz, whom I met as a fellow employee at the United States Weather Bureau in Portland, Oregon, was a bombardier on a B-24 Liberator bomber. Why were the bombers not notified that their bombs were falling short? Obviously, there was a lack of proper communication between the U.S. forces.

- - -

As I stepped out of my foxhole I saw a hole made by a dud less than eight feet away. An unexploded one thousand-pound bomb was at the bottom of the hole. Had this bomb detonated I would have been destroyed. When a dud hit the ground it made a perfectly round hole so deep the bomb itself could not be seen. These dud holes were scattered in numerous places between the bomb craters and one could only guess how many more were obscured by dirt thrown on top by nearby explosions. I had no idea there would be that high a percentage of duds.

As we moved forward we encountered small-arms fire, but many other Germans came forward with arms raised in surrender. We motioned for them to keep their arms raised and slowly move toward us as we took them prisoner. Many were wounded and most of them who surrendered were badly shaken and some in serious shock. Ernie Pyle wrote that he did not understand how a man could live through that bombing and not go completely insane.

We advanced almost one mile on July 25th and were now about four miles west from St. Lo. We learned from the prisoners that

Bomb craters after St. Lo breakthrough [Operation Cobra]. American front line bombing of the German positions which also hit the 8th Infantry Regt.

the German Panzer army opposing us was horribly shattered. Horace Sisk informed me early the next morning after the July 25th bombing that the attack which was to follow at 11 AM was called off because Col. Rodwell decided our heavy casualties left us too depleted. The decision was not made until nearly 11 o'clock. Following earlier orders, B Company had moved out sharply at 11 o'clock, thus they did not hear anyone call that the attack was canceled. When Rodwell heard this, he said we had no choice but that we all had to go, and the attack order was given. Sisk said the breakthrough was considered successful. Later he told me the 4th Division was pushing southward in the hole we created. This opened up an area that the U.S. 3rd Army, under Gen. George Patton, could attack through. Patton, himself, landed in Normandy on July 31st, six days after he ordered his troops forward.

Passing by the town of Marigny, on July 28th, 1944, we moved to six miles west-southwest from St. Lo against lighter German resistance. Altogether we gained about four miles that day. On the 29th we were about 10 miles southwest of St. Lo and attacking slowly toward the southwest. In the meantime the tanks of the 3rd Army were ordered to attack toward Avranches and then to take the city, and push another five miles southward before swinging west into Brittany.

The Germans Left behind a pile of barbed wire and stakes in their hasty retreat of Marigny

The Germans were alarmed by the sudden push to the south and west, but Hitler saw it as an opportunity to launch a lightning thrust into the American salient, reaching the west coast of the Cotentin Peninsula near Avranches. This would, in effect, slice the American salient in two leaving the south portion completely cut-off from their lines of supply.

Hitler ordered some of his best troops, two Divisions of S.S. Panzers, to lead the attack. This would have been a masterstroke and a disaster for the Allies had Hitler had the power to pull it off. The Germans had moved toward Mortain and captured it by August 7th. In the meantime the 4th Division had been moving toward Mortain and advanced to 9 miles northwest of there by the 5th. On August 6th our command post was five miles northwest of the city as we fought bitterly to stop the German advance. Thus the Germans were stopped about 10 miles short of their objective, the sea. Hitler had again brought on disaster by overextending himself.

When the retreat began, the German salient extended to the west for 40 miles but in places was hardly more than 20 miles wide. The British, under Gen. Montgomery, attacked southward from near Falaise, which is 18 miles south southeast from Caen. The Americans attacked northward from Argentan, closing the gap to 15 miles on August 14th. A panic retreat began by the Germans

American troops passing through Marigny

A German Tiger Tank knocked out by 8th infantry anti-tank forces

with the remnants of some 50 odd divisions racing for the gap, which was being held open by the 12th S.S. Hitler Youth Division. The majority did not make it and were killed, while a minority of survivors escaped through the gap and hurried back to form a defense line near the German border. By August 19th, they had crossed the Seine River and were on their way back. The space through which the survivors escaped became known as the Falaise Gap and the salient thrust within which the Germans were partially trapped became known as the Falaise Pocket. The carnage was indescribable. Fields were littered with dead humans and animals. Roads were crowded with dead Germans and destroyed vehicles. On the 14th we were fighting in an area about 12 miles south by east from Mortain. As the last of the German survivors escaped through the Falaise Gap, we began moving toward Paris.

Chapter 7

PARIS IN THE SUMMER

The last time I saw Paris,
Her heart was warm and gay,
I heard the laughter of her heart in every street cafe.

"Lady Be Good", Oscar Hammerstein II

By August 24th, we had moved to 20 miles south southwest from Paris pushing through several villages on the way. The pattern was almost the same in each case. When we moved in the French would round up the collaborators that were among them. The men would be shot, sometimes on the spot, and the young women who had affairs with Germans were brought to the center of the village and put up on a platform hastily constructed for the occasion. Their hair would be cut off to the scalp, and then a German swastika painted on their heads in black paint. Occasionally they would be stripped to the waist and a swastika painted across each breast. Then the girl would be transported on a cart somewhere outside the village.

While on the way on August 20th, some of the men in our company encountered a shot-down Canadian flyer that had been hidden by the French since he parachuted in on June 8th, two days after D-Day. They immediately brought him to me since we were both from Seattle. He was dressed in French farmer's clothing and his hair was long. We stared at each other for a moment and I felt there was something vaguely familiar about his face. He recognized me first and rushed to me and threw his arms about me saying "Hockey player!" I cried "Bobby!" It was Bobby Dodds whom I had played hockey against in Seattle. We had tangled in the last game we played against each other, but now we were the best of long lost friends. He told me of being hidden by the French and of fighting along with the French Underground. He told me of encountering

On our rapid advance toward Paris, infantry GIs often rode on tanks. The soldier in the foreground is carrying an anti-tank rocket launcher commonly called a bazooka

German soldiers who thought he was a Frenchman and sometimes giving them lights for their cigarettes. He also told me the French Underground said they had a way of getting him back to England but he opted to wait for us since he knew we were moving inland. After he was found by men from our company, American officers told him that he would soon be sent to England. At the earliest opportunity, I wrote my parents that our company had found him. My mother phoned his father and told him, whereupon his father notified the *Seattle Times* newspaper. They immediately published a story about our meeting and included both of our pictures.

He was returned and honorably discharged from the Royal Canadian Air Force and he came back to Seattle. Living in the United States, he was required to register for the draft. Shortly afterward he was drafted into the United States Army, but while still in basic training, the war ended and he was discharged. After the war I went to see him at a Ben Paris restaurant in Seattle where he was working as a bartender. He died a few years after our meeting.

- - -

During these few days while we were south southwest from Paris, we encountered a fabulous chateau with beautifully landscaped grounds. A French family was living there and a lovely young blonde lady invited some of us in. I was impressed with the huge recreation room near the front entrance. There was a magnificent billiard table and elegant furnishings with a most impressive landscape oil painting that covered most of one wall. Outside was a separate building that was a grotto filled with vaults. The names on these vaults were nearly all Casanovas, and I wondered if this were the famous Italian nobleman's chateau. He had at one time been head of the Paris lottery and built a chateau somewhere near Paris. I did not have time to find out more since our Company was preparing to move.

As we neared Paris I saw an old castle off to our right. Since the Company was stopping for a while, I hurried over to the castle, which obviously was very old, as it had a moat and a drawbridge. I was fascinated. I saw no sign of anyone there but knew I had to be very careful in case there were Germans hiding out. I went over the bridge and cautiously peaked inside. The structure was in excellent shape and had been well maintained. Most of the furnishings were still in place, yet it seemed to be vacant of inhabitants. On the second level there was a small room with papers littering the floor as though that room had been ransacked, but the other rooms appeared untouched. From my knowledge of French script, I deduced that the papers were lists of supplies for the castle. Each paper was signed by M. Chatelaine, whom I took to be the caretaker or a custodian of the castle. All the papers were dated in the 18th century. I was fascinated, but knew I could not stay in case the Company was ready to move again. The name and exact location of this old castle remains a mystery to me today.

- - -

The Germans were retreating rapidly now, and as we neared Paris during these days in late August, we encountered wildly enthusiastic welcomes at each village. Flowers were strewn in front of us and thrown over us. Girls ran for us with hugs and kisses. Wine was offered to us freely and what I remember best was a big, red, juicy tomato thrown to me by a pretty girl. I had not had a fresh fruit or vegetable since I left the U.S.

The French national anthem, "La Marseilles," was sung over and over again from morning until night. Before being taken into the Army, I had studied singing for the previous eight years and I had performed at numerous public affairs. I made an effort to learn all the words of the anthem, and singing it made me very popular with the French people. This was the Liberation and it was an enormous contrast from conditions in Normandy where there had been many pockets of German resistance. Across the front of some businesses in big letters was the word COLLABERATEUR, designating those who had done business with the Germans. Across the front of some other shops was painted ACHTUNG JUDEN as a grim reminder of the Nazi occupation calling attention to Jewish ownership. Most of the few passenger automobiles that were operating had the letters FFI painted across the sides. This was a designation of the French Underground organization that actively resisted the Nazis. They called themselves the Free French or the French Force of the Interior. It seemed to us that many Frenchman suddenly became members of the Underground when the Liberation took place. This is not to say that there were not many extraordinarily courageous Frenchman who took a very dangerous and active part in Underground activities before we arrived.

- - -

On August 24th we moved to where we were just three miles south of where the Paris airport is now. The weather was pleasant, and above a small dam near the town was a beautiful lake. The water surface was smooth, the scene was tranquil, and all I could think of was having a swim. I stripped down to my G.I. shorts, dove in and swam out to the center of the lake, and noticed a small dock along one shore. A girl was trotting toward it and waving at me. She wore a flowery, flowing skirt and sat on the dock next to the water with her legs dangling over the edge. I swam toward her looking up now and then, and saw that she was continuing to flirt. I saw a G.I. come running out of the woods as if he had been with her. She hoisted her skirt a bit for my benefit and he came charging toward the edge of the dock and almost plunged headfirst into the water trying to get a look, whereupon she laughed, jumped up, and dashed away. He caught up to her at the other side of the field, but she broke away running for the nearby woods with him after her. I saw no more of them and I continued my swim.

- - -

We were deliberately held near Orly for a couple of hours to allow the French Second Armored Division under General LeClerc, to reach Paris before we did and have the honor of being the official liberators of Paris. They took so long to get there, apparently partying along the way, that Gen. Bradley lost his patience and ordered the 4th Division to move into at least the southern portion of the city, thus making us the first American unit to enter Paris in World War II. The French Second Armored Division finally moved in and headed toward the center of the city and led the Liberation along the Champs d.'Elyses. Only one 4th Division Regiment was allowed to participate in the Liberation parade, but ours, the 8th Regiment, was ordered to move to where there were still a few pockets of Germans. Fearing that we would kill them anyway, these Germans chose not to surrender, and the result was street fighting. No civilians were on the streets during the fighting, but as we moved into the eastern part of the city there were no more Germans apparent, and crowds of Parisians were out to welcome us.

In the crowd I spotted a beautiful girl with long black hair, sparking dark eyes and a delightful smile. I saw that our company was moving into a park just ahead, so I pointed to her with one hand and pointed at the park with the other as I called out, "Meet you there!" She nodded in agreement. We stopped in the park. I badly needed to shave and clean up a little and asked if she would come back and meet me. She indicated she would and laughed when I took off my helmet and said I had more hair on my chin than I had on my head. I was delighted that she came back as she promised. She was definitely the most beautiful girl I had or would see anywhere in England or Europe. We chatted a bit and then I got the word our company was going to stay in the park for the night. I was

Rescue Told By Seattleite

JOHN C. CAPELL   SERGT. ROBERT DODDS

First details on how Sergt. Robert Dodds, former Seattle hockey player, was aided by the French Underground in escaping capture by the Germans after being shot down in a Halifax bomber have been received by a Seattle family.

Word of Dodds, a Royal Canadian Air Force machine gunner, came from Pvt. John C. Capell, a fellow hockey player in the junior hockey league here, now stationed in France, in a letter to his parents, Mr. and Mrs. Thomas Capell, 3722 38th Ave. S. W.

Capell, a West Seattle High School graduate, wrote in part:

" . . . Some of the men in our company picked up a flyer who had been shot down. When I heard he was from Seattle I wasted no time in meeting him. What a surprise it was to find that it was Bobby . . . He joined the R. C. A. F. in '41.

"We didn't recognize each other for a minute; then it dawned on us both at the same time. (The youths had played on different teams against each other.) He had changed a little . . . heavier if anything and had his hair cut to look like a Frenchman . . .

"He . . . hid out . . . with the French Underground . . . lived with a family who took good care of him. He became a member of the Maquis and lived comparatively free until we came and the town was liberated.

"He had . . . been to local cafes and bars . . . had even given lights to Germans who asked for them."

On September 21 Dodds was reported in a press dispatch to The Times as having been rescued. At that time his father, Capt. George Dodds, 240 W. Bertona St., pointed out he had expressed confidence in his son's ability to "take care of himself" when a previous announcement was made that Dodds had been shot down over enemy territory June 8.

ER 5, 1944.

Sergt. Dodds Back in Seattle, But It Seems Like a Miracle

It seemed no less than a miracle to Flight Sergt. Robert Dodds, popular young Seattle amateur hockey player and Royal Canadian Air Force tail-gunner, that he should be having dinner with his family last night in his home city.

It was so different from what might have happened that Sergeant Dodds gave all the credit for it to a kindly Providence.

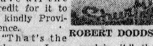

ROBERT DODDS

"That's the only way I can explain it," the young airman remarked.

For Sergeant Dodds was forced to bail out from a shattered Halifax bomber the night of D-Day plus-2, barely escaped capture, disappeared into the mysterious channels of the French Underground, fought with the Maquis and finally was able to rejoin his own outfit after Paris was liberated.

Bailed Out Near Paris

It was after 1 o'clock in the morning of June 8, when the invasion was well under way, that Dodds and six other men in the crew of his plane bailed out into the darkness somewhere south of Paris.

"I had the good fortune to land in an open space, some sort of field," Dodds related. "There were Jerries less than a city block away. I could tell that from the ack-ack, but managed to elude them. With my compass I made out which way was west, and I started out.

"Toward 5 o'clock in the morn- heard bells ringing, and I was near a village. There some men in the street, but ng told m not to ask them tions.

en I c to a house, a a re mansion, in fact, I went in. I made no mistake there. They took me in, and that was my introduction to the French Underground."

Joined Band of Maquis,

Dodds remained hidden there until searching Jerries came. Then his hosts helped him escape—how he will tell when the war is over —and thus he was escorted from village to village by kindly French patriots.

"They supplied me with clothes, brand-new clothes, too," Dodds said, "and when the opportunity came I joined a band of Maquis fighting the Jerries from the woods and in what they call mountains over there. And they were brave fellows, too. Just to illustrate their spirit, there was a young 19-year-old boy who declared his life was worth 20 Nazis, and he was out to get every one of them before he was through.

"We lived on raw meat and uncooked food, for the Jerries were too close for it to be safe to build fires. And when things got too hot for this Maqui warfare, we took refuge for a few days in some village."

Returned to Own Outfit

Dodds lived this life for nearly two months until advance reconnaissance units of the American Army appeared in the village which was then Dodds' headquarters. He rode to the outskirts of Paris in a jeep, and there encountered a Seattle friend, Pvt. John C. Capell, a former fellow player in the junior hockey league here, who last month wrote to his parents of the meeting with Dodds.

It was not many days later that Sergeant Dodds returned to his own organization. During a brief leave, he had an opportunity to visit in Gorebridge, Scotland, where his parents, Mr. and Mrs. George Dodds, and his sister, Mollie, were born, and where his grandmother still makes her home. He arrived in Seattle Friday night.

Dodds is a former Queen Anne High School pupil. His parents live at 340 Bertona St.

elated when she offered to show me some of the city. We started out together and got just over a block away when one of the men from our company came running toward me and said we were about to move out. I said, "OH NO! NOT NOW!" I thought about it a moment, and called back to him, "I'll catch up to the company in about two hours." He said, "You don't know where we're going any more than I do."

He was right and I wasn't about to lose the Company, so I made an agonizing decision. I turned to the girl and said a quick, "A'VOIR," and went running back to the Company which was already beginning to move. We moved to the town of Chelles, which is 10 miles east and a little north from Paris. We stayed at Chelles for two days and I was assigned to assist the Company mechanic doing minor repairs on our vehicles. It had been raining and crawling under the vehicles and lying in mud puddles had given the mechanic a case of pneumonia, so I had to take over. Early one evening I watched a French civilian truck park across the street from where I was working. Civilian vehicles all used alternative sources of energy usually charcoal gas, and most of them were trucks, each of which towed a small two-wheeled trailer. This carried a small stove that had a compartment above the wood-burning firebox in which to heat charcoal. The heated charcoal gave off a gas that was carried to the engine in hoses that ran along each side of the vehicle and into the engine. Later that night the truck was still there and appeared to be parked for the night, so I watched for the driver to come out early the next morning. When he came out he was carrying an armload of wood which he took to the trailer and did some things I couldn't quite see, but I saw smoke coming out from the stove. He did a few other things around the truck and then stepped in and drove away. Amazingly, the whole thing took less than five minutes.

- - -

We moved to the north and northeast from Paris and from September 2nd to the 4th we stayed near Itancourt, or about 5 miles to the southeast of St. Quentin. This was a lovely little town almost completely undamaged by the war. Here we were stalled while waiting for supplies to catch up with us. We had little to do during that period and enjoyed the three days we had there. First we checked around the area for Germans and found some in the woods nearby. A couple of Germans were shot and the rest made

Northern France, Southeastern Belgium, and Northern Luxembourg

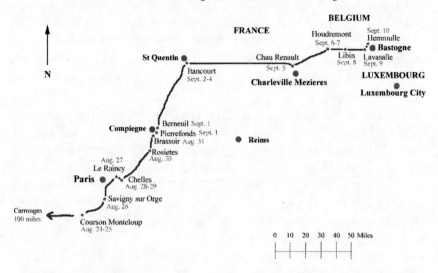

a fast exit. They left motorcycles behind and I decided to try one with a sidecar. I had plenty of experience with bicycles, but never a motorcycle and I thought it would be fun. Gene Redfield was there and got on a two wheeler while I rode the one with the sidecar. We were on a trail in the woods and I came to a fork in the path. I attempted to take the left fork but the three wheeler would not lean as a bicycle would. I was inhibited from turning, thus I went straight ahead and crashed into a tree. That was the end of the motorcycle with a sidecar.

Gene and I met a couple of 18-year-old girls, and one with auburn colored hair was especially attractive. We spoke to them with my limited French. I had picked up a very old French-English dictionary from wreckage in Normandy and I asked them to sign their names and where they were from on a blank page in the back. They did and added short notes, which I still have (shown below). After the 50th anniversary of D-Day I had a French Canadian hockey player friend, Mike Donaldson, prepare a letter to them or anyone in their families. I wondered if they were still living and if so if either one or both remembered meeting me. I enclosed copies along with short notes to the mayors of the French towns from which they were refugees. I mailed these to the mayors but never received a response. I thoroughly expected to at least hear from a family member or someone who knew them, especially when I sent copies of the notes they wrote describing who they were and where they had come from. I have never received an answer.

I then had a bit of a blow, which was completely unexpected. I was being transferred out of the Wire Section and into the Orderly Section. I would have welcomed being moved to the I and R Section but not to the Orderly Section. The latter was much safer and had better food and living conditions, but it was not as challenging. It also made me wonder whether I was being transferred out of the Wire Section for some reason. A couple of the orderlies assured

me that an officer had selected me, because that's the way they had gotten there. The orderlies all seemed like nice guys, and they were. The big problem was that Sergeant Charles Murphy was in charge, but from what I could tell Sergeant Bill Halsel, the staff officer's cook, did all the supervising and made all of the decisions. Sergeant Murphy did absolutely nothing, which is what I expected from what I had heard. He was a con man who secured the safest job in the Company, and for an enlisted man, had the best living conditions. Murphy was quick to tell me that I had been assigned to him. I told him I knew about him and that I had no respect for him. "So f---- you Murphy and don't try to give me any illegal or unethical order because I won't take it. You are a sergeant and I am a private so I must take your commands except for those!" Murphy said no more at that point and walked away but afterwards he was quite congenial and abided by what I said about unethical orders.

I was assigned to an officer who just came to our regiment. My job was to dig his foxhole, inflate his air mattress, and lay out his sleeping bag. I thought this ironic since I had done a lot of camping in civilian life and never had an air mattress or sleeping bag. I also did his laundry for him. After about a week he was moved to another regiment and I was temporarily without an assignment. However, Halsel requested that I drive the weapons carrier because it was very difficult to drive. The vehicle had to be double-clutched when shifting down and one had to double-kick the clutch when shifting up. Unlike the Jeep and most other army vehicles, some of these Dodge ½ and ¾ ton trucks did not have syncro-mesh gearing in the transmission. Whenever we moved from one command post to another, all the officers' equipment and supplies as well as their kitchen had to be moved. We used a captured four-wheel German trailer to carry this huge load, which had to be towed behind the straining weapons carrier. This required a trained driver and I welcomed the chance to use my skill.

Chapter 8

TARGET SIEGFRIED

Now that we have breached the great Atlantic wall,
comes now the Siegfried, the deadliest barrier of them all,
and on which the west defense of Germany relied,
Built by Nazi slaves, whose bonds held fast until they died.

Capell '03 On the attack on the Siegfried Line, September 1944

Murphy had somehow manipulated the acquisition of the ¾ ton Dodge weapons carrier for the Orderly Section. Whenever we changed command posts a vehicle of that size and power was required, but it was not necessary for any other Orderly Section duties. I realized the Company was badly in need of a vehicle like it for other jobs. I presented the idea to Bill Halsel that the weapons carrier be turned over to the Company for whatever duties it was most needed. It could still used by the Orderly Section when a command post move was made and also once each day to pick up the food for the officers' kitchen. I also proposed that I stay with it as driver. Halsel liked the idea and said he would immediately propose it to the Company officers whom he was sure would agree. My idea was accepted and was to be put into effect and I would no longer be assigned as an orderly. I was delighted and looked forward to the upcoming adventure, not realizing how dangerous it would be. I was also kept extremely busy barely squeezing time enough to sleep and eat. There were prisoners to haul, water to be obtained for the Company, and supplies and ammunition to be delivered.

Almost every day I made the rounds of the Company picking up water cans and carrying them to the water point, which was at a different location almost as often as we moved. The water point was equipped with a pump and filter, which would be set up next to a stream or river. The assembly was mounted on a trailer towed by a 2½ ton GMC truck. I would check with one of the company officers each day to get its latest location, which he got from Division Headquarters. Sometimes I would be shown a map but usually I had to commit to memory the directions. Should I make a mistake or get faulty directions, I could easily be in enemy territory. I got very accurate at following the directions because my life depended on it, but I was helpless when given inaccurate directions.

Most war prisoners taken by our regiment were gathered at Regimental Headquarters and picked up by the Division MPs. However there had been several MPs killed coming up to our Company, and insisted that we bring our own prisoners back. Now I would be taking over on that job. Often we would have prisoners to take back every day. There were many other missions to which I was assigned, so I stayed quite busy. When I took prisoners back I realized that being alone I was at great risk. Since the prisoners were sitting in the back of the vehicle directly behind me with nothing between us, the nearest prisoner could reach forward and strangle me. I was not allowed the extra protection of an escort or rifleman until some time later. However, it was partly my fault because I did not ask for one. I soon learned how to handle these prisoners by being very firm and confident. I completely avoided getting physical with them except one time when, impulsively, I struck one of them when he refused to obey. I was shocked at what I had done but did not dare show any outward sign of fear. I expected his associates to attack me so I had some anxious moments before I realized I would be safe, at least temporarily.

Prisoners were taken in bunches after we had made a successful foray. Late one morning there was a large number of them collected at Company Headquarters. I was urged to take back as many as possible, and was given sixteen of them. Since the back of the vehicle could seat just six men, and eight if squeezed in, I said I could possibly take ten but that would be all. The response was, "You have sixteen of them. Get them back anyway you want but get them back." Often when prisoners were particularly difficult to get back to a compound they were simply shot and killed, but I absolutely refused to do that. After a couple of minutes I came up with an idea that might work. Fortunately there were three Italians among them who must have been working in a German labor battalion. I felt they could be trusted, as the Italians had no love for the Germans now. One of them spoke fairly good English and said he had lived

Jack Capell with the weapons carrier to which he was assigned for the last six months of the war in Europe. The tarp over the back is the one he made and in bright sunlight clearly shows swastikas on each side. Also, the pistol he is carrying is the one he took away from a German shortly after D-Day and used as a sidearm in addition to his M-1 Garand rifle. The picture was taken a few days after the war ended in Europe

in Brooklyn, New York. One of the others carried a three-quarter life-sized, wooden carved statue of Jesus Christ. Facing forward, it was masterfully painted and looked uncannily realistic, showing Him nailed to the cross.

I said, "You can't carry that with you, you know." Whereupon, the Italians burst into impassioned pleas for the salvation of Christ. The Italian with the statue broke into tears. The Italian from Brooklyn said, "He would rather give up his life!"

I thought for a moment, then began ordering Germans into the back of the vehicle. When one layer was in, I sternly ordered the others to pile on top. One man understandably turned and faced me in protest. I stared directly at him and very threateningly ordered him to pile on. He did, and with the additional weight some of the others groaned in pain. I directed two of the Italians to sit in front with me. I told the one from Brooklyn to instruct the man with the crucifix to sit up on the hood with his feet on the front bumper and carry the statue on his lap. With the sacred icon looking forward he held the statue around the waist. Anyone watching us would see Christ in the lead with his followers, first the Italians and then two layers of Germans. The Germans, uncomfortable as they were,

Prisoners going to Division Headquarters MP compound led by Christ on the Cross. The one on the hood is an Italian as were the two in the front with me. 13 Germans were piled in back

strained to see the sight. Some even smiled. I started the truck and began heading back to Division Headquarters. We attracted attention and someone must have phoned Division that we were coming. As we neared the Headquarters, men lined the roadway. Some took their caps off and crossed themselves; some dropped to their knees. Some just laughed.

- - -

Going back to Division Headquarters to get supplies for the Officer's Kitchen was a daily task. The job was easy enough but was somewhat overwhelming to me when I saw fresh food reserved for officers. I longed for some fresh food that I had not had since I left the States, with the exception of the tomato near Paris. There was one huge stack of big delicious oranges, I decided since it was near the exit to snag one on the way out. The cross-eyed storekeeper was watching me. I never knew which way he was looking. He yelled, "Drop that!" I yelled, "The hell I will and mind your own f----- business!" There were some MPs just outside the tent and they immediately came in and I grudgingly dropped the orange and left. I was surging with anger but then philosophically said "THIS is the Army."

When I went to the water-point and on various other missions, I often went through unfamiliar territory. I knew the enemy could be anywhere and when I came to a house or a building near the roadway, I kept my pistol aimed at windows, doors and the far edges of the buildings. If the enemy were there and armed with a rifle, I would not have stood a chance. Fortunately no one did shoot at me from one of the roadside places. I was lucky but I didn't know how long my luck would hold out, I needed an escort.

- - -

We left Itancourt by September 5th and moved east, moving once every day for the first half of September. By September 7th, we crossed into Belgium and were about 13 miles north from Bouillon, France. As we moved along this area and near the Meuse River we encountered a series of trenches dug in World War I. They were considerably eroded and looked like long, deep ditches. We had seen other World War I trenches when we were in the vicinity of St. Quentin. I felt a bit of a thrill to think I was participating in a part of history just as the men who manned these trenches. I mused over what those ditches would have looked like 25 years before.

Much was different for the doughboys of that war compared to the
GI's of this war. We both experienced the mud and filth, the torn
and shot up bodies, and the absolute misery of war. "War is hell,"
said Sherman and how right he was. In World War I the doughboys
operated in groups, whether in the trenches or on the attack. In
World War II, GIs were taught to always remain dispersed so that a
shell or a grenade would not kill more than one man. The grouping
together idea of World War I was a carry-over from previous
wars and probably has its roots in the idea of the Roman phalanx.
Tank warfare was not yet much of a factor, for the development
of tanks was in its very beginning. The horse-mounted cavalry
was no longer effective, but many generals were trained when it
was still an efficient tool, and it was still a factor in their thinking.
The idea of being physically together led to war songs being sung
together. Therefore, songs like "Over There "and "Tipperary" did
not develop with us.

As we moved across northern France, reaching Belgium on
September 7th, we encountered no organized resistance. The
Germans did, however, continue firing at us using mostly heavy
guns but no rifles or machine guns. We began seeing more of a type
of German weapon flying overhead. It was their newly developed
"buzz bomb" or V-1; an automated and unmanned flying bomb.
From each launching site the bombs would be launched at the rate
of one per hour. They came low overhead, so close that we shot at
them with our rifles. One time an American fighter plane swooped
down and buzzed one of them so closely that the prop wash from
the plane turned the bomb around and headed it back toward
the Germans. As the bombs came over they wobbled wildly and
zigzagged in their path until their guiding mechanism got them
under control and directed toward their target. Their targets had
been somewhere in England but now as we pushed eastward they
were often directed at larger cities to our rear such as Antwerp,
Belgium. They were propelled by a ramjet, which was very noisy,
and controlled by a gyroscope navigation system. The V-II was a
rocket-propelled bomb launched from farther behind the German
lines. It flew so fast and so high I was never able to see one. Other
men in our company, however, said they could see them. Neither
of these flying bombs was ever a direct threat to us.

The next of Hitler's new wonder weapons was the jet propelled
fighter and bomber airplane. When one came over it was the first

pure jet plane I had ever seen. It flew high and very fast and also seemed to be no threat to us. Later they came over almost every day, sometimes several at a time. They rarely fired at troops near the front lines and we didn't even bother to take cover when they came over.

I was very busy during this time since I had to move the officer's trailer and the orderlies and their equipment almost every day, as well as retrieve the officer's food from Division. I also had to find

Larger streams and rivers were often forded by the use of pontoon bridges established by combat engineers

the new water point, which moved nearly every day. We passed through Bastogne, Belgium on September 10th with little resistance. Then we moved on to the east, passing south of Malmedy and by the infamous road-junction at Baugnitz, Belgium on September 12th, 1944. Later on during the Battle of the Bulge, it was here that the Germans massacred a large number of American prisoners of war.

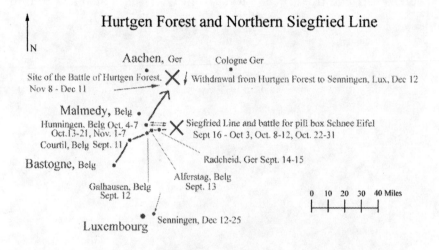

Hurtgen Forest and Northern Siegfried Line

We continued on until we reached the German border on September 14th and crossed 16 miles southeast from Malmedy, Belgium. Here we met heavy German resistance as we moved closer to the Siegfried Line, the nearly impenetrable line of defense, which extended all along Germany's western frontier. The rain continued for much of that time and the mud was horrible. Combined with the mud, the smell of the dead was sickening. Anti-vehicular mines were buried in the roadways and eventually removed. Some GIs had removed a number of mines and stacked them along the edge of a roadway that was at the bottom of a muddy hill. If a GI vehicle slid on the mud and went just a little off the road it would be the end of that vehicle plus a sizable part of the landscape. We now moved into the Schnee Eiffel Forest of Germany, which is an extension of the Ardennes Forest of France, and a section of the Siegfried Line ran through these forests.

The Siegfried Line, which ran for 940 miles along Germany's western frontier from near Kleve in northern Germany to near

Americans at the back door of a captured German pillbox on the Siegfried Line

Basel, Switzerland, consisted of a backbone of approximately 20,000 "pillboxes", tank dugouts, and trenches.

The pillboxes were essentially bunkers for one or more guns which could fire through the front of them. Their walls and roofs were at least ten feet thick of reinforced concrete and shaped like a huge half clamshell, although more steeply sloped upward in front. To the best of my recollection the overall dimensions were about 40 feet on a side and at least 20 feet high in back, which was a straight up-and-down wall. These installations were usually built on a hillside sloping downward toward the enemy and molded into the terrain, so that they looked like part of the slope. With vegetation growing over them they were hardly distinguishable even from a short distance away. There were ports in the front of them through which the guns fired, and in the back of the pillbox at the bottom there was an entry port which consisted of a steel or iron door. In the rear part of the box there were sleeping quarters with steel bunks that were hinged so they could be swung up against the wall. The description I have just given is typical of the first pillboxes I saw and I believe all of the others in this part of the Line were similar, wherever they could be molded into the slope of the land. Trees that interfered with the field of fire were removed. The pillboxes were designed so that together their guns would cover every inch of terrain in front of them.

In between the pillboxes were covered machine gun nests and all of the area in front was heavily mined. A short distance in front of the line of pillboxes and machine gun nests were the "dragons teeth", anti-tank defenses which were a series of concrete obstacles, each one in the shape of a tetrahedron or a four-sided pyramid about four feet high, as I remember. These were in rows about five or six deep and were continuous along the Line, except for periodic openings to allow the Germans access to both sides of the Line. If enemy tanks were to pass through, they must go single-file in the narrow openings that were left. The narrow line of tanks would be exposed to heavy fire from the pillbox guns.

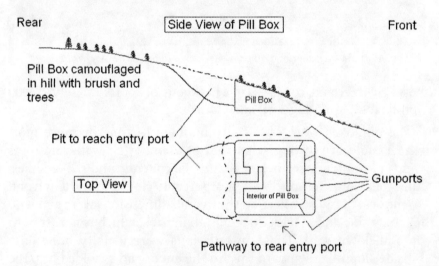

Attacking such a formidable line of defenses was not easy. Bombing even with direct hits would only crack but not shatter the pillboxes. And shelling, even with heavy guns, could not destroy them in a reasonable length of time. Flame-throwers could be effective but would require a man to get close to the pillbox and that was almost suicide. However, some men did just that. Another method was to use a pole-charge which required a man to mount TNT or dynamite on the end of a five or six foot long pole, fuse it,

Dragon's Teeth form a line in front of the pillboxes

prop it against one of the open gun ports, light it and try to take cover or run back. This was, of course, extremely dangerous and could only succeed if the riflemen with him kept a continuous and heavy rifle and machine gun fire against the pillbox. The first pillbox to be captured was taken by one of the regiments of the 4th Division which was able to move a 155mm gun close enough to get a line-of-sight shot at an open gun port on the pillbox, and then followed it with more shots. The Germans inside were killed, knocked senseless or badly shaken and easily taken prisoner.

In less than 24 hours after attacking we had penetrated the highly touted, so-called impervious, solid line of Hitler's western defenses, the most formidable line of defenses ever concocted in the history of the Western World. The 1st Division also claimed the distinction of being first as they also broke through the Line the same day, which was September 16th, 1944. We remained on or near the Siegfried Line for about 17 days and were in an area centered about 19 miles southeast from Malmedy.

Pillboxes were favored spaces to locate the Regimental Headquarters because a more secure spot could not be found, and since our company had the captured German generator truck, the pillbox could be equipped with lights. It was necessary, of course, to block any light that might get out through a port or a crack in the pillbox. I went into the first pillbox we captured to prepare it for the officers to move into. This meant checking for any hazards, particularly unexploded ordinance or booby-traps. There was a crack right down the center of the roof and I rigged a tarp to direct any water that leaked through off to one side where it could be caught in a can or a bucket.

The name of the man who ran the generator truck was Virgil McGehe. He was a friendly easy-going guy who asked me to periodically leave him a can of water when I returned from the water point. I was happy to accommodate him and in appreciation he showed me where he had a cache of brandy stowed and said I was quite welcome to have a drink any time I wanted it. As I said before I was very cautious about having a drink whenever we were in combat but a small swig was enjoyable. I crawled up into the truck and made my way forward, being very careful to avoid touching any of the machinery although in complete darkness, I found the brandy and had a drink. Suddenly a bright flashlight was on me. Startled, I quickly turned. "Do you know what you are doing Capell?" It was the voice of Captain Glaze, our Company Commander. WHY DID HE SAY THAT? WHAT WAS HE LOOKING FOR? Then I noticed that on the control panel one of the switches was slightly open, I quickly realized that I must have bumped against the switch when I moved by, knocking it a little out of position and the lights in the pillbox went out. Hoping my guess was right I responded, "I think I have found the trouble, sir, and should have it fixed in a moment." I quickly closed the switch I suspected and breathed a great sigh of relief when I heard a voice from near the pillbox call "LIGHTS ARE ON!" Fortunately, Captain Glaze thought I was in the truck looking for the problem and had no idea why I was really there, nor did he suspect that I was the one who caused the problem. Over 50 years later I had an enjoyable dinner with Frank Glaze in Seattle and asked him if he remembered the incident. When I told him the real story he said he never suspected what really had happened.

- - -

The weapons carrier I was driving had a removable wooden set of frames over the cargo bed so a tarpaulin could be stretched over it. The cover was so ripped that it served little purpose. I found a large piece of blue-gray canvas in a German warehouse. Earlier I had found a large needle that I had saved for just such a purpose. Then, after fashioning a sail maker's palm out of a piece of leather I was ready to sew. After cutting the German canvas to size it made a very neat fitting cover with a flap to go over the driver and passenger. I was very proud of my job until the first time I took it out. When I came back, men in the Company area laughed and said you had better not take that out again. I got out to see what they were talking about and discovered that when about 50 feet away, with the light just right, one could discern a large swastika painted on each side. After all my work I decided not to abandon it, but because the swastika was very faint and could only be seen in certain light, I chose to ignore it. At least I was sure I had the distinction of being the only driver of an U.S. Army vehicle with big swastikas painted on each side during World War II.

The fact that I was busy with the weapons carrier sometimes from sunrise to sunset did not excuse me from doing overnight sentry duty. When it was quite cold it was miserable duty, but nevertheless it was extremely important for the safety of everyone in the Company. One sometimes had to use every faculty to keep awake and alert, even when one felt dead tired with eyelids weighted down by window sashes. One night when the Regimental Headquarters was located in a pillbox I was assigned to sentry duty by its entry port. With but a single sentry available to guard the pillbox, I thought this was not only an extremely dangerous place to be, but it was of little protection to the occupants of the pillbox. Behind the box where the entry door was, the ground was hollowed out, and the forest grew right up to the edge of the hollow. The Germans knew the immediate area well since they had just left there, and a patrol could easily find their way through the forest even in the dark and come right up to the rim of the hollow. From there they could throw a grenade down to the back door if they knew the guard was there, or much worse yet, they could throw a lighted flare and open fire on the sentry, then rush down and into the pillbox and slaughter every occupant in it. It would have been much wiser to have the sentry posted at the top of the hollow near the pillbox, and especially so if he were in a hole at least partially camouflaged. It is true that the near complete darkness may have prevented him from seeing someone approaching the rear entrance, however, if sticks were spread around the entrance way it is not likely that a person approaching would not be heard.

It was about midnight when all of these concerns were flashing through my mind. I was standing guard in the back of a pillbox. It was very dark and I could see absolutely nothing, but was listening very intently and heard nothing. SUDDENLY I WAS STRUCK VIOLENTLY ON THE SHOULDER! I was knocked to the ground and my rifle flew out of my hands. I frantically searched for the rifle in the darkness, and hurriedly pointed it toward a sound of scrambling around on the ground. I was a split second from firing at the noise when I thought I detected a faint sound that did not sound like German. Just in time, I held my fire and again I heard a sound, this time it sounded like a faint, breathless and raspy "MAJOR ". Pointing my rifle directly at the sound I moved toward it. I still could see nothing but whatever it was on the ground was squirming as though it were trying to get up. Then I distinctly heard, "Major Todd—--- I fell!" Then I realized it was Major Todd of our Regiment and he had fallen. The only place he could have fallen from was the top of the pillbox, and that was at least 20 feet above. The breath was knocked out of him and I helped him to his feet. I then assisted him into the pillbox where the staff officers had been sleeping. Since I had been yelling, "HALT!" at the absolute top of my voice, I'm sure they were all quite wide-awake by that time. I said, "Major Todd has fallen and may be hurt. Will someone please tend to him?" I heard someone come to his side so I went back to my sentry post. My adrenaline was still flowing fast and I'm sure those inside the pillbox got quite a fright.

It was a terrifying thing to think I had nearly killed one of our staff officers, although it would have made little difference whether it was an officer or an enlisted man. It would have been a horrible burden for the rest of my life. I was gratified that I had not panicked. I was relieved that I acted as I did. Therefore it was a shock to hear a story that was circulating around the Company. The word was going around that an officer had walked up over the top of the pillbox and fallen off the back right on top of the guard, who went running into the pillbox screaming. When I heard that I seethed with fury. I could not imagine how such a story could have gotten started. Had I gone running into the pillbox I would not have heard Major Todd identify himself nor would I have been at his side immediately to assist him. No one thanked me, nor did anyone seem to know that I was the guard who was involved in the incident. I realized now exactly what had happened. Major Walter Todd, who was the Regimental G2 (Intelligence) Officer, had been visiting another headquarters when in the darkness he tried to find his way through the forest to the Regimental Headquarters pillbox. When he got to it he did not realize he was there, so instead of walking around the side of it, he walked directly up over it and plunged off the edge. He happened to be right in the center of the top and therefore fell directly on me.

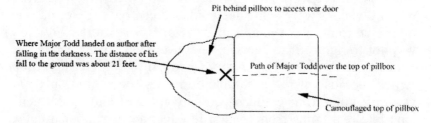

Pit behind pillbox to access rear door

Where Major Todd landed on author after falling in the darkness. The distance of his fall to the ground was about 21 feet.

Path of Major Todd over the top of pillbox

Camouflaged top of pillbox

When I re-established contact with Frank Glaze many years later, I asked him if he remembered the incident. He said indeed he did, and surmised at the time that the occurrence was just as I described, and he commended me for my presence of mind in not killing Major Todd. I felt much better after hearing Frank Glaze's opinion. I knew that Walter Todd had survived the war because I saw his name listed in the "Ivy Leaves," the publication of the Fourth Division Association. I got his address from another member, Leo Jereb. I then prepared an audiotape recounting the incident and mailed it to him. I was curious to know whether he remembered. Immediately upon receiving the tape he telephoned me and said he knew what the tape was going to be about as soon as he started it. He said it was his most frightening and harrowing experience of the war. He was sure he was going to be shot and credited me for saving his life.

- - -

We moved back from the Siegfried Line to a town called Hunningen, which appears on some maps as Hunnange, in Belgium, where the Germans were still holding out. It was a daily chore for me now to haul back German prisoners. Hunningen is located about 12 miles east by south from Malmedy, or about 11 miles northeast from St. Vith, Belgium. These names were both quite well known later on in the Battle of the Bulge. We were near Hunningen for a miserable 33 days. Death and destruction were everywhere. The rainy season had started and the mud was pervasive and deeper in places than I had ever seen it. Because there was fighting in the same general area for so long the smell of the dead was horribly sickening. The days were getting shorter and the nights much longer since it was November 7th before we moved out of that area.

As usual, we had no idea where we were moving, and the Division command made an intense effort to keep the Germans from finding out. We were being shifted to the Hurtgen Forest, where whole divisions were being depleted. Secret from the Germans and unknown to us, was a phantom army of U.S. soldiers whose job it was not to fight but to deceive. They were the 23rd Headquarters Special Troops of the 12th Army Group; often called the "Rubber Army" because of the inflatable dummies they commonly used. Dummy tanks that could be quickly inflated and assembled to look like real tanks from even a few feet away, rubber inflatable artillery guns and different types of realistic looking Army vehicles were used to look like they were all part of a real army. They often were used to impersonate the 4th Division in which cases they were painted with 4th Division markings. Many of the men in the unit had, in civilian life, been trained as artists such as Ed Biow, thus were quite capable camouflage experts. All of this was accompanied by realistic sounds such as tanks moving or whatever was appropriate. I knew nothing about this special unit even though they impersonated us many times until I received a phone call from Ed Biow, who was living in Lake Oswego, Oregon at the time. Ed Biow was one of these Special Troops from the time they landed in Normandy until the end of the war in Europe. He had been trained as an artist. On November 7th, 1944 the 23rd Headquarters Special Troops were busy confusing the Germans while the 4th Infantry Division was preparing to move into the Hurtgen Forest. In Early December, just prior to the outbreak of the Battle of the Bulge, this phantom Army was again impersonating the 4th Division but were withdrawn just before the German counterattack began. Had they not been withdrawn, they may very likely have all been killed or captured.

Chapter 9

The Black Forest of Death

*Beautiful that war and all its deeds of carnage
must in time be utterly lost.*
"Reconciliation" by Walt Whitman

The bloodiest battle, in which the 4th Division was engaged, with the exception of Normandy, was the battle for the Hurtgen Forest. This was a German forest, the center of which was 13 miles east-southeast from Aachen and is a northeastern extension of the Ardennes and Schnee Eiffel Forests. It was hardly more than 50 square miles of fir trees and hardwoods planted closely in rows. Just beyond its eastern edge is the Valley of the Roer River where dams had been built probably by the Germans. These were considered a serious threat to our advance if the Germans opened the dams and flooded all of the low-lying land downstream. Therefore it was felt to be essential that we capture them before that could happen. We could have attacked the dams indirectly by going around the forest, or we could go directly through. However, the forest itself was a formidable defensive obstacle. The defender had a great advantage over the attacker because of the thick trees, the steep hills, the deep gullies, the wet and stormy weather and the blindingly dark nights. It took the U.S. 1st Army over three months of heavy fighting and thousands of dead and wounded. More than 10,000 men of the 4th Division alone were lost during the month of November. At least three other American Army divisions also fought in the bloody forest with thousands of their own casualties. The countless numbers of Germans who died there is a figure that is unavailable, but it must have been staggering.

We thought of how much easier it would have been to bypass the forest and attack outside the edge. It was fairly open country and would have been much harder for the Germans to defend. The only reason I had ever heard that would explain why the Command chose to go through the forest was that they were simply mistaken on how difficult it would be for us to take it. There may have been some concern that if the forest were bypassed, the Germans could keep an Army concealed there. Once the German Army was bypassed, they could have attacked us from the rear after cutting us off. No matter the reason, it was simply a blunder to do what we did.

- - -

Although the first of the divisions of the American 1st Army started fighting in the Hurtgen in early September, they were followed by two more divisions, yet little progress had been made by the time the 4th Division began moving in on November 7th. The area was very sparsely populated with a few small villages and some tiny hamlets connected by narrow, mostly unpaved roads. The hardwoods were mixed with a type of fir common in Europe, normally 75 to 100 feet tall, but when we arrived most were broken and mangled from shellfire. The first of the 4th Division regiments to move in was the 12th Infantry, followed a day later by the 8th. By that time the 12th was already in serious trouble with two of their companies surrounded by Germans. One of their men was wounded and found by Germans. They stole the food and cigarette rations he carried and then wired his body to a booby-trap and left, obviously expecting to blow up the medics or anyone else who came to help him. Cold, wet, and unable to walk, this man lay wounded for 72 hours. Incredibly, he was still conscious enough to warn his rescuers of the booby-trap. According to MacDonald, who recounts his story in his excellent book "Battle of the Hurtgen Forest," the man survived.

There were but a few narrow, muddy one-lane roads through all of the forest and some firebreaks through which a vehicle smaller than a truck could squeeze between the trees. The Hurtgen Forest was cloudy nearly every night while we were there. The tiny bit of skylight that faintly hinted at illuminating the clouds was almost entirely blocked by the trees. The only possible way to navigate a vehicle was to look straight up at the sky, instead of straight ahead. I found I could often discern enough skylight between the trees to follow a firebreak (a narrow roadway through the forest for fighting fires).

I was never called upon to do sentry duty while in the Hurtgen because I think the Command realized that no one could find his way in such complete darkness. Except for the almost continuous artillery shells bursting in and above the trees, not much else happened during the night, which lasted almost 16 hours. The high elevation of much of the forest made it vulnerable to sleet and snow and especially miserable at night.

American medics treating a wounded GI in the Hurtgen Forest

One late afternoon while moving to a new location in the forest, I passed a woodcutter's house. I noticed there was a barn and a chicken house nearby, so when I reached the place where I planned to dig my hole for the night, I walked back to the house and into the barn and gathered a big armload of straw. I then remembered that I should check the chicken house before leaving, so I set down the straw and looked for an egg. I found one and, as usual, I cracked it on the bridge of my nose and dropped the contents into my mouth. An egg, even though raw, was a delicacy since I had not had a fresh egg since leaving the States. They were issued to the staff officers but the enlisted men got only small tins of canned ham and eggs in the K-rations, or on occasion when the kitchen truck was with us we sometimes got powdered eggs.

I picked up my armload of straw and continued. When selecting a place to dig a hole, except for the broken branches and treetops that littered the forest floor, one had only to avoid the old stumps, which were cut off even with the ground. This was because whether it be peacetime or wartime not a splinter of wood was wasted by the woodcutters or the peasants. I quickly dug a hole and then borrowed the crosscut saw we passed around for such purposes. I proceeded to cut a small tree and cut it into lengths to lay across the top of the hole. First I lined the bottom and the sides of the hole with straw and laid a blanket over the straw. Then I laid the wood I cut over the hole, leaving an opening for me to enter. All I had to do now was to shovel a layer of dirt over the wood as a protection against shell fragments and shrapnel from shells hitting in the trees, or what we called "tree bursts." I now had the finest hole I had ever prepared in all the time I had been in combat. Being mid-November there was a long night ahead and I was going to be warm, comfortable and safe. It would be pure luxury. Eagerly I climbed into the hole and it was perfect. I quickly settled down and went to sleep, but then awoke realizing that I had not relieved my bladder for the night.

Disgusted with myself I climbed back out of the hole and realized I could not leave it without losing it in the darkness. I decided to lean as far away from the hole as I could but I kept my left toe hooked on the edge. However, I lost my balance and pulled my left toe forward. DISASTER! I LOST THE HOLE! I reached back with my toe and the hole wasn't there. Frantically I dropped to my knees and searched with my hands. IT WASN'T THERE! I searched and searched and searched and it wasn't there. In despair I gave up and sat down leaning against a tree. In the meantime with tree bursts firing their fragments and shrapnel downward, I spent the rest of that very long night exposed. It was the best, safest and the most luxurious hole I had ever prepared and I HAD LOST IT! At daybreak there was enough light for me to find the hole. It was about 30 feet away from the tree against which I had been leaning for the previous hours of darkness. It was too late to use it, for the company was preparing to move to a different location in the forest, and I spent the next day busy with assignments on the weapons carrier. Late on the following day I had to hurriedly prepare a hole without even getting time to go back and get the straw.

- - -

Most of our regiment suffered horribly in the forest with the type of fighting we had to do. My assignments spared me much of that. Finding the water-point and going back to Division was not comparable to the misery being suffered by our rifle companies. My job was not without danger, however, considering that I was traveling alone much of the time, through a forest infested with the enemy, and with shells exploding in the trees and casting fragments and shrapnel down and all around me. Of the three regiments in the 4th Division there were 36 Rifle companies, twelve in each regiment, and it was among these men that the highest casualty rate occurred. In just one five-day period ending on November 20th, some of our Companies were down to less than fifty men able to fight, which meant that less than 30 percent of their men had survived. Our regiment, the 8th, and the 22nd had suffered about 1500 casualties during that five-day period, and about 500 more of what were called "non-battle" casualties, which included trench foot and battle fatigue. Men with battle fatigue or shell shock were absolutely useless and often dangerous, and had to be removed

Two walking wounded heading for an aid station in the Hurtgen Forest

from the fighting. Those with trench foot could not even stand and therefore were evacuated. Rarely did we ever see them again.

Many of the men who suffered from trench foot had their toes and sometimes their feet amputated. Even Sergeant Charles Murphy did not escape the trench-foot problem and had to be evacuated. As did many of the men, Murphy did not take his shoes off for days at a time for fear of the enemy breaking through, he was afraid that without shoes he would not being able to run as well. I neither saw nor heard any more of Sergeant Murphy after that until I read of him in Ernie Pyle's book *Brave Men*. I made it a point to take my shoes off every night for a while. I also always kept two pair of socks, one on my feet and one inside my shirt to dry, and then switched them periodically. Since dampness and cold were the cause of the malady, the system seemed to work, however, I did come close to having a problem a couple of times when my toes began to darken. Massage seemed to help, so I made a special effort to do it as often as possible and my feet eventually improved back to normal.

- - -

A forest always had brought to my mind aromas of pine needles and pleasant memories, being accustomed to the coniferous forests of the Pacific Northwest. The Hurtgen Forest was a coniferous forest but there the similarity ended. In peacetime no doubt it was similar in that it had that same delightful forest aroma and lovely appearance. The trees however were smaller and there was absolutely no underbrush. I think the lack of underbrush could be attributed largely to the fact that the local population gathered all burnable material for their stoves, including the pinecones. An immense transformation took place when the peaceful forest was turned into a battlefield and a scene of horror.

Once stately firs that stood straight and tall were now bent and broken with grotesquely mangled branches. No tree escaped unscathed, and, instead of forest underbrush, there were bodies of dead men, smashed helmets, discarded articles of bloody clothing and empty shell cases. And there, a quite usable blanket, except for the blotch of dried blood in the middle of it. Charles B. MacDonald in his book *The Battle of the Hurtgen Forest* tells of a man in the forest who kicked a bloody shoe out of his path and was horrified to find a foot was still in it. Nearby was crumbled concrete, once part of a German gun emplacement with its tangled, distorted reinforcing rods pointed upward. This was once the pristine pine forest of ancient times that later on became the park-like domain of the woodcutter, dense with trees on sharp and rugged terrain, but natural and beautiful. Now after just a little more than two months of fighting it was a hideous scene of death.

- - -

My travels in the forest were nearly all done during the daylight hours, for it was virtually impossible to move around in darkness. Headlights were a luxury only to be used when there wasn't an enemy watching. Our vehicles were equipped with blackout lights but even they were not advisable unless one wished to make himself a target. One day our Mess Sergeant came up to the Company for some reason and stayed too long to get back in daylight. The kitchen truck stayed back just to the rear of Division Headquarters since it was not used during any of the time we were in the Hurtgen. The cooks, having no other job to do at the time, were used in the Graves Registration Unit (GRU) picking up dead bodies of both Germans and Americans. After a quick attempt to check their identification they loaded the bodies on quarter-ton trailers towed by jeeps. The Sergeant was concerned about getting back to where he was staying by the kitchen truck and asked for help, so I was assigned to get him back. I started back on the narrow muddy road to Division. There was one spot where the roadway was cut along the upper portion of a steep ravine and I knew it was going to be very difficult to navigate in the darkness.

I cautiously made my way along the first half of it when suddenly the vehicle plunged forward, tipped to the right, dropped down in front and leaned precariously. Obviously, a large artillery shell had taken out a section of the road. The Sergeant made a hasty attempt to abandon ship before rolling down the bank, but when he started to step out he realized there was nothing below him. His grasp on the seat frame went into a death grip as his feet dangled below and the frequency of his cries of alarm increased.

I realize that if I reached over to try to pull him back into the vehicle it would likely tip over. I had to abandon his rescue until I could secure the delicate balance of the vehicle. I needed to get to the winch cable on the front bumper and drag the cable out to a tree and secure it. If I stepped out, however, the removal of my weight from the left side of the weapons carrier might be enough to send it tumbling down into the ravine. I very carefully climbed around the windshield and on to the left front fender, then stepped onto the left corner of the front bumper and from there released the winch cable. Now the problem was there was no tree or anything within ten feet to which I could secure the cable. There was nothing left to do now but to get to the nearest tree as fast as possible hoping that the teetering vehicle would not roll over. Luck was with us but, in the meantime, the Sergeant had died a thousand deaths, and how he had wished he had joined the Navy. By using the winch I got the vehicle past the bad spot and onto the road again and we continued our nerve-wracking journey. After delivering my passenger I still had to find my way back. When I got to near where the road was out, I proceeded ahead on foot until I found its exact location. When I got as near to it as I dared, I winched the vehicle to trees in order to pass over the destroyed roadway.

- - -

The Battle of the Hurtgen Forest ended a little less than three months after it began, and the 4th Division fought for nearly all of the last two months. From the time the Division first entered the forest they tediously moved from one edge of it all the way to the other. From a high point one could see the Rhine River Plain and the towers of the city of Cologne, Germany. Replacements for the Divisions could not keep up with the casualties so finally the 4th Division was to be withdrawn. By that time the battle for the Forest was nearly over. The officers' kitchen was disassembled and loaded onto the four-wheel trailer along with the officers' bed rolls, bags and supplies. We hitched the weapons carrier to the trailer. Bill Halsel and I climbed in front as Johnny Cotts, Jerome Nowak and Watkins loaded in back along with their blankets and packs. At last we were leaving the Forest, and leaving no fond memories behind.

Chapter 10

WACHT AM RHEIN

Whoso sheddeth man' s blood, by man shall his blood be shed.

Genesis ch.9 v.6

We left the Forest and traveled up and down the steep hills on a narrow muddy road that finally led us out of the Hurtgen. As happy as we were to be moving out of the area, it was a miserable trip. We towed a heavily overloaded trailer behind a straining little truck on a slippery and very muddy roadway. Obviously the brakes were not designed for such heavy work, and it wasn't long before they were seriously overheated. I was forced to travel much faster than I wished in such mountainous terrain in order to keep up with the rest of the convoy. The brakes became so hot their braking effect was almost completely gone and we couldn't notify the vehicles ahead of us because they were traveling much faster than usual and we couldn't catch up. The convoy was hurrying along a road that ran along a ridgeline that, in places, was quite visible to the enemy. I was just very lucky that I had such a congenial group of men with me. Nobody griped and they all seemed to realize that I was doing the best I could. At least three times the vehicle ahead of me slowed so suddenly that, without any braking ability, I could not slow fast enough to prevent smashing into the vehicle ahead. I was forced to drive off the road into the bushes and small trees to stop. Fortunately they were not large trees and we were able to continue after getting back on the road. The men in the truck behind us knew we were in trouble, but we had no way of notifying the vehicles ahead. Had I pulled out of the convoy, since none of us had any idea where we were going, we probably would have gone into enemy territory and all been killed or captured. All of the men with me agreed that we should try to stay in the convoy. At long last the terrain began to level a bit with lower hills further apart. Finally the brakes began to cool enough that some braking action returned, and we all breathed more easily.

- - -

The trip had taken us nearly the whole day. It was evening on the 12th of December, 1944 when we arrived at our destination, which was near Senningen, Luxembourg. The first job, of course, was to dig a hole and cover it. We were now six miles east northeast from the center of the City of Luxembourg. A little farther to the east was the German border, which ran by the Moselle River and was along a portion of the Siegfried Line of German defenses. The Germans who manned this portion of the Siegfried Line, according to what we were told, were very low-grade troops. They were from a Penal Battalion, which were men released from prison to fight as infantry and were very poor soldiers. Therefore, sending us opposite such a weak force was like a vacation from heavy combat. This was designed to give us a chance to get replacements for our depleted companies and rest a bit. Later on when I saw the mangled, dead bodies of some of these Penal Battalion men I reflected on the thought that they had traded a life in prison for death. We too had some men in our company who had chosen to take their chances as combat infantryman rather than spend their life in prison. Their identities were kept secret from the rest of us unless they, themselves, chose to talk. One of them I became friendly with. He seemed quite cheerful and affable and confided in me that he had been serving a long sentence for manslaughter and was offered probation on the condition that he serve as a combat infantryman.

- - -

I then got some very exciting news! I was going to get a 48-hour visit to a hospital camp in Arlon, Belgium where I could get hot showers, hot kitchen-cooked food and a cot with sheets and blankets. I was elated at the thought. I was to go on December 15th and 16th. There were eight of us selected to go, all veterans of the Hurtgen Forest and several previous battles. I, like most veterans in our Company, had not had a single day off since before going into combat. The last day I had free was in England early in May, over seven months before. With a little bribery (a carton of cigarettes worked well for this) we convinced the driver from the Quartermaster Corps, who came up to get us on the afternoon of the 14th, that we should leave as soon after 9 PM as possible. It would be between 35 and 40 miles to Arlon over roads marred by shell holes and bomb craters. We should be there by midnight and this would give us a comfortable sleep for a few hours on a nice cot before getting up to a warm shower and an early morning hot breakfast. Our stay at Arlon was to be for just two days but it might as well have been for the duration. I was so happy about the prospect of two days in paradise.

We were able to leave shortly after 9 PM and it was a happy bunch of guys that headed toward Arlon, bouncing over the war-scarred roads that night. The hospital camp was in a sturdy stone building, neat and clean inside and furnished with individual cots with sheets, blankets and pillows. I had almost forgotten there was such a thing as a pillow as I had not used one for over six months. I was so excited by all this luxury that I did not know if I could even get to sleep, but I found it to be absolutely no problem and I think I was asleep within seconds after I hit that lovely pillow.

First thing in the morning was the hot shower, and it was to be my first indoor hot shower since I had left the United States a year before. And then on to a delightful breakfast of pancakes and cooked fresh eggs, and it was the first time for either of those in at least the last six months. Strange why a man would want to leave this paradise even for a few hours, but I was curious to see what the town of Arlon was like. "Hound Dog" Jones had the right idea however. He valued what he called his "quiet hour," and there was nothing that Arlon could offer that would be better than where he was. Not following the sage advice I got from Hound Dog, I wandered into town after breakfast, and found nothing of particular interest except for one shop where I was able to buy some souvenirs of the town to send home. I had saved a couple of cartons of cigarettes from my rations, which could easily be converted to Luxembourg money. Very few shops were open and those that were had little to sell to anyone who did not have ration tickets. There were a couple of saloons and I had a beer in each. I found out that at least one of them had a brothel operating upstairs. I had absolutely no desire to give them my business nor do I think any other fellows I was with patronized a brothel while we were in Arlon.

We had superb noon and evening meals, and after dinner I spent the evening writing letters. There were other activities right there at the camp such as chess and table tennis. I played a couple of games of the latter before going to that nice inviting bed. I had another wonderful sleep and got up to a hot shower and headed down for breakfast. All eight of us arrived about the same time and sat together. We were all eagerly looking forward to the day, but sad that it would be our last. Most of us agreed that there was no better place to be that day, other than home of course, than right there in the camp. There were various challenges at chess and at table tennis for we had a busy day planned. There was also a nice library in case one wanted to relax with a book. Happily, we went on back to where our cots were and there was an officer who had just come in.

"I have orders from the commander of this camp that all of you men are to immediately load up on a truck that is waiting for you outside," he announced.

Like water blasting through a bursting dam, we simultaneously blurted out words of protest to the effect of,

"WE HAVE ONE MORE DAY HERE!"

"ATTEN-SHUN!" the officer shouted. "I am sending for the Colonel." The officer left and shortly afterward the Colonel arrived.

"I don't know what the problem is but something is happening at the front and you are needed immediately."

A couple of our men voiced their protests audibly. "I'M NOT GOING BACK! WE WERE PROMISED TWO DAYS HERE!"

With a stern countenance the Colonel announced "The orders I have don't leave any room for argument. If you don't go out and load on that truck immediately you will be considered deserters. In that case YOU WILL BE TAKEN OUT AND SHOT!"

That was enough to get our attention, and we gathered up our things, went out and climbed into the truck, but were not happy. Even Hound Dog, who seldom used profanity, seemed to have quite a stock of it for this occasion. The weather had turned cold, very cold quite suddenly, and with the wind blowing through the tarpaulin over the back of the truck we were miserable. This was the beginning of the coldest winter in Europe for many years. The day was December 16th, 1944. This was the date Hitler had selected for his great counterattack, which he called "Wacht am Rhein" and what became known to us as the Battle of the Bulge. We knew nothing of this and continued to bitterly gripe about our two-day rest being cut to one, and about the biting cold wind blowing into the back of the truck. We were not issued winter clothing and, in fact, none of us who were veterans ever had been.

Soon we were to stop at a fuel dump, which was a place where gasoline was stored and made available for refueling. There was a shack there and the men inside had a little stove to keep them warm, so we hustled in to get a little heat. They had a radio playing that was reporting something about a major German counterattack and one of the American divisions that was reported annihilated was the 4th Division. We could hardly believe what we were hearing. The town of Echternach was reported captured by the Germans, and we knew it was in the 4th Division sector. We all immediately began quizzing the driver who said "I just got my orders. I don't know anything about anything else." We all wondered where we were going if our Division was wiped out. Obviously the report was erroneous, although the company that was in Echternach had nearly all of their men killed or captured. The Quartermaster Corps driver, who incidentally was a black and, I'm sure, didn't know anything about the situation as he probably wasn't told any more than we were. The broadcast we heard was supposedly the British Broadcasting Corp (BBC) but their information was obviously wrong.

- - -

The reason I mentioned our driver being a black man was that we seldom saw any, being at the front most of the time and among infantrymen. The Army was completely segregated at that time, and there were none in our entire Division, or in any other infantry division that I ever saw. Most of them, I believe, were used in the Quartermaster Corps and various supply and railroad divisions. I well remember one black artillery unit firing eight-inch Howitzers that targeted on us for hours one night. White officers, however, were directing the firing. The black men felt bad about their shells falling on us, even though it wasn't their fault, and shared their nice hot pancake breakfast with us. The reason for blacks not being used in the infantry (at least as far as I ever saw or knew of) I never understood. At least they did not have to serve as infantry GIs, who had the most dangerous, lowest paid, poorest fed jobs, with the worst living conditions in the U.S. Armed Forces.

- - -

We loaded back onto the truck in a much more pensive mood. We no longer felt the cold as much, nor did we think as much about leaving our comfortable hospital camp. My mind was swirling with concerns about what might have happened to my friends - Redfield, Braun, Sisk, Kakoski, Cotts, Halsel, Sepic, Kuhn, Jetton, Leon Wall, the wonderfully talented producer of oil paintings, and the rest I felt such an affection for and had bonded with over our many days of combat. We had no way of verifying the BBC report. It wasn't until long after the war had ended that I learned much of what had happened that day. The 106th Division which was one of the three divisions just to the north of us had so many men killed and captured that there were not enough left to rebuild the Division with replacements. The other ones nearest to the north of us retreated and had severe casualties. The 4th Division had heavy casualties but did not retreat and held fast on the southern flank of the German breakthrough. But all of this we didn't know as we rode back in that truck. However, as we got closer we heard the sound of guns getting louder, and now besides the almost continuous firing of artillery we could hear the sound of machine guns and rifles. When we left to go back to the rest camp, the guns were relatively quiet but now we were listening to the sounds of a full-scale battle. To our surprise we returned to Senningen, Luxembourg which was the identical area from which we left. We had not retreated one inch and no one that I knew of in our Company was killed. Furthermore, the entire 4th Division had not given up any ground anywhere, although there were heavy casualties in and around the town of Echternach.

Frank Glaze, who was our company commander at the time, said the commander of our Division; General Barton issued a strict order that there would be no retreat in the 4th Division at any time under any circumstance. In other words, we were under strict orders at all times to fight to the death. Glaze feels that this was an important factor in the 4th Division having the highest casualty rate of any American Division. Statistics on casualties were recorded by the Service of Supply and the figures they give for casualties in all of the 65 divisions that fought in Europe show the 4th Division as having the greatest number, which was approximately 35,000 men. Not only did we have a strict policy of fighting to the death, but also were used as an assault division in the major battles of Western Europe.

We were taken to near the center of the little town of Senningen, which was just six miles east-northeast from Luxembourg City, and there we were met by a dozen or so men from our Company. That was when we learned we had lost no men from our Company and had not retreated. The 22nd Infantry Regiment of the 4th Division, which was in and around the town of Echternach, had not retreated either, but they had many dead and wounded.

We were almost immediately herded into the cellar of a building where an officer briefed us on the situation. We were informed that the Germans had broken through to the north with armored columns and so far had not been stopped. The 4th Division had not retreated but there was danger that we would soon be surrounded on three sides. We were essentially cut off from the rest of the 1st Army, of which we were a part. Communication with them was extremely limited because radio contact was difficult to establish, and if it were the enemy could easily jam it. Telephone wire communication could not be maintained because Germans surrounded us. I was very concerned that I could not get a letter home since I was afraid that my parents might have received the report I heard on BBC. I later found the mail was not getting through and my father, on his deathbed at the time, had no way of knowing the report was wrong. My parents did not know if I was wounded, dead or captured.

The officer who briefed us ordered us to inspect our rifles carefully and make sure they were in perfect operating condition and, if not, get new ones. The Supply Sergeant was there with a supply of rifles to be issued if needed. From a stack of hand grenades we were to take as many as we could carry. We were also to take six one-pound blocks of TNT and a small supply of dynamite caps. In order to explode a block of TNT, a fused dynamite cap must be inserted. The fuse is then ignited. The explosive was used to loosen frozen ground so a foxhole could be dug. One dynamite cap was then taped to the outside of the water-filled canteen bottle that hung over our hip and was secured to our ammunition belt. Since a man need only carry one block of TNT at a time, the extras had to be stored, so I let the men in the Orderly Section use the compartment just behind the driver's seat in the weapons carrier. The reason for the dynamite cap being taped over the outside of that water-filled canteen bottle was that it would explode very easily if something struck it. If one fell backward on it, it would almost surely explode. We felt it better for it to explode on the outside of a water-filled can than directly against one's rear end. We knew we would soon head toward the front, which obviously was not very far away judging from the sound of the small arms fire and intense shelling. A serious battle was raging just ahead of us. Consequently, as soon as we were briefed we were sent forward to fight.

It wasn't until after the war that I learned what had been going on behind the German lines just before we left for Arlon. The penal battalion, which was opposite us, was a subterfuge to mask what was really happening. For the previous few nights the Germans had been moving in some of their best troops opposite us. They were mostly SS units and Panzer battalions which included the best of what Hitler had left. Civilians who came over to the American side reported on all these troop movements, but amazingly, the American Army Command chose not to believe them or to attach sufficient importance to what was going on. The German plan was for these units to suddenly attack on the morning of December 16th and thrust in one massive tank attack to reach as far as Antwerp, Belgium. This was Hitler's last great gamble. The 4th Division was the southernmost division in the path of the German attack. Largely because of our "no retreat" order, we yielded no ground to the powerful German attack. Our units, particularly those in and around Echternach, were determined to fight to the death. Our casualties were heavy but the 4th Division held its ground. Thus the thrust toward Luxembourg City was stopped dead and the Germans were denied this important communications center.

There was absolutely no opportunity for me to write a letter even though I was very concerned about how my parents were handling the news. One could not write in the darkness of night and with only eight hours of daylight during which we were busy every minute, what chance was there to write? And then there was the problem of whether mail was even getting through. I asked Redfield if he knew and he said he had no way of telling, except that there was none coming in. I thought of the last time I had seen my parents which was just one week short of a year before. I saw them for just a matter of hours and I had to go "AWOL" to do it, but it was well worth it as it was the last time I would see them before going overseas and into battle.

Things were going well for the 4th Division on the battlefronts from what I heard the next day. Furthermore, I got some good news personally. It wasn't like getting a letter from home but it certainly solved a problem for me. I was to have a man to ride with me, and that was going to be a great help on some of my more dangerous missions. His name was Mike Cammarote, a sergeant from E Company of the 8th Infantry's, 2nd Battalion. Mike had been wounded in action and after leaving the hospital he was sent to a replacement camp where he heard about what I was doing. He volunteered to ride along with me as "shotgun" and was surprised I had not been killed trying to do what I was doing. I realized I had been very lucky so far and considered Mike to be literally a "lifesaver." When going through a town or by a building near the road, Mike and I devised a system. As we approached a building, Mike kept his rifle trained on its far corner, then just before getting to it, I would slow down and he would run around the back of the vehicle. He stayed crouched down as he got to the hood, all of the time keeping his rifle trained on the left side of the building. If there were any Germans waiting to ambush us, Mike would have a very good chance of getting them before they got us. We used that system a number of times. And in several instances Mike had to shoot. However, we agreed that if they showed any sign of surrendering we would take them prisoner, and fortunately for all concerned most did surrender when they were caught by surprise. Mike came from New Jersey and was a tailor before the Army took him. He was a jolly fellow and a great companion and undoubtedly he saved my life on more than one occasion.

- - -

The weather stayed very cold and windy but dry from December 16th through the 20th. I finally got a chance to talk to Horace Sisk on the 17th to find out what he knew. He told me the situation was extremely serious to the north of us and that we were essentially cut off completely from the rest of the 1st Army. The American 3rd Army, commanded by Gen. George Patton, was headquartered in Luxembourg City just six miles away from where we were. Sisk said he believed the 4th Division was now, or soon would be, considered to be in the 3rd Army under Patton (officially, I believe, the transfer would be made on December 19th). Sisk said that from what he overheard, it had been determined by our intelligence that there were an estimated 25 different German divisions including 11 panzer (armored) units with some being SS panzers. The notorious 2nd SS Division was a part of the attack force. Also, among the panzers was the crack Panzer Lehr Division. The breakthrough had taken place along about 50 miles of the Ardennes front and was mostly into Belgium and northern Luxembourg. The breakthrough area extended from near Monschau in the north, southward to just north of Echternach, Luxembourg where the 4th Division was able to hold and form a southern shoulder. Of course, after all these years, there is no way I could remember exactly what Sisk had told me, but I have surmised from later reading about the battle that the facts related above are completely truthful or very close to it.

Just before it all began on December 15th, 1944 there was very little action along the 4th Division front that we knew about. Opposite us was the German Penal Battalion. To the north along the Ardennes Forest front there were five American divisions thinly spread out along a 50-mile front. Two of these divisions were badly depleted from having just suffered many casualties in the Hurtgen Forest. The weak German units on their side of the line were deceptions, a fact completely unknown to our command. Also unknown were the troop movements going on behind the German lines, such as the tanks, armored vehicles, artillery and parachute and infantry divisions being amassed in the forest under the cover of darkness. There were a total of 25 divisions of the best troops Hitler had available to him, including SS units—panzer and parachute divisions. Because Hitler's Wacht am Rhein had fallen far short, by not reaching Antwerp, Belgium where it would have secured an Atlantic seaport and divide the Allies, it was a disaster to the forces he had remaining.

- - -

The snow began on December 20th and continued for most of the time through Christmas Day. The sky remained too cloudy for effective aircraft operations until after December 25th. To the north of us Germans were advancing rapidly westward, led by their tank units (the huge and powerful German Tiger tanks mounting 88 mm guns were especially deadly). We were astounded at the viciousness with which the Germans fought, and at the equipment they still had, such as the Tiger tanks and the 88 mm guns.

The weather also became an important factor for it not only eliminated our air support but it also slowed us down in such things as digging our foxholes. No wonder we were so surprised to hear that in the Army newspaper, the "Stars and Stripes," an article stated that all U.S. service personnel would be served a kitchen-cooked hot turkey dinner on Christmas Day. We laughed to think that some reporter thought such a thing could be done for an infantry outfit that was holding the line against the Germans. We also knew that some public relations staffs got quite imaginative at times, especially those of General Patton. As Christmas Day got closer however the rumor persisted, and to our astonishment our company kitchen truck arrived, and parked in the snow about 3/8 of a mile back from where we were.

Early on Christmas morning, even though it was snowing lightly, I could see the kitchen truck behind us in the valley. There seemed to be plenty of activity around it and now I was sure there was indeed going to be an attempt at Christmas dinner. Obviously we couldn't all leave our positions and go back and have dinner together, so what was the plan? I soon found out. A non-commissioned officer came up and gave us orders to walk back to the kitchen truck one by one. When the first man got his food, the second one would be selected to go back. Of course that meant the first man could not eat his food until he brought it back to his hole. When my turn came I took my canteen cup and mess kit lid (which is all we normally kept, except for the knife and spoon), slung my rifle on my shoulder and headed back. At the kitchen truck I got a couple of pieces of hot turkey, a scoop of reconstituted dehydrated potatoes with some sort of gravy from a mix, a scoop of turkey dressing and a serving of cranberry sauce as well as a canteen cup full of coffee. Indeed! WE DID GET OUR HOT TURKEY DINNERS. But there was a catch. The mess sergeant, in no uncertain terms, ordered each one of us when we got our dinners to go immediately back to our holes before eating anything. Now that was going to be a challenge. That meant I would have approximately 3/8 of a mile to travel up and down on a rugged, rocky forest floor over low but steep hills, covered by snow and ice on top of broken trees and branches. After a very cautious, tedious trek I arrived at my hole with everything relatively upright, spilling only about one-third of my coffee. I set the mess kit of dinner down on the snow beside the canteen cup, while I set the rifle down and brushed away a little fresh snow to make a place to sit inside my hole. That once hot dinner was history as such, but I was hungry and it looked good, although I may as well has just taken it out of a refrigerator. However, I was not expecting the cranberry sauce to be frozen to the bottom of the mess kit. The short German SS bayonet that I carried for a trench knife helped chisel it out.

The Germans must have been having their Christmas Day also because, although their artillery fire continued mainly to let us know they were still there, the machine-gun and rifle fire was almost nonexistent on both sides. I'm sure many of those German soldiers thought of the happy Christmas times they had had when they were boys growing up and how they missed their families on this special day. Christmas was always a huge holiday for my family, even though my father had to be at work on many of them during the Depression. My mother and I sometimes met him where he worked, just to be with him, and then ride home with him. As a boy, Christmas was the happiest day of the year for me and, I suspect it was for my mother and father also. I was deeply homesick, but treasured those past days so much I felt warmth inside when I thought about them. How ironic and how wrong it was for us to be fighting and killing on that or any other day.

- - -

When the sun rose on December 26th there was an appreciable amount of blue sky showing. How we had longed for a clearing sky throughout all of those cloudy days since the Germans began their breakthrough on December 16th, for now the Air Force could help us. As the Germans advanced, now almost 50 miles beyond where they started on the 16th, their supply lines were being stretched and certainly by now they were in dire need of gasoline and ammunition. Now that air power was on the scene the Germans' supply problem became enormous. They had relied upon capturing Allied gasoline dumps to refuel from, but now the Americans were burning the gas before they could get there. Air power was attacking the German lines of re-supply. The German fortune had turned. Hitler's Wacht am Rhein had failed!

Now instead of losing part of just one army, Hitler was losing a sizable portion of five. He was nearly back to where he started the attack on December 16th in just a little more than one month. The day after Christmas, now in Patton's 3rd Army, we made a rapid move toward the German border and took a number of prisoners, which kept Mike and I busy for most of the day bringing them back to the Division MP compound. Our Regimental Headquarters that evening was now at Wecker, Luxembourg which was 14 miles east northeast of Luxembourg City. The city itself was now completely out of danger of being captured by the Germans, as was Hitler's initial plan. The Luxembourgers rightfully showed their gratitude to the men of the 4th Division for saving their city, and erected an impressive monument in the city to those men. Men who were in the 4th Division in World War II, who have visited the city even in recent years, are still treated like heroes when they visit.

- - -

The weather remained cold through December 27th, and then began to moderate. My hole was dug on the eastern outskirts of Wecker and over half a mile from the nearest German defenses. It was close to a rather nice Luxembourg house. Since the Allied planes were back flying again on December 31st, I thought little of it when a fleet of eastward-bound heavy bombers began appearing. There were high, thin clouds but the first planes were quite visible and appeared to be American B-17 heavy bombers. I thought this a good opportunity to heat up some water and shave. I went into the house and found a small pot in the kitchen and intended to put in some tap water and take it outside to heat it over a small can of burning gasoline. However, the sound of bombs whistling down caught my attention while I was pouring the water. Since I was one-half mile or so west of the nearest Germans, I thought it very strange that the bombers should be releasing their bombs already. Suddenly the entire house shook as a bomb struck nearby. Pans and dishes came falling off the shelves. I ran outside the house and back to my hole. Our own bombers were bombing us again. Could they be our own pilots too?

Now the bombs were falling directly on the town of Wecker where most of our Company men were. We later learned that our own bombers had hit us again. In our Company alone two men were killed and eight others wounded. One of them who was killed was my good friend Sepik, from our Company's I & R Platoon. He was also one of the first men I met when I joined the Company in England. In this bombing, all of the bombs dropped on us, none reached the Germans. On July 25th we were hit so hard because the smoke line drifted over us, but with regard to the shortfall on this bombing I know of no explanation.

New Year's Day, January 1st, 1945 was bright and sunny, but we were in no mood to celebrate after our loss of such fine men on the previous day. The New Year's Day weather being so fine, the Air Corps was out again, this time with twelve P-38 fighter planes. They came swooping down over us. THEY WOULDN'T DO IT TO US AGAIN, WOULD THEY? We weren't sure, so we ran for the big cloth panels with the brightly colored American insignia, and spread them out. But they DID IT AGAIN! This time they strafed us with their guns, and in spite of the panels, they did it AGAIN AND AGAIN! We never heard a further explanation on that one either.

Obviously, we had a love-hate relationship with the Air Corps. We loved them when we needed them, and hated them when they made us their targets. In all seriousness, we did feel very bad when we saw an Allied plane get blasted out of the sky and go down in a trail of smoke and flame, and cheered when we saw parachutes open.

There is a sequel to the incidents of December 31st, 1944 and January 1st, 1945. The first I learned of anything about the incident was just a few days later from Horace Sisk who was in Regimental Headquarters at the time. He told me that within a couple of days after January 1st an unmarked command car came up with a load of officers in American uniforms but with no identifying insignias. Sisk told me these officers were from the Air Corps and for their own protection their identities were kept secret. It was over fifty years later when I found out from Frank Glaze that Lieutenant Rooks, in command of the I & R Platoon, was so upset about losing one of his best men that he came charging toward the Regimental Headquarters with pistols in both hands. Capt. Frank Glaze and Major Walter Todd restrained and calmed him. Feelings ran high when people on our own side killed our men.

- - -

We held our position near Wecker for the first week of January 1945 during which time the cold weather and blizzards began again. Early one morning Mike and I went out to start the weapons carrier and had no problem getting it started, but when I went to drive away, it would not move. The vehicle had four-wheel-drive and had chains on all four wheels but we were frozen to the ground. One wheel on the front and one wheel on the back were turning when I put the vehicle in gear, and although the wheels turned, it went nowhere. Mike and I used our trenching tools to chisel away the ice from around the wheels and we were soon on our way.

The 4 -wheel-drive ¾ ton Dodge weapons carrier was the best wheeled vehicle we had in adverse weather, such as deep mud or snow. It carried a winch on the front bumper to get out of really bad situations, or to assist other vehicles. It was far more versatile than a jeep, which was underpowered in pushing through deep mud or heavy wet snow. The ¾ ton Dodge had a relatively wide traction tire which was good for getting a grip in mud or snow, but, because of the large tread, it was poor in getting traction on a hard, slippery surface, such as ice. During blizzards, Mike and I spent much of our time winching jeeps out of snowdrifts.

Some of the land in the area of the western Rhine Valley was a floodplain and there were dikes with narrow roadways on top. These roadways became nothing more than a surface of ice after a few vehicles passed over them. Mike and I were driving along one of them when a 2½ ton GMC truck came toward us from the other direction. There was scarcely room to pass, and, being on ice, no chance to stop. I steered as far as I could to the right without slipping over the edge, although I was dangerously close. I thought that if the GMC driver would do the same, we might squeeze by. He didn't, and we struck portside to portside and our vehicle went over the bank, turning end over end. The little truck hit hard on its left side! Mike came crashing on top of me. We had up to a dozen one-pound blocks of TNT plus numerous dynamite caps stored in that compartment directly behind me which was what I immediately thought of as we were dropping over that bank.

"Mike, are you all right?" Mike responded that he was okay. "In that case, look around and see where we are. Does it was look like Heaven or Hell? Or maybe the TNT didn't blow up!"

"OH MY GOD! I had forgotten about that! Well, one thing I am sure of, it's the same old world BECAUSE IT'S JUST AS COLD AS EVER!"

The truck that knocked us off the road was not at all polite about it, and he didn't even check to see how we were doing. If he had, he would have found us with the vehicle lying on its left side at the bottom of a bank, and with me half buried in the snow and Mike on top. The next problem was to figure out what to do to get the weapons carrier out of there, and on the road again. I told Mike to release the winch cable and take it up the bank, and see if he could secure it to a tree on the other side of the roadway. Luckily he found one just where we needed it. Now, if we were lucky, the engine would start even though the truck was on its side. It did start just long enough that I could take up on the winch and pull the truck over onto its wheels. Now that it was upright, I knew I could start it, even if I had to add a little gasoline to the carburetor bowl. Now it was just a matter of starting the engine again and using the winch to pull the vehicle up the bank. The men in the Orderly Section immediately noticed the truck with its battered left side when we came back. Mike said, "You guys don't know how lucky you are! We didn't blow up any of your TNT!"

Chapter 11

THE FROZEN KINGDOM OF NIGHT

After winter's long black forest night,
Comes springtime's early morning light,
Yet guns of war more death will bring
Until peace is back and birds will sing

Capell '03 In memory of the infantrymen who lived
or died in the final months of WWII in Europe, 1945

Some of the coldest weather of the winter was early in January, and then again just after the middle of the month. Once again frozen feet and fingers and trench foot took a heavy toll of our men. Standing sentry duty in a blizzard in the middle of the night was unbelievably miserable. Many of us did not have overcoats so we wrapped ourselves with strips cut from burlap bags, so much that sometimes we looked like mummies. The Germans also wrapped in burlap, even though most of them had overcoats. As mentioned before, much of the newly developed winter clothing never made it to the front. When the war was finally over and we saw rear-echelon troops again we saw that most were wearing the new warmer winter clothing, such as the insulated shoes. It was a shock to realize how many cases of frozen feet and trench foot could have been avoided had these shoes gone to the men who really needed them. General Omar Bradley in his book, "A Soldier's Story" admits he made a serious error in sending so much ammunition to the front instead of winter clothing during the cold weather of 1944-45. He admits his error cost many American lives. He has to be admired for his frankness and honesty but there is no excuse for those responsible for allowing special warm clothing to be issued to rear troops who did not need it as badly.

With the January days still quite short, arriving at a new location late and without time to prepare a proper shelter before dark, ingenuity was needed to find a way to keep warm. One method I often resorted to was to select a large manure pile, throw a couple of boards on it, and sleep on that. Strange as this may sound, it was a way to keep warm. The fermenting manure generates enough heat to melt the snow on it. The problem was that the pile was also emitting steam and gas, which I presume, was methane. Breathing soon became almost impossible and I had to jump back out into the cold again.

One night while groping around in the dark to find a place to sleep I came across a shed with a smooth concrete floor. The floor felt somewhat warm, and was just what I was looking for. Without a second thought I laid my blanket down and went right to sleep. A while later I felt a furry leg push against me, and then I realized I was sleeping with a cow. Since the cow was nice and warm I was very happy to stay there, and the cow didn't seem to mind at all.

Another night during a rather steady snow, I formed a wall of snow around me and stretched a shelter-half over it, and then crawled under. Soon new snow covered the shelter-half enough to block out any light that might escape. I put a little gasoline in the bottom of an empty ration can and lit it. With the heat from the burning gasoline and with the snow sealing out the cold wind, it became reasonably comfortable.

Sentry duty was normally assigned only during the hours of darkness. Each man assigned was to be on duty for one hour, and when his hour was completed, he would go to where the next scheduled man was sleeping. After calling him he would go back to his hole or shelter for the rest of the night. It was the responsibility of the man who was called to immediately take over on sentry duty. If he did not, or if he fell back to sleep, the chain would be broken and there would be no one on duty. Woe be to the man who broke the chain if he were discovered. But, as Frank Glaze said, what could you do to a man for punishment? What worse situation could he be in than the one he was in already? You could shoot him, but then you have lost a man. His only punishment was his own conscience, and for most men, that was plenty.

The best arrangement for sentry duty, especially in a dark forest, was to have all the scheduled men sleeping in the same hole. Then the man whose time was up would simply call out the name of the man who was to relieve him. This system worked very well, and what amazed me was that I would hear my name called and wake-up immediately, but would not wake up to anyone else's name. The capability of the brain to perform certain functions astounded me. It seems as though I could program my brain to react to some sounds, and ignore others. An example was when I could hear footsteps approaching my hole, and yet sleep right on through the sound of guns and explosions blasting around me.

Perhaps the most miserable time I had on sentry duty during a blizzard was one night when I saw through the blowing snow what appeared to be a corner of a blanket from which the snow had blown off. Desperate to find anything that might help protect me from that biting wind, I pulled it out of the snow and put it around me. Immediately however I detected a horrible stench, and realized there was a huge blotch of dried blood on it. Apparently I pulled it off a dead body. At the moment, however, the most important thing was protection from the blizzard. I kept the blanket around me for the rest of my time on duty. Afterward I regretted that decision. The smell remained in my clothes for weeks afterward, and no matter how sickening and disgusting that odor was there was no way I could wash it out until the weather moderated.

Mike and I spent much of our time assisting other vehicles, mostly jeeps that were stuck in deep snow or had slid off the road. American Sherman tanks were vulnerable to slipping sideways on ice or hard packed snow. We watched a column of American tanks attempt to traverse an icy side slope on a ravine. As the commander of the first tank started out he opened the hatch while the tank immediately started slipping sideways. It suddenly rolled over and he was crushed. The following tanks stopped and obviously were afraid to continue. A Company of infantry was nearby, and they were summoned to assist. The tank men had a couple of long ropes one of which was attached to the back of the tank and the other to the front. About 50 of the infantrymen spread out along the rope in back, and about 50 more along the rope in front. They then performed a tug-of-war with the tank in the middle. Suddenly a man would lose his footing on the icy slope and trip the man below and, like dominoes, all the men below would fall and slide downhill on the ice until somehow they began to get their footing again. Thus the tank would be brought forward a few feet before the tripping and slipping began again. It was a tragic but comic scene and again illustrated the interdependence of tank and foot soldiers.

- - -

Mike was being given other assignments much of the time now because the companies were getting short of men again. Finally he was assigned back to E Company which is where he was when he was wounded. I missed him not only because of my own safety, but he was also a great companion. There were several occasions that, had it not been for Mike and his quick and accurate rifle work, we would not have survived.

By mid-January we were beginning to gain back all of the land to the north of us that was lost in the German counter-offensive. We were now moving north in Luxembourg and by January 17th, we were 10 miles west of Echternach, Luxembourg, where the 4th Division had been able to hold the line against the German attack. By the 20th of January we had passed to nine miles east of the city and near the German border.

We were getting close to the same battlefields near the Belgian-German border that we first fought on in September. Many of the dead animals had been lying there for months. When the snow was not on the ground, the dead humans were picked up whenever they could be located. However, since snow was on the ground from December 20th for most of the time until the end of January there were many bodies lying in snowdrifts that were not found. Also, when the ground was frozen and when there was snow on top of it, the human waste was not dug in, and all this filth was continuing to accumulate. By the third week of January a sudden thaw had begun, and the filthy-looking streams were running full with the melting snow mixed with human waste and discharges from human and animal carcasses.

8th Inf. Regt. CPs during the German counter-attack
starting Dec 16th, 1944 (Battle of the Bulge)

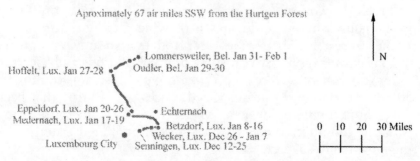

Aproximately 67 air miles SSW from the Hurtgen Forest

Lommersweiler, Bel. Jan 31- Feb 1

Hoffelt, Lux. Jan 27-28   Oudler, Bel. Jan 29-30

Eppeldorf, Lux. Jan 20-26   Echternach

Medernach, Lux. Jan 17-19

Betzdorf, Lux. Jan 8-16

Wecker, Lux. Dec 26 - Jan 7

Luxembourg City   Senningen, Lux. Dec 12-25

N

0   10   20   30 Miles

I picked up the Company's water cans to refill them at the water-point set up by Division Headquarters. I got directions to a swollen stream that looked as filthy as all the others, and there drawing water out of it, was the pumping unit. The water they were pumping looked as dirty as the water in the stream. Astounded, I asked the attendant, "What in hell are you using for a filter? It looks as bad coming out as it does going in!" His amazing reply was, "Oh, I can't use a filter, because it clogs up almost as soon as I put it in." I said, "WHAT?" His response was "Don't WORRY about it, I'm putting in enough chlorine tablets to kill a ton of bugs!"

Having run completely out of water myself I was terribly thirsty, and since this was the only water available, I hoped what he said about the chlorine was at least somewhat accurate. I drank some, and soon suffered the consequences. I went directly back to the Company and reported to the Sergeant. He was very relieved that I had not filled the cans. He went to a staff officer who ordered the Intelligence and Reconnaissance Section to find a wine warehouse nearby where we could fill the water cans with wine. We then had wine for drinking and anything else water might be needed for, but I was too sick for it to do me any good. I couldn't even take a drink of wine. There was absolutely no water available so I hoped I would be able to get some orange juice or something like that from the mess sergeant, but he said he didn't have any.

I was becoming more dehydrated than I had ever been or have been ever since. I had almost continuous dysentery, and now to add to my misery, another blast of very cold air and snow came back. The blizzard this time was as bad as any that winter, and I spent much of my time outside of my shelter with my pants down. Misery like that needs no further description. I considered trying to walk back to the medical aid station, but I just felt too weak. I could have yelled for a medic but they were all busy caring for wounded men, and I felt the wounded should have priority. After a day or so I got to the point where I could sip a little wine, and by that time my friends were able to boil some water from melted snow. After three or four days I was able to eat some of my K-Rations and I seemed to make a fairly fast recovery. When my paralysis was coming on 30 years ago, one of the suspected causes was a virus that been dormant in my body for many years. If a virus is the cause of my paralytic condition, then that incident with polluted water seems the most likely suspect.

Chapter 12

THE WAR-RAVAGED VALLEY
OF LEGEND

The legendary River Rhine, home of Wotan's golden Shrine,
Where Rhine maids guarded gold from base design,
Modern war still reigns as greed and hate prevail.
Man's search for love and peace, is yet to no avail.

Capell ' 03 based on Richard Wagner's opera "The Rhine Gold"

Certainly the Valley of the Rhine River is the most romantic and legendary geographic area of Germany. This was the legendary home of the Rhine Maidens and the gleaming Rhine Gold. But though we had not yet seen the Rhine River we were once again back in its western valley. Before the end of January we were fighting to recapture the same land in Belgium for which we had fought so hard in September and October of 1944. We fought in the familiar battlefields east of Bastogne and southeast of Malmedy. It was an area of small towns and villages, hamlets, and scattered farmhouses.

On February 5th we crossed back into Germany again, this time about 10 miles east southeast from Malmedy, Belgium. While in this area I made a trip back to Division Supply to get food for the staff officers' kitchen and passed several farmhouses from which the German civilians had just left. One of them was well kept, and out of curiosity I entered. I checked a couple of dresser drawers and found they were mostly full of clothing. I shoved them closed and thought to myself how they would be completely ransacked within a few hours once the rear-echelon troops arrived there. I had not completely closed one drawer, so I turned back to push it closed. I wanted the place to look exactly as I found it, then I would have nothing on my conscience. However, I noticed a hinged wooden box partially showing under the clothes. I thought it might be a jewelry box so I checked. To my astonishment it was full to the top with silver coins. The family must have left in a frantic rush, probably because we were attacking the village.

Now I had a dilemma. I was determined not to have looting on my conscience, and yet if I left the box there, it would surely be quickly taken by rear-echelon troops. There was a small vegetable garden behind the house, so I thought if I buried it in a shallow hole, there was a very good chance the family might eventually find it when they returned to see what was left of their house. I felt good about it, knowing that I did about all I could do. I wish the story had ended here, but sadly, I made another trip back the next day to pick up supplies.

I made a quick check of the house and garden. It was no surprise to me to find the house ransacked, but I was sickened when I looked in the garden and found a freshly dug hole where the box had been. Someone must have been watching me, and I was completely mystified as to where that person might have been.

Vandalism disgusted me, and there always seemed to be a few morons that would do it. I mentioned it being done by rear echelon rather than front-line troops, but that was probably only because they had the best chance. Combat troops were too busy trying to stay alive to worry about such stupidity as vandalism. I checked another house in the area and that one was ransacked as well. However, it was very disturbing to see empty American Red Cross cartons there. Red Cross cartons were sent to the German prisoner of war camps to help keep American prisoners from starving. How did these cartons get in the house, and did their contents ever reach American prisoners? It was unpleasant to think about.

- - -

We stayed in the western Rhine Valley area for the rest of January and into early February. Most of the time we were just west of the Siegfried Line along Germany's western border. The Germans were putting up a much stronger defense than we expected, and undoubtedly it was because they were fighting near the border of their homeland. I'm sure that many of them had no enthusiasm about fighting for Hitler at that time, but many would fight to the death for their homeland.

The mail was finally getting through again by mid January, and it seemed the news regarding my father's health was better. I felt very guilty about not having written my parents very much since the German counterattack took place on December 16th. The limited hours of daylight left us with almost no time left to do anything but carry out assigned duties. With the news my parents got about the 4th Division being in the center of the German attack, they had no way of knowing whether I was dead or alive. For a while, at least, no mail was getting out from our Division, since we were blocked on three sides by the Germans. Once it was dark we couldn't do anything that required light because the enemy could see even a well-shaded candle or a lit match.

From what I learned later, my father was making some progress recovering from the stroke he had in June, and by November was able to drive his car a limited amount. However, the worry about what was happening to their only son must have been devastating. It wasn't until after the war I learned from a good friend of my mother how my parents watched and waited for the mailman each day. Nearly six weeks after the German counter attack my letter finally reached home. On February 2nd my father had another major stroke from which he did not recover. He died just a few days later. My mother saved all of my letters, so when I got home I was able to see when I had written them. I found that I did write two letters later in December and two more in early January, but it wasn't until January 29th that any of them reached home. My mother assured me that my father knew I had survived.

Gene Redfield was a treasured friend. He was the one who brought me the letter with the bad news and seemed to sense what was in it. My father had died on February 5th and I learned of it just over two weeks later when Gene brought another letter from my mother. He asked me if the news was bad and I told him it was. He was the only man in the company I told. He said he would do whatever he could that might help me, and offered to use his connections at the Division post office to bypass the censors and expedite a letter home for me. I was very appreciative and used the opportunity to write a letter to my mother. I remember writing that letter by the light of a small amount of gasoline burning in the bottom of C-ration can. Fortunately we were in a place where I could do it. We were in the Schnee Eifel Forest of Germany and right on the Siegfried Line. Three of us built a structure together by cutting down a couple of trees, cutting them into logs, and constructing a shelter. We chinked all of the cracks or openings between the logs with a combination of mud and snow, since the ground was thawing now. We used a couple of folded shelter-halves to seal the entrance opening. Thus the structure was lightproof and windproof. My mother had sent me a very small pocket size Bible in which I found comfort after writing the letter.

As February came to a close and March arrived, the news from home was weighing heavily upon me. There was also more bad news from home. A very good childhood friend had been murdered, but my mother held that information from me for my sake. I had also lost some close friends in the war, which she did not tell me about until later. One of them was a young fellow, which she also was very fond of. His name was Paul Wendolyn, who was an unusually kind and personable fellow as well as being an outstanding athlete in baseball and football. The friend who was murdered was from a family that was very close friends with my parents. They had two daughters, one my age and the other a couple of years younger. Her name was Frances Radecop, a pretty and very intelligent 18-year-old who was about to enter the University of Washington. She was found clubbed to death after she discovered an intruder in her bedroom. The murder was not solved until more than six years later.

The American Red Cross sent doughnut wagons to the "fighting fronts" to serve coffee and doughnuts to the "boys who were doing the fighting." The fact was that they did not get close to the fronts, but stayed a safe distance back, which to us who were at the front was very understandable and quite logical. Granted they were close enough to hear the guns and were within the range of very long-range artillery. There was also a small threat from German V-l or a V-II flying bombs. The Red Cross girls presence did us little good unless arrangements were made to take us back to where they were. I did get that opportunity once when a truck took a dozen or so of us back to a doughnut wagon. It was a memorable occasion. There were four Red Cross girls serving coffee and doughnuts to a line of GIs. It wasn't the coffee or the doughnuts I remember; it was the girls. I had not seen an American girl for over a year, and it was exciting. They all looked quite pretty, but one of them really impressed me.

I would have had much happier memories of the incident were it not for what happened the next night. We were back in reserve and

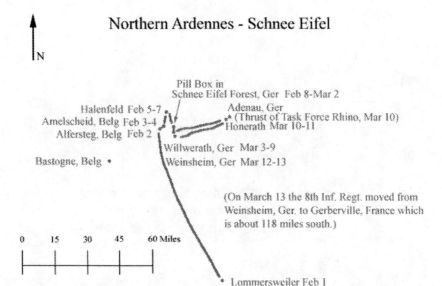

Northern Ardennes - Schnee Eifel

N

Pill Box in
Schnee Eifel Forest, Ger Feb 8-Mar 2

Halenfeld Feb 5-7
Amelscheid, Belg Feb 3-4
Alfersteg, Belg Feb 2

Adenau, Ger
(Thrust of Task Force Rhino, Mar 10)
Honerath Mar 10-11

Willwerath, Ger Mar 3-9

Bastogne, Belg

Weinsheim, Ger Mar 12-13

(On March 13 the 8th Inf. Regt. moved from
Weinsheim, Ger. to Gerberville, France which
is about 118 miles south.)

0   15   30   45   60 Miles

Lommersweiler Feb 1

not right on the fighting front for a couple of days, and yet I was
still called out that night to stand sentry watch. I was to stand at the
entrance of a bunker the Germans had built. It seemed absolutely
ridiculous because we were well behind the line. Having not been
given a reason for guarding this bunker I began to get angry as well
as puzzled by it all. I found the sergeant that had been assigned the
duty of picking the sentries, and asked him exactly what he knew
about it. He said all he knew was that a staff major carrying some
food and a couple of bottles of wine went in there with a Red Cross
girl earlier in the evening.

Whenever in ancient times the concept of rank was conceived
in a military organization, an inseparable adjunct to it was an
accompanying privilege and power. The misuse of that power
is, no doubt, as old as the concept itself. However, in itself, rank
does not justify selfish behavior. The major involved shall remain
anonymous. The girl involved did no favor to the countless number
of fine young women who seriously desired to assist the war
effort by joining organizations such as the Red Cross. They were
much appreciated by most servicemen. Others who volunteered
in the health services and in such organizations as the United
Service Organization (USO), and the various canteens such as the
Hollywood Canteen in Hollywood, and the Stage Door Canteen in
New York City were also appreciated.

Chapter 13

SIEGFRIED ENCORE

But when the blast of war blows in our ears,
Then imitate the action of the tiger:
Stiffen the sinews, summon up the blood.
Shakespeare, King Henry V, Act 3

We were making very slow progress in the Siegfried area this time, and apparently morale in some of the rifle companies began to suffer. One morning we were quite surprised to see troops move up through our area with insignias we did not recognize. A couple of hours later, three 2½ ton GMC trucks came by. Shortly afterward they returned full of unarmed GIs and from all appearances the men were under arrest. One of our officers told us they were being taken back to be shot for desertion. This was not hard for us to understand since there was nothing else that could be done to a GI that was an infantry rifleman. If he were sent to prison, he would be much safer, have a cot to sleep on, and would have regular hot meals, all of which would be quite a luxury to a combat infantry man.

Soon after the trucks went by, another man was brought back in a jeep. He wore no insignia and was unarmed, but wore better quality clothes as though he had been an officer. Unlike an officer, however, he looked as though he had not shaved for three days. He sat in the front seat next to the driver with an officer I did not recognize sitting directly behind him. They stopped at our Regimental Headquarters and got out and for the next day or so the man was kept in a nearby stone building under guard. The entire incident was kept so secret that none of the men in our company I talked to knew what had happened, other than the fact that there was a small mutiny in one of our battalions. Some of the men refused to attack when ordered, saying they were short of ammunition and food, and were just plainly exhausted. According to a Stars and Stripes article that I remember reading, there were approximately 150 men shot as deserters in Europe. If that were true, then this one group would have accounted for over half of them. Most likely the men in the trucks were not all shot as we were told.

In addition to morale problems that developed among a few of the men, Fred Braun and I stumbled upon another disturbing situation that was apparently developing. It happened as result of Fred chasing me through the forest when he found out that I had a package his sister sent me in the mail. It started when I saw a photograph of a beautiful blond girl among his pictures and asked him who she was. He said it was his sister and gave me her address. I wrote her a nice letter and told her how impressed I was by her picture and I thought I was in love with her. After all the flattering words I finished the letter with bold letters saying "PLEASE SEND ME A BOX OF HERSHEY BARS—WITH ALMONDS!" And now came the package with the Hershey bars and a letter from Arlene who lived in East Orange, New Jersey. When Gene Redfield brought me the package I told him to tip off Fred that I had a package from his sister. When Fred came rushing over, I ran away into the forest, carrying the package as Fred came chasing after me. Suddenly I almost ran onto the body of an American GI. Bodies were not at all uncommon but this one seemed out of place. Our playful chase stopped abruptly and we examined the body.

I did not immediately see the wound that killed him. I felt his skin temperature to see whether he had been dead very long and I deduced he had been dead for less than an hour. He was lying face down and I found the bullet entrance wound over his right kidney. We turned him over and found a rather large exit wound as though he was shot in the back with a 30-caliber rifle, the same as we carried. He had been shot from behind and we were very sure there had been no Germans in that area for hours. We concluded that another American killed him. We found "dog tags" around his neck, and when we saw some other men in the woods a short distance away we called them over to examine him. They said they knew him and that he was in their company but that he was not the man who matched the dog tags that were on him. I asked if he had been carrying his own pistol and they said, "Yes, he had a nice German Mauser." I said, "It sure looks like murder to me. Somebody wanted his Mauser. Are you going to report it to your company commander?" They said they certainly would.

The discovery of this particular murder may have prompted action by the command, although other cases like it may have been discovered at the same time. It is quite possible that the murders were committed by a single man who collected foreign pistols to sell to new replacements. Within a few days we were sent forms upon which we were to identify our pistol, including any serial numbers or markings. We were also required to write in the name of the man in our company whom we willed the weapon to in the event of our death, which meant someone we knew and trusted. Failure to comply with the registration order was punishable by death. The idea worked and I saw no more evidence of murders for weapons. The reason these foreign weapons were in demand was that an enlisted man was prohibited from carrying an American-made handgun, and yet they were very useful for close-up protection. We could however carry a weapon of foreign make which we usually obtained from Germans who were dead or captured. Only officers could carry American handguns so the only way an enlisted man could get one was from the body of a dead officer. This was to protect officers from enlisted men who might kill them to get their weapon.

- - -

During the last few days of February we were on the Siegfried Line 11 miles to the east of St. Vith, Belgium in the Schnee Eiffel Forest. We were seeing few of the V-l "buzz bombs" compared to what we saw earlier, probably because the Germans were relying on the V-ll rockets which had a much greater range. The Luftwaffe was not very active although we were seeing more jet bombers and fighters coming over. They were never as big a threat to the infantry as compared to "bedcheck" Charlie. Occasionally, a German fighter-bomber came over such as occurred one evening shortly after I took over on a sentry post.

The hillside where I was posted had a fairly open field of fire with just a few bushes and small trees ahead of me. However, at the bottom of the hill was a wooded area where the Germans were holding a defensive position. Often, when we had a clear field of fire in all directions, the sentry post would be staffed by just one man, since there was little danger of the enemy coming in on the flank without being seen. The sun was disappearing over the horizon when I took over. I was equipped with a BAR (Browning Automatic

Rifle), which is actually a light machine gun. Suddenly, from over the treetops at the bottom of the hill came a German two-engine fighter-bomber at high speed. It was headed directly toward me and just high enough to clear the terrain.

Author firing on JU-88

The BAR was already pointed almost directly at the aircraft, which was a Junkers-88, and I had but a very slight correction to make to fire directly between the two engines and at the pilot. However the aircraft had a machine gun at the nose which was pointed almost directly at me. There was a split second of suspense before it was determined who would fire first. Fortunately it was me who put a burst of BAR into the aircraft which apparently struck the pilot. The aircraft streaked over me like a rocket, and almost faster than I could comprehend, it went into a clump of trees about 75 yards behind me. There was a crash but no explosion and no large fire. The aircraft did not get off a single shot at me or our company. ALL SEEMED INSTANTANEOUS!

I saw the crash behind me and felt curious to check the wreckage, but at the same time I did not want to see it. There were usually about four men in a crew and I was certain there were no survivors. However, I had a very good reason for not looking even if I had wanted to. I still had 40 minutes left on the sentry post, and could not leave. Once I was relieved it would be too dark to see much of the wreckage anyway. I was reasonably sure I had shot him down since there were no other guns firing at him. I fired a few rounds only from the BAR. The plane was coming directly at me and the

JU-88 downed by author

pilot was in a very exposed position. I went back to my hole a little uncertain as to exactly what had happened.

The scene remained fixed in my mind for some years afterward. It became vivid again when Gene Redfield, whom I had kept contact with over the years, offered me a group of small snapshots that he had brought back. He didn't know who took them or anything about them, and nothing was marked on them. But there it was! There was a picture of the crashed Junkers-88 just as I saw it the next morning when I strolled up to look at the wreckage. I expect someone had picked up a camera out of a German house and shot the remaining film and it was brought back to the States for developing.

German Fighter-Bomber Junkers-88

It was just within the last few years, I discovered our company commander, Frank Glaze, clearly remembered seeing the airplane going down. He said there were just a few rounds of light machine gun fire that got it and did not realize exactly where they came from. Now after discussing it together, we both agree that it was the shots I fired that brought it down.

- - -

We were still near the Siegfried Line after the end of February, and on March 2nd we were about three miles from the German city of Prüm. For the next six days we were stalled by moderate German resistance three miles northeast of Prüm near a place called Willwerath. While at Willwerath we were given a briefing on a special operation in which we were to take part. The 8th Infantry Regiment, along with a few other support units, was to embark on an assignment called Task Force Rhino, which was to make a sudden thrust over the Rhine plain in the direction of the Rhine River. We began the attack on March 10th and the Germans began rushing in reinforcements to stop us, but before they succeeded we advanced 21 miles towards to the Rhine River.

Germans taken prisoner by 8th Int. Regt. and gathered at Adenau

The name of the town we reached was Adenau on March 11th and the attack lasted just a little more than a day. Many Germans were killed and about 50 prisoners taken, they were being held at the town of Adenau and I was told to use my weapons carrier to take them back to the M.P. Temporary Compound.

I was ordered to take the prisoners back within the four or five hours we would have before dark. I protested that I could not do that unless I was given at least 2 more men to help me but I was allowed only one. Fortunately, he was a good man, although I can't recall his name now, and we did manage to complete the order on time.

The day after the attack we passed within a couple of miles of Prüm, and spent the night of March 12th near Weinsheim,

Prüm, Germany

Germany. We were briefed on a long move we were to make to the south. On a map the distance shows as 114 miles, but by road it was much farther. Trucks had to be brought in to carry the men such a great distance in one day.

- - -

For some years after the war I had no particular interest in remembering the incidents described above, however, on about the 40th anniversary of D-Day there seemed to be a revival of public interest. After doing interviews and contributing to books about the war, I took a renewed interest in remembering as much as I could. I re-established contact with other men in our company, such as Gene Redfield, Fred Braun, Horace Sisk, Stan Kakoski, L.A. Wilson, Louis Norris, and Hugh Jetton. There were other men in our regiment who survived and were still alive at that time as well. Two others that lived in the Portland area were Harold Cross and Francis I. Smith who were in other companies of the 8th Infantry Regiment. Shortly after the 40th anniversary, Richard Mosby of Portland initiated the Northwest Chapter of the 4th Division Association. The memories came flooding back, and especially after reading all I could about our Regiment and Division, as well as the war in Europe in general, I developed a greater interest than I had ever had before.

Chapter 14

Sunrise at Last

Hark, hark the lark at Heaven's gate sings
As Phoebus 'gins to rise.

Shakespeare, *Cymbeline*

After a full day of traveling we arrived at our destination which was in the former province of Lorraine. At the time of Napoleon it was French, but after the Franco-Prussian War it became part of Germany. Under the conditions of the Treaty of Versailles after World War I, the provinces of Lorraine and Alsace were awarded to France. After Hitler invaded France they became German again. Now that the Germans had withdrawn, they were once again French. Somehow these people lived together relatively peacefully in spite of such varied ethnic dominations and persecutions in their quite recent modern history.

In our move south we traveled through the broad western valley of the Rhine, a route that passed through the region of the Saar, so named because it includes the valley of the Saar River. Most of the men in the division went by rail in the notorious "40 by 8" box cars (40 men or 8 horses). Collecting stamps helped make geography and history come alive for me, and this was particularly true when we moved through the Saar. I remembered clearly when the last of that country's stamps were issued. In 1935, a plebiscite was held at which time the population voted as to whether they wished to remain an autonomous and independent country, or become a part of Germany. The voters chose the latter, and the Saar no longer existed as a country. It had once been German, but after World War I, the Treaty of Versailles created it as an independent autonomy. It was a busy coal-rich industrial area and a valuable prize for Germany to regain. It had a predominantly ethnic German population, and as the Nazis rapidly gained power in the late 1920's and early 30's, the outcome of the plebiscite was no surprise.

Gerbervillers in Lorraine was our destination. It was 7½ miles south by east from Luneville, or 21 miles southeast of Nancy, which is the largest city in Lorraine. We stayed there for nearly six days at the time and, being behind the fighting front, it was an opportunity for us to repair equipment, bring in replacements for our losses, and have a bit of a rest. We fully realized this was all in preparation of crossing the Rhine River itself. I spent part of each day repairing and maintaining vehicles but had a considerable amount of spare time. It was a good break and appreciated since, with the exception of the day I was at the hospital camp on December 15th, I had not had a day off in the last ten months.

Apparently most of the civilians had been evacuated because we saw almost no one in the streets and only a few shop keepers. Before we arrived in the town, there had been and still were a rear echelon unit of Quartermaster Corps soldiers who were black. We were ordered to have no contact with them as might have been expected with the Army's policy of strict segregation at that time. We were also told that several of them had been convicted of rape and were under a sentence of death. We were also warned not to fraternize in any way with the civilians. To be caught talking to a civilian would be punishable by a $75 fine. This was a sizable amount considering I drew only $35 of my pay each month, all of which I had automatically sent home. The army sent the remainder of my pay to my mother and matched the amount as a contribution towards her dependency allotment.

Nearby was a little town of Saint Remy aux Bois, which had been headquarters for a group of FFI. During the occupation a German soldier was shot and on September 5th, 1944, the town was destroyed by the Germans in reprisal.

Gene Redfield and I spent much of our spare time together but there was little of interest to do other than to wander around town where most shops were closed, and those that weren't had little to sell without ration tickets. It was an excellent opportunity to write letters. One evening Gene and I were invited to join some of our friends who had found a small supply of wine and brandy in the cellar of a partially wrecked building. It was a good chance to party since I didn't have to be concerned about doing sentry duty.

In the mean time, another party was going on in a nearby building among a group of men whom we referred to as the Rebels. They

Saint Remy aux Bois

carried on the tradition of the men I described in chapter 5. They were strong segregationists and bragged about how they kept "the niggers in their place." Although most of the Rebels referred to in Normandy had been killed or wounded by the time we reached Gerbervillers in March, there were enough replacements of the same persuasion to fill out their ranks. There were more than enough of them to indulge in their passion to brawl among themselves.

Gene and I decided to leave our party long enough to invite another friend who was staying on the second floor of a building about a block away. We didn't find him but as we were leaving the building, we encountered a very drunk Rebel about to enter. He was armed with a German machine pistol, commonly called a "burp gun". We tried to convince him the guy he was looking for was not there but he started upstairs anyway. We had just seen the man he was looking for upstairs and knew there would be trouble if we didn't do something. Gene and I both rushed him at the same time knocking him down the stairs. We took his machine pistol and threw it far back into some bushes where we were quite sure he would not find it. The guy was very drunk and barely conscious. We didn't think there would be much chance of the Rebels finding each other so we went back to our party, which was about two blocks away. Within about ½ hour we heard the sound of a rifle shot followed by the sound of a burp gun, and after a few more rifle shots, all was quiet again. We were puzzled as to how that drunken Rebel could have gotten that burp gun again, if indeed he did. We decided to leave it up to the Rebels to take care of their own situation that night and minded our own business. The next day the Rebels were all sobered up and everyone seemed to be healthy. We never did find out what went on that night. Apparently they had a very successful session of R&R because they had their fun, and nobody got killed.

On March 21st we loaded up again and moved north into the province of Alsace to a place called Dauendorf, France. It is 20 miles north by west from the city of Strasbourg, France which is near the Rhine River and the German border. By March 27th we moved back into Germany to Bad Durkheim, 15 miles to the west of Mannheim. Early in the morning of the 28th we began our move in preparation for crossing the Rhine. The long-awaited day had finally arrived.

Chapter 15

STRIKING THE HEARTLAND

A budding blossom rises by River Rhine
With flowering glory in its time,
With Nazi madness doomed by force divine
A budding Germany with hope shall climb!

Capell '03 in remembrance of spring 1945

The move toward the Rhine began early on the 29th of March and the beauty of the Rhine Valley impressed me. As we moved toward the north, we followed closely along the Rhine River. On the other side of the river, which was occupied by the Germans, some of the hills rose up steeply from the River like mini-mountains. On one the hill-tops there was one of the most beautiful castles I have ever seen. From my vantage point, it appeared to be old but well preserved. We reached the Rhine near the town of Worms and crossed it on a pontoon bridge built by the U.S. Army Engineers. The Germans put up surprisingly light resistance against our crossing except for nearly continuous artillery fire. I was not aware of any of our men being hit during that operation.

We were about 15 miles by road from where we left near Bad Durkheim to where we began our crossing of the River. Because of the bottleneck created by having only one bridge with one lane, it took hours to reach the other side. Once across we were blocked by vehicles ahead while the companies in front of us were clearing out pockets of German resistance. There also were many areas that needed to be checked thoroughly before the column was allowed to proceed. Sometimes we waited over an hour before moving. Other times we might stop for no more than a couple of minutes. After many hours of alternate waiting and moving, nearly everyone began falling asleep. After 24 hours the officer assigned to our group, Lieutenant Halluba, was spending all of his time running back and forth, trying to keep drivers awake. After more than 30 hours the problem was even worse. I admired Halluba's perseverance in keeping us awake. Actually most of us tried very hard to keep the column going by trying to stay awake ourselves and switching drivers frequently. When we were moving it wasn't as much of a problem as it was when we stopped, and drivers would start falling asleep in seconds. Altogether we were in the vehicles for 36 hours without a break, and the distance we traveled was about 70 miles. We finally stopped near a little town called Erlenbach, which is about 30 miles southeast of the German city of Frankfurt.

The satisfaction of driving so deep into the heart of Germany made up for the grueling session of the past couple of days. By the sound of the guns to the northeast of us, however, the fact that we had struck at the heart of what had been the Nazi homeland did not kill their desire to fight. We moved to the northeast and by April 1st were near Reichenberg, just 4 miles south of the city of Wurzburg. I was immediately ordered to get water for the company and was given verbal directions as to where to locate the water point. As I said before, I always felt it would have been wiser for me to have gotten the directions by telephone directly from Division Headquarters rather than have them relayed through a Company officer. The Army way, however, was to have everything go through channels and it didn't work well at all in this case.

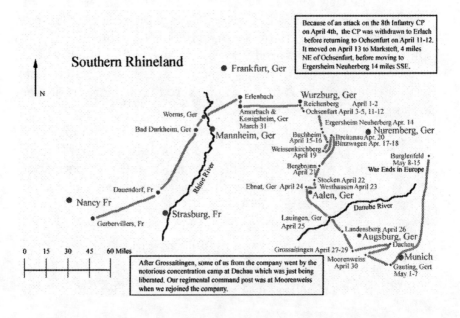

Because of an attack on the 8th Infantry CP on April 4th, the CP was withdrawn to Erlach before returning to Ochsenfurt on April 11-12. It moved on April 13 to Markstelt, 4 miles NE of Ochsenfurt, before moving to Ergersheim Neuherberg 14 miles SSE.

Southern Rhineland

N

Frankfurt, Ger
Erlenbach
Wurzburg, Ger
Reichenberg   April 1-2
Ochsenfurt April 3-5, 11-12
Worms, Ger
Amorbach & Konigsheim, Ger March 31
Ergersheim Neuherberg Apr. 14
Bad Durkheim, Ger
Mannheim, Ger
Nuremberg, Ger
Buchheim April 15-16
Breitenau Apr. 20
Binzwagen Apr. 17-18
Weissenkirchberg April 19
Burglenfeld May 8-15
War Ends in Europe
Bergbronn April 21
Dauendorf, Fr
Nancy Fr
Stocken April 22
Ebnat, Ger April 24
Westhausen April 23
Aalen, Ger
Danube River
Gerbervillers, Fr
Strasburg, Fr
Lauingen, Ger April 25
Landensberg April 26
Augsburg, Ger
Dachau
0 15 30 45 60 Miles
Grossaitingen April 27-29
Moorenweiss April 30
Munich
Gauting, Gert May 1-?

After Grossaitingen, some of us from the company went by the notorious concentration camp at Dachau which was just being liberated. Our regimental command post was at Moorenweiss when we rejoined the company.

Certainly I should have been given a map with the water point location marked. Since I was normally given nothing but verbal directions I became very careful in thoroughly understanding and remembering exactly what I was told. My life often depended on it. I was given nobody to ride "shotgun" with me, which I was not happy about since we had just moved rapidly into this area, and I had no idea where the Germans were. I followed directions carefully and came to the road junction where I was told to turn left, which was the exact opposite of what I should have done. Soon the road became lined with houses and buildings as though I were entering a town. It did not look right at all and I knew I should turn back as soon as possible. However, the street was narrow and I would have had to stop and go back and forth a couple of times to get the vehicle turned around. If I were in German-held territory I would be an easy target if I stopped. I saw no soldiers, German or American and the streets were vacant of civilians.

Immediately I saw white flags hanging out of windows in the buildings ahead and knew I was in the "no man's" land that exists when the Germans are leaving, or have just left, and the Americans have not yet arrived. It was a very dangerous place to be, and not daring to stop to turn around, I drove as fast as possible, hoping to find an intersection where I could turn and head away from the center of the city. By traveling fast on a narrow street lined with buildings I was not such an easy target. Finally I approached a street that came in from the right, and looked as though it angled somewhat back. It appeared very promising and I quickly turned onto it and raced back in the direction I was hoping to go. Then I saw a couple of tanks in the road. Were they American or were they German?

My heart was pounding when I recognized American markings, and I realized I WAS SAFE! The lead tank pulled farther into the center of the roadway as the hatch opened and the commander popped his head out while pointing his pistol directly at me and yelled, "ARE YOU A GERMAN?"

"NO, I AM AN AMERICAN!"

"THEN WHAT IN HELL ARE YOU DOING COMING UP THAT STREET?"

"I'M FROM THE 4TH DIVISION AND I AM TRYING TO GET

OUT OF THIS DAMN CITY. I WAS LOOKING FOR THE WATER POINT AND WAS GIVEN BAD DIRECTIONS."

The tank commander apparently believed me and was sufficiently assured I was not a German attempting to lead their tank column into a trap. He called me over next to him and listened to my explanation of where and why I had been there. He asked me in detail what I had seen and I assured him I saw no tanks or vehicles anywhere along my route or even in sight from where I had turned. I told him I saw no guns or soldiers or even civilians, but plenty of white flags hanging out of windows. He said, "This is absolutely unbelievable because we have been fighting for that street for the last couple of hours. A few minutes ago there was a tank up there firing at us. They even had a couple of heavy artillery guns there within the last half-hour."

"You have nothing to worry about now; they're all gone!" Jokingly, I continued, "If I was wearing a star on my shoulder, I would order your whole column forward and get this f----- war over with."

"Well thank you, private, for the advice. Of course if you're a spy or something and not telling the truth, we'll have to shoot you. But if you're not lying, you can tell your girlfriends that you lead the attack that captured Wurzburg. Oh yeah, about the water point, go down this road behind us for about a mile and a half and take the road that turns off to the left toward the river and you will start seeing signs as to where it is. Good luck, you sure had it so far today or you'd be dead. As for your information I'm going to assume that you are right. And you had better be right! I'm moving the whole column forward now and we're gonna chase some Nazis!"

Following the tank commander's instructions, I found the water point without difficulty. I decided not to mention anything to the officer who obviously told me to turn left when I should have gone a few yards further and taken the road that went toward the right. When I learned that Wurzburg had surrendered the day after I was there, I definitely felt I made my contribution, but then whom could I brag to if no one would believe me, except for my close friends. When I realized what day it was on the calendar I had another little surprise. The date was April 1st, 1945 - APRIL FOOLS' DAY!

Chapter 16

THE NIGHT VISITORS

Made quiet by wine, so soundly I slept
'til flames outside the window leapt,
and Nazi boots ran by my head,
While comrade Harry outside lay dead!

Capell '03 In memory of the killing of Harry Kuhn April 4, 1945

We remained in the vicinity of Wurzburg through April 2nd, when the city fell to the Allies. We searched the surrounding area for German soldiers who apparently not only left the city, but also the nearby towns. On April 3rd we moved to a place called Oschenfurt, 10 miles southeast of Wurzburg, which was almost completely undamaged by the war, and had a number of sturdy concrete and stone buildings lining its main street. The sounds of war were nonexistent and it seemed as though the enemy were miles away. Finding a place to sleep was easy. I found a spot by a window on the second story of a building located on the main street. There I laid down my blanket and looked forward to a peaceful night's rest. I was ready to settle down for the night, when some friends downstairs yelled at me to join them with champagne they had just found. The sentries had already been assigned, and I wasn't one of them. Since we didn't know where the enemy was, posting sentries was a good idea but I really did not expect any problem that night and decided to relax and enjoy our party.

We found a couple of candles and blacked out the room so no light would escape. When I went back to my blanket, I was completely ready for a good quiet night's sleep, and fell asleep almost immediately although my head was cloudy with champagne. Shortly afterward I was instantaneously startled awake by gunfire and flames leaping up outside the window and then the sound of hobnail boots running by my head. ONLY THE GERMANS WORE HOBNAIL BOOTS! A German had just run by me and nearly stepped on my head—WHY DIDN'T HE SHOOT ME?

I quickly looked around the room, which was well lit by the flames outside, and saw the window shot-out and glass and debris on the floor, but no one was in the room except me. I jumped to my feet and, after grabbing my rifle, peered into the hallway. Outside the sound of small arms fire continued unabated. It was too dark to see anything so I found my way down to where we had partied the night before, and called. There was no response. I ran to the door on the main street. Outside and to the right flames were leaping up from a jeep, while across the street, in a stairwell, men from our Company were waving at me and calling me over.

I ran across the street and joined the others firing at Germans retreating up the street to the left. Two of the men in the stairwell were leaning over Harry Kuhn, looking for signs of life, but he was dead from numerous bullet wounds. He had been assigned to the light machine gun that was still there. Obviously the Germans who raided us were successfully withdrawing to the north end of the street that ran in front of the building. They all made their escape although at least one may have been wounded badly. Another was burned by gasoline and was last seen running away with his clothes on fire. Harry was the only one of our men that was killed and as far as I know he was the last man in our Company to be killed in the War.

It was determined by our I & R platoon that the Germans were a squad of paratroopers. They targeted our Regimental Headquarters that was located on the main street a block or so north of the building in which I had stayed. Frank Glaze tells of having been in the Headquarters building when they came. Part of their group targeted our vehicles by pouring gasoline on them and setting them afire.

Besides the two men who had been checking on Harry there were two others firing rifles at the rapidly retreating Germans. I ran across the street and jumped in the stairwell and began firing also, until someone up the street yelled, "HOLD YOUR FIRE!" Men from our Company came rushing out of the buildings to the north of us to pursue the fleeing Germans. We were told to stay back where we were. The Germans apparently disappeared into bushes that bordered the town.

With the Germans gone the questions came pouring forth, mainly directed at me. They could hardly believe I came out of that building alive. They said they had been firing at Germans in the building just moments before. When they told me a German was sighted just inside the window of the room where I had been sleeping, I realized he had to be the one who ran by my head. He had apparently just come in the room when his comrade in the street below ignited gasoline poured over a jeep. Flames leaped by the window and lighted the room including the German, whereupon my comrades sighted him and fired. He obviously ran for his life right by my head and out the door without taking time to shoot me, apparently assuming I was already dead. By that time I was coming out of my champagne-induced sleep and scrambled to my feet. Ironic as it was, the champagne no doubt had saved my life. Had I awakened sooner when the German first came in the room he would've killed me. My strict rule to avoid alcohol while in combat certainly did not save my life this time. In fact the effect of alcohol probably saved me.

The most bothersome thing about the whole incident was the question of what happened to the rifleman supposedly guarding Harry. Why was Harry dead and he was not? Where was he?

We looked in the adjacent cellar, and there he was. He vehemently protested that Harry was killed first, and several Germans, some armed with machine pistols were converging on him. I found no evidence to back his story. There were no shell casings from the type of rifle he carried, and thus he apparently fired no shots. He would normally have been standing on Harry's right side[*], and guarding that side, but that was where the shots came from that killed Harry. Some of our men were willing to give him the benefit of the doubt, but I was not. Harry was my friend and I was sad and very angry at what I thought had happened. I recalled the time in Normandy when Harry was shot completely through the forearm with a sniper's bullet, and refused to let me call for a medic because he said they needed to treat men who were more seriously wounded. I choose not to mention the name of the man who was with Harry for the sake of his living family members and for the lack of complete evidence. I will probably never know what really happened, but circumstantial evidence indicated that he had deserted Harry.

---

[*]Harry was positioned in a stairwell but exposed on his right side, therefore, needed a guard to protect him from the enemy approaching from his right side.

We suspected the Germans retreated to a hiding place, but we didn't know where. We thought there was a good chance they might attempt another raid the following night. Additional sentry posts were assigned, and I was picked to stand the first watch. Nicholas Storey was to guard my right flank with an M-1 rifle while I manned a BAR. Storey was a very likable New Jersey farmer and I knew I could trust him, however, when we began our watch at twilight he got nervous. We were on the sentry post that overlooked the grove of trees from which we expected the enemy to come. As it got darker he began to visualize movement in the trees. He burst out with, "If they come up that hill, I'M GITTEN OUTA HERE!" In reaction I pulled my pistol and pointed it at his head, "I need you here, and I'll see to it that you stay, dead or alive!" He calmed down and somewhat apologetically insisted he momentarily panicked and that he wouldn't think of leaving me there alone. I said, "Sorry friend, I know you wouldn't."

The Germans did not come out from the trees below and all was quiet for the rest of the night.

Chapter 17

SIFTING THE ASHES

From the ash of a Nazi funeral pyre
and the death of Adolph Hitler's Final Solution,
Will grow a glorious peace empire
without the Nazi mental pollution.

Capell '03 In memory of the collapse of Hitler's Nazism, spring 1945

After remaining two days in Ochsenfurt, during which time we kept a close sentry watch for any further attacks, we moved our command post about 2½ miles closer to Wurzburg. We surmised our regimental command had decided to spend a few more days scouting the area in case there were more nearby units of top-grade German troops. However, there were many small groups of low-grade German soldiers that quite willingly came in as prisoners. These were nearly all from Volksturm regiments and some of them were boys barely in their teens. Hitler's forces were so badly depleted by that time that he was taking anyone that could fire a rifle. Some of these individuals were so pathetic looking I felt sorry for them as I was taking them back to the MP prisoner compound. Our regimental command post was at Erlach, 7½ miles southeast of Wurzburg, from the 6th to the 10th of April, during which time I was busy with my usual duties of bringing supplies and water, and taking back prisoners.

We couldn't help but feel the war was over for us but none of us wanted to take chances. In some ways the fear of death was even greater now because there was something horrible about the prospect of being the last man killed in our war. We had no way of knowing, but it had already happened in our company with the death of Harry Kuhn. This was one reason I felt so bad about Harry. Close calls were a daily experience in Normandy and I accepted it, but now the sound of a shell coming in, or a bomb falling was very frightening. I well remember one night when some of us decided to sleep on the second floor of a frame house. We were all assigned to sentry duty that night, and thought it would be easier to call each other. We didn't expect enemy action but when German bombs came whistling down I was extremely nervous. That was the last serious threat we had, even though the war would not officially be over in Europe for another month.

Strangely, we moved back to the town of Ochsenfurt, the town where we were raided on the night of April 3rd. Our regiment scoured the area for a couple of days before moving south at the rate of about four miles per day, passing about 30 miles west of Nuremberg. Our regimental command post moved 19 times during those 30 days of April. That meant finding a new place to sleep almost every night. There was no need to dig a hole in which to sleep as nothing was being fired at us. I didn't sleep in or on a bed because of the prevalence of bedbugs and lice. A reasonably clean and smooth wood or concrete floor was usually my choice, but one night I found a smooth concrete slab in a basement morgue. I could not have found a more peaceful place.

Certainly that was not the case the next night when I unwisely used a room in an insane asylum. I hesitate to call it a mental hospital, considering the Nazi policy of eradicating the mentally deficient. Apparently the staff had departed, but most of the

A destroyed bridge in southern Bavaria

inmates remained since they had no place to go. The screaming and moaning of the inmates got worse as the evening progressed. It was a horribly depressing place to spend the night. The Nazi policy of treating mental illness was to eliminate those who had it and thus purify the race.

The weather became quite pleasant for much of the latter part of April. I stayed quite busy since I had to get the supply of food for the staff officers' mess, water for the company, and usually help take back prisoners. Nevertheless, I could often find a few minutes most days to explore the countryside. One sunny afternoon, I went for a stroll by myself. This was a lovely part of Bavaria, covered with green hills and beautiful valleys and not heavily populated. I found a most enticing stream that formed a pool deep enough to swim in and wasted no time stripping off my clothes and diving in. I had

A scene in southern Bavaria

such a pleasant swim that I vividly remember it to this day.

Another time I saw a castle on a hill and hurried up to explore it. It was vacant and apparently had been for some time, and next to it was the ruins of an even older castle. Nobody seemed to be around and after I finished exploring, I sat in the sun next to the castle and enjoyed the view for a while. I was reminded of Beethoven's 6th Symphony, "The Pastoral." It was running through my head, as this was the perfect setting for it. A vision of that lovely scene of hills, valleys, and pastures runs through my mind every time I hear that music. The castle and the adjacent ruins presented a peaceful vision I shall never forget.

On the 25th of April near the town of Lauingen we crossed the famous Danube River. It was a disappointment after imagining it from Johann Strauss Jr.'s "Beautiful Blue Danube Waltze." The river was swollen from the spring runoff and anything but blue, certainly very muddy. The closest large city from Lauingen was Augsburg, 25 miles to the southeast.

There were great numbers of German soldiers wandering about the countryside either in groups or individually, and nearly all wanted us to take them prisoners. Whenever I went out in the weapons carrier I would encounter them walking with their arms up hoping I would take them as prisoners before they were shot. I would indicate to them to walk toward our command post with their arms up, and pointed to where they should go. Later we grouped them together in a large open field and by the end of the day, there must have been about 5,000 of them. Our Company Commander, Frank Glaze, ordered them to be guarded by keeping them within a rectangular group. He had us post machine gunners at the opposite corners of the rectangle with orders to fire at any of them that stepped outside the designated boundaries.

Finally, a Division supply truck came up with cans of C-rations which contained such things as beef stew and hash. I helped pass out the food which we did by ordering the prisoners to walk by in groups of three men and giving each group a single can which was to be shared by all three. Each can was a size that would hold about six ounces of liquid measure. We had no way of getting sufficient water to the prisoners and there were no latrine facilities. A small number of them were women and we kept them grouped in one corner of the rectangle. With no desire to be assigned to a machine

German soldiers captured and placed into a rectangular field

gun where I might have to shoot prisoners, I volunteered to check them for anything that could be used for a weapon, such as a straight razor. One gave me a fine six-inch slide rule in a beautiful leather case. He insisted I take it even though I said he didn't have to give it up because it wasn't a weapon. We left the next day as a contingent of men from another division took over. It seemed negligent to me that the Army had not made arrangements to handle large numbers of prisoners taken at once, and I wondered how long it would be before these miserable remnants of Hitler's armies would get more food and water.

We were still about 10 miles west of Augsburg when we stopped just north of an airport where it was believed a number of German troops were located. I dug a foxhole in case of a skirmish. The ground was very wet and I had to put sticks and boards in the bottom of the hole to keep out of the water, and then put twigs on top before laying down my blanket. That evening a passenger aircraft took off from the airport and flew very low over my head and continued north. It seemed obvious to me that it was an important Nazi making an attempt to escape, but why would the plane be heading north? My understanding was that everything to the north was held by allied forces until somewhere south of Berlin. That led me to the conclusion that the escaping Nazi was headed for Berlin. This escape attempt remained a mystery to me for years after the war until I discovered some facts that helped explain what could have happened.

One set of events that has been described in books about the last days of Hitler's Germany I first found in William L. Shirer's book *The Rise and Fall of the Third Reich*. Hitler was in his bunker in Berlin when he received a telegram from the commander of the Luftwaffe, Herman Goering. In the telegram he said he was prepared to take over leadership if Hitler were to decide to relinquish power. Hitler was furious and declared Goering a traitor and stripped him of his Luftwaffe command. Hitler immediately selected General Ritter von Greim to take his place and telephoned von Greim, who was somewhere in the vicinity of Munich. The Germans still had telephone communication between the two cities by running the lines a little to the east and between the Allied and Russian advances. Von Greim was ordered to report to Hitler in the Berlin bunker at once. He ordered the famous German woman test pilot Hannah Reitsch to fly him there. Hitler did not tell von Greim why he

wanted to see him. He could as well have given him the information
by telephone and saved them from the extremely dangerous trip.
The flight passed over terrain that was being rapidly conquered by
the Russians who fired upon von Greim with anti-aircraft guns as
he passed over. Von Greim was wounded severely and had to be
carried on a stretcher when he met Hitler. Only then did he learn
of his meaningless promotion.

- - -

Early the next morning I made a water run for the Company,
and as I was delivering the water cans I was told we were about to
capture the adjacent airport from which the mysterious aircraft
had apparently left. My foxhole was dug a couple of hundred yards
outside a runway opposite the airport buildings. The captured
German generator truck was parked nearby. It was used to light the
regimental command post whenever the post could be located in a
bunker or structure that could be blacked out. The operator of the
truck, Virgil McGehe, had parked it with the back end in a deep mud
puddle and had left the generator motor running. He should have
connected the ground wire to a steel stake driven in the ground, but
he did not. When I took him his water can and hoisted it onto the
truck while standing in water, I supplied the ground for a 115 volt
current, my body being the conductor. I went completely numb and
fell down flat on my back into the water. I had no feeling but I could
see the 50 pound can of water falling through the air and landing
on my chest. I felt no more than if a feather dropped on me, but
afterward I felt stunned by the blow. Nobody was around and I don't
know how long I laid there with my mouth barely out of the water.

Gradually I came to my senses
but had to wait to overcome all
of the paralysis before I could
get up. I told McGehe to keep
the truck grounded or he would
get no more water.

I started back to my hole
when I was struck with the
most violent concussion blast
I experienced since we were

*Photo of an oil painting by Leon Wahl of
our company, showing the weapons carrier
author used*

bombed near St. Lo. The entire airport exploded at once. I had had enough shaking up for one day. The Germans had been storing quite a large number of bombs at the airport, and when they gave up hope of being able to defend it, they fused all the bombs together and set them off.

Chapter 18

THE NAZI LEGACY OF HORROR

Hitler's Reich of a thousand years
to myriads brought death and tears
and to his Aryan super race
Brought its demise and its own disgrace.

Capell '03 On the occasion of Hitler's self-inflicted death. April 1945

Early on the 30th of April we moved toward Munich. When we were about 15 miles northwest of it we neared the town of Dachau. We knew there was a infamous concentration camp there. I had read and heard about it by the time I was in high school, but that still did not prepare me for the extent of its horror. At the edge of the camp was a railroad siding lined with railroad cars. Most were boxcars with their doors open. One of the first cars I saw, however, was a gondola type which was filled to the top with a stack of naked human bodies, a preview of what we were to see in the boxcars. We stopped and examined them. Besides the gondola car, I counted 40 boxcars and all were loaded with dead humans. Whereas in the gondola car the bodies all appeared to be naked, those in the boxcars wore scraps of ragged striped uniforms and all were very emaciated.

We had no way of finding out whether the cars had just come in or were about to go out. Years later I found that a long time friend, Eudora Delo nee Eudora Radecop, was married to Perry Delo who had been in the 42nd Infantry Division which, along with the 45th Infantry Division, had been the first to open the camp on the previous day. Delo had picked up a small camera and taken a number of pictures in and around the Camp as well as the boxcars and their contents. 40 years later he generously offered them to me because I was so interested in seeing pictures of what I remembered so well. Perhaps for him it was a relief to get rid of them. I felt the war had left a serious emotional scar on my friend.

Bodies in boxcars at Dachau

Bodies in boxcars

Pile of bodies ready to be put into the incinerator

Ladislav Aigner, a Holocaust victim, was living proof that not everyone who came to Dachau in the boxcars was dead. He had been in one of the cars and was rescued when they were opened. His story, as told by his son is as follows:

Ladislav was a happy, 15-year-old Czechoslovakian boy who enjoyed working with his father who owned his own drayage business. Ladislav lived at home with his mother Anna, father Julius, and two sisters Erika and Marika. However, his family was Jewish and by 1938 the Czechoslovakian government was controlled by the Nazis, which meant disaster for Jewish families. His father's business license was revoked, as was the case with all Jews under Nazi domination. He succeeded in obtaining a position as a billiard equipment salesman. Later that same year the Nazis forced the family to move to a dreaded ghetto in Budapest, Hungary while Julius was sent to a labor camp in Russia. The ghetto was located in a section of Budapest next to a Nazi factory to serve as a human shield in order to deter Allied bombings of German industry.

The ghetto was a horrible place where Jews, who had been taken from their homes, were crowded together with inadequate food and water. Some were forced to labor outside the ghetto, but were severely punished should they try to smuggle food back in to the ghetto. All of the younger, healthier men, however, were already taken away to labor for the Nazis and only old men and children remained. Many died from illness and starvation. Except for infants, every Jew was required to sew a yellow Star of David on their clothing to wear at all times.

The family's stay in the ghetto soon ended when cattle car trains began crowding Jews, including the Aigners, on board and headed for an unknown destination. Buckets of water and containers of food were occasionally shoved in the cars. Their toilet facilities consisted of a barrel with a couple of boards on the top. The stench was so severe that the car occupants crowded the cracks at the edges of the doors seeking a tiny bit of fresh air. Eventually the train reached Auschwitz, Poland. The family soon realized their destination was Auschwitz Concentration Camp, which was designed and built as a "death camp".

After being ordered off the train, they were paraded in front of Dr. Mengele who selected those who would die and those who would be assigned to labor. Ladislav, already numbed by the events of the past week, watched with horror as his mother and his sister,

Marika were directed to a line which led to the "showers". They would be ordered to undress and enter a "shower" room. After being crowded in, the door was locked and poison gas canisters were inserted through the ceiling. Ladislav would never see them again. This was Hitler's "final solution" being carried out at Auschwitz, one of the camps built for that purpose. Such was planned to be the ultimate fate of all Jews, Gypsies, homosexuals, political or dissident Protestant leaders and anyone else undesirable to Hitler and his Nazi hierarchy.

Ladislav was considered by Dr. Mengele to be healthy enough to perform labor. He was 15 years old and had survived the starvation conditions of the ghetto and the cattle car. His other sister, Erika was removed from the line but he did not know of her fate at the time. He was taken with the other laborers and with a group of five men he was given a bowl of thin potato broth to share between them. The men were then assigned to work, Ladislav being sent to the kitchen. Certain Jews were known as "Zonder Commandos" and were given special privileges such as a little more food than the others. They had the horrible duty of removing the dead from the gas chambers, which meant they often dealt with their own family

Dachau Prisoners Released. Undoubtedly these were either new arrivals or Zonder Commandos

members and friends. They also policed the barracks and picked up those who died during the night and during their laboring work.

Working in the kitchen gave Ladislav occasional opportunities to filch a little extra food which, although it helped ward off starvation, resulted in him being caught by a guard when he attempted to get a bit of cabbage. The guard threw a pitchfork at him, which pierced his foot. He sought medical care and was sent to the camp hospital when his foot developed an infection. It was in the same camp hospital that Dr. Mengele carried out many of his infamous and horrible experiments. Dr. Mengele abided by the slogan "An injured Jew is a worthless Jew and therefore a dead one". Dr. Epstein was a Jewish doctor assigned to the hospital and treated Ladislav kindly during his second visit for the same infection. One day Dr. Epstein ordered him from the hospital. He was puzzled at the change of attitude of Dr. Epstein toward him until a few days later when he realized all the remaining patients were removed and sent to the gas chambers.

Even with his foot still getting worse he was sent back to work. He encountered an inmate who was being transferred to another camp but wanted to stay near his family at Auschwitz. He traded uniforms with the man and took on his identity so he would be transferred instead. That caused him to be moved to a camp at Landsberg, Germany where airplane bunkers were being constructed. Ladislav's injured foot was accidentally scorched by water, which magnified the pain. Due to this incident he was sent to Landsberg Hospital for treatment. After one week with the terrible conditions at the hospital he had contracted typhus, lice, and a fever that led to periods of unconsciousness.

In the meantime, the Russians were closing in on the eastern front and the allies, including the 4th Infantry Division was approaching on the western front. Hitler ordered the slave laborers to be removed from the fighting front probably because he did not want the allies, especially, to see the conditions under which the laborers were forced to work. Those at Landsburg, including 15 year-old Ladislav, were to be shipped to Dachau and loaded into cattle cars. Three American infantry divisions, including the 4th, were getting near and the guns of battle could be clearly heard at Landsburg.

On the way to Dachau American fighter planes strafed the train and some of the Jews were killed and wounded. With part of the

Wall and electrified fence surrounding the camp at Dachau

Dachau guards executed by American soldiers

roof of the cattle car torn off, Ladislav made his escape, but he was shortly afterward recaptured by the Germans and put back on a cattle car. Thus what became known as the "Death Train" was on its way to Dachau. We (the 4th Division) arrived at Dachau at the end of April 1945, less than one day after the train arrived there.

As we neared the camp the first thing to come into my view was an open-top gondola type of railroad car loaded with naked and obviously dead bodies. On the track next to it were a series of boxcars, 40 in all, each with its door fully or partially opened to reveal dozens of bodies. Some were so emaciated they were little more than skeletons, and all wore striped concentration camp uniforms. Men from the 42nd Infantry Division had arrived some hours before and had opened the cars and found a few survivors who had been removed by the time we arrived on the scene.

By the camp and lying in front of a concrete wall were a number of dead Germans in Army uniforms who had obviously been lined up along the wall and apparently executed by the troops who first entered the camp. Perry Delo, a member of the 42nd Infantry Division, described to me how these Germans were rounded up and shot. In the meantime, the camp inmates attacked the camp guards and were stoning them to death. According to Ladislav Aigner, the American troops forcefully restrained the inmates and took their victims away as prisoners.

Upon his rescue from amongst the bodies in one of the Death Train cars, Ladislav was taken by American troops to a hospital where he was not expected to survive. However, after a prolonged hospital stay he recovered and learned that his father and sister Erika had been located by the Red Cross and reunited in Budapest. Eventually he joined the remaining members of his family in Budapest. During the Hungarian revolution against the Russians in 1956 he escaped, which is a story in itself, and finally boarded a ship for the United States. He took the name Leslie Aigner and now resides in Oregon with his wife Eva, herself a victim of the Budapest ghetto.

Many of the inmates were still in the camp when we left. We were ordered to move on and continue to scour the countryside for remnants of German forces. We were told we should not attempt to assist the inmates because special troops were being brought in that were trained to deal with them. Many of the prisoners, however, had left and were lingering in the vicinity.

The author, left, with Eva and Leslie Aigner

Our kitchen truck had arrived in the town of Dachau and was ready to serve us a hot meal. After filling my mess kit with food I sat down against a nearby tree. I noticed some young children in striped suits in the bushes not far from where I was. I was astounded by how young they were. Before seeing them I did not know that children were among the prisoners at Dachau. At that time I was under the impression that the concentration camp was for political prisoners and did not realize that it was mainly for Jews, Gypsies, some Christian theologians and a number of other populations not considered suitable to the Nazis.

As soon as I sat down to eat, a few of these children wandered toward me, and one stood directly in front of me staring down at my food. They would not speak and certainly would not smile or even change their expressions. I offered my food, but not even the boy in front of me would reach out to take it. I finally pushed the mess kit into his hands, whereupon he silently turned and carried it away into the nearby woods. The boy showed no emotion and said nothing. He was so emaciated I could not tell whether he was six or fifteen years old. Leslie Aigner told me that since the boy was in Dachau, he was probably about fifteen years old, which was Aigner's age when he was first taken to Auschwitz. The emotional impact of the sight of those children with their blank faces and sunken eyes remains with me very strongly today.

That afternoon we moved to Gauting which is 10 miles southwest of Munich. It is quite picturesque and has a good view of the Alps along the southern horizon. Even though it was quite close to Munich there was no conspicuous evidence of war damage. Our kitchen truck had moved into Gauting and was setting up to serve an evening meal. Since I had given away my previous meal, I was looking forward to some food. About that time a friend in our company drove by me in a 2½ ton GMC truck and asked me to join him. He had been ordered to pick up a group that included the mayor and leading citizens of Dachau, and drive them to observe the horrible scenes inside and around the concentration camp. I knew it would be an experience I would never forget, but I also knew I would get no food until the following morning. I was very hungry, so I declined the invitation. I still regret missing that opportunity.

For the next few days we remained in Gauting. Few of the residents were still there, thus nearly all of the houses were empty of their occupants so plenty of beds were available, but rather than sleep in a house I preferred to sleep in a park-like field. After ten months of sleeping outside, the park appealed to me. The house next to the park was obviously the most expensive residence in town and I suspect belonged to the Nazi Gauleiter, or governing leader of that area. The fact that he apparently fled, or more probably had been taken into custody by the U. S. Army tended to confirm my conclusion. Therefore, I felt quite justified to enter the house and find a single-size bed mattress to take outside to sleep on.

Not long after I laid the mattress down I got a visit from a sergeant I did not recognize, but suspected he was from Division Headquarters. He said: "Where did you get that mattress?"

"Why do you want to know?" I responded.

"You got it out of that house didn't you?"

"So?"

"Take it back!"

"The HELL I will!" I responded angrily.

"You'll take that back or I'll get half a dozen MPs up here and they'll take it back!"

Disgustedly I retorted, "What's all this to you?"

He replied, "I have my orders."

"I get the picture now. That house belongs to a big-time Nazi and you guys are protecting him, but don't give a damn about an ordinary German citizen."

I began to realize what the Army command was doing. They wanted to get complete cooperation from the Nazi leaders in the area so they could get better access to records of the displaced persons and various types of information about the local government. The Nazis also had access to records of the slave laborers who were issued to various businessman and farmers. In addition, there was also the Nazi program of placing the blonde and blue-eyed children they had taken from conquered countries, with German families to be raised as Germans. The U.S. Army wanted all the information the Nazi leaders had about these children.

Chapter 19

IT'S OVER

The guns are silent but Berlin burns,
Though chaos reigns, the peace returns,
Families head back to what once were homes
Where a desperate outlaw gang now roams,
At last the war is over, we may celebrate
And dedicate ourselves to love not hate.

Capell '03 on the occasion of the armistice May 8,1945

We entered Munich on May 7th, one day before the war officially ended in Europe. The city was in more complete ruin than any city I had seen so far. Looking in any direction it was difficult to find a roof intact and few complete walls were still standing. The streets were so filled with rubble we had difficulty getting our vehicles through. The one building that I remember as being intact was the Buergerbraukeller. This was the beer hall where a bomb exploded after Hitler's speech in an unsuccessful attempt on his life. It was also the site of the 1923 Beer Hall Putsch. Much of the city was still burning and I wondered where those hundreds of thousands of people were. How many were hiding in those ruins? Forty years later I met one who was. Victoria Hylla who as a child lived in Munich was there during the destruction of the city. She was in the basement of a building that was still burning, and had to leave when the heat got too intense. She later married Heinz who was then a prisoner of war held by the Americans. He had been in a parachute division that fought directly against us when we landed on Utah Beach in Normandy. He and his wife and my wife and I became close friends after Heinz and I met following being interviewed on a D-Day anniversary television feature, as I described in chapter 3. He was a POW in Germany, and, when the war ended, settled in Portland, Oregon, after being sponsored by an American officer.

Buergerbraukeller in Munich at right

Gene Redfield, at left, brings the official word from Division Headquarters

When we got news the war was officially over we were near a town called Burglenfeld, about 20 miles north of the city of Regensburg. For us the war had been over for days. The last shot I remember firing was on April 5th at Ochsenfurt. After that time there was one German air raid and some occasional German artillery, but even that died out before the end of April.

From Munich we traveled on the Autobahn for a few miles although much of it was impassable due to bomb craters. It was the first chance I had to see one of Hitler's touted super highways. I knew of none in the U.S. like that until years later. We didn't know it at the time, but later learned the Armistice was being signed. There was no celebration because for us we had considered the war over for at least a week. In reality, most German soldiers had given up long before.

We settled in near Burglenfeld for the night. This was a pleasant wooded area about 25 miles to the east of Nuremberg. After returning from a water run I was asked to take a corporal to one of our First Battalion Companies to pick up some supplies for our kitchen. I was given a map showing the exact location, so we started out and soon saw a sight that grabbed our attention. We had just turned onto a narrow tree-lined road when there ahead of us was a very attractive, well-dressed young lady. She wore a stylish jacket and skirt with high-heeled shoes and silk stockings. She had dark attractively styled hair. She was walking in the same direction as we were going, and the corporal immediately said "Let's pick her up." I stopped and used the limited German I knew to ask her where she was going. She indicated the next town where her parents lived about six miles down the road. I said we could take her for about 4½ miles before I turned off the road. She was a little afraid at first but finally began to trust me. I told her to climb up and ride in back. I thought of helping her but was afraid she would be frightened if I moved toward her. As she stepped up her skirt rose along with my pulse.

The corporal knew I had a stash of cigarettes in a compartment under the driver's seat. When he asked me how many I had, I surmised what he had in mind. I didn't like it at all and told him so, but there was not much I could do to prevent him from propositioning her. He was a corporal and outranked me and I was assigned to him for this mission. He took a handful of cigarette packages and ordered me to drive off the road into a small clearing in the forest. I said, "If she says no, or if she resists you in any way you leave her alone or I'll make you!" He knew I meant business and dropped the cigarettes. She realized what we were arguing about and she screamed, "NEIN!" She scrambled out of the vehicle while calling the corporal a swine, and thanking me. I grabbed six packs of cigarettes and shoved them at her and said emphatically, "Weiter Gehen!" while pointing to the road. She understood and when she saw the corporal was not moving toward her she looked at me, smiled and said, "Danke!" When she got to the road she turned, waved, smiled, and continued on her way. Surprisingly, the corporal apologized for his conduct and admitted she had reason to call him a "swine."

Cigarettes were much in demand for purposes of barter and were as good as money. Both the corporal and I laughed about how the young lady might explain how she "earned" the six packs of cigarettes. I sent all of my pay home but if I had been paid in Europe I would have been paid in "invasion money" which was printed by the U.S. government in the denomination of the country. The purpose of this was to prevent inflation in the various countries. On the currency black-market in Paris, an American 1-dollar bill was worth 5 dollars in the currency of the country. While the war was on we were threatened with capital punishment for carrying American money in the European countries. The capital punishment threat was the only effective punishment for many infantry riflemen. They could not be busted in rank because they were already at the bottom, and their pay was so low they did not draw enough money to be able to pay much of a fine. However, I'm sure the army was not interested in killing off its own men so I doubt if the threat was carried out very often.

We stayed in Burglenfeld for about a week where the staff officer's mess was in a building with hotel rooms upstairs. In one section of rooms there were girls who were in their late teens and early twenties. There were mostly Poles and Russians and those who had been taken from their families by the Germans. They were placed with German farm families to be raised as Germans and help on the farms. They were preferably blond and blue-eyed. The plan was to return them to their real families. I would come to the building each day to pick up the garbage and one Polish girl would always talk to me as best she could considering the language barrier. One day I was to pick up something from our kitchen truck, which was no more than a mile away and I thought there would be no harm in letting her ride along. As we neared our destination she suddenly started yelling and jumping around while pointing at a house. I slowed to see what she was yelling about and she quickly jumped out and ran into the house. I came right after her and found her hugging and kissing a woman and man. She said, "Papa and Mama!" I knew she was Polish and they were Germans, and then realized they were the ones who had been taking care of her after she was brought to Germany. I felt terrible to have to do it but I knew I had to forcibly pull her away and drag her back to the truck. All I could do was to return her to the building where she had been kept, and hope for the best for her and for her real parents, as well as the ones who adopted her. It was another case of the devastation the Nazi inhumanity brought to so many people.

Every day I loaded the garbage from the staff officer's mess and took it to the area designated as a dump. Starving people from around the area had already discovered it and were waiting when I arrived. I had been instructed not to let them have any for fear of spreading disease. Being alone on the truck there was no way I could prevent them from getting at it without shooting them, which I refused to do. I jumped into the back of the weapons carrier and knocked two of them down and off the truck. There already was at least a dozen of them pushing against the back of the truck and more coming. The situation was desperate, and as another old man tried to climb on, I punched him, and felt sick in the stomach for having done so. Many of the people were holding out containers. I tried to dump the can where they could get it, but there was so much desperate pushing and shoving, with some of the people down on the ground being stepped on, I just dumped the can's contents on top of them. It was a horrible experience, and I had to go through similar experiences each day for the rest of the week.

It was no wonder I became so angry when, after I returned to the U.S., I heard people complaining about us sending food to the war-torn parts of Europe.

Bamberg was a moderate sized city about 35 miles to the north-northeast from Nuremberg and it was to be our company's home for the next five weeks. We were told we would soon be heading back to the U.S. I was also told I would be one of four men from our company who would be given a 24-hour pass to go to Paris. Even better was the news that Gene Redfield would also be going along with another friend, Stan Kakoski. I had been anticipating getting a pass now that the war was over. Since it had been over a year since I had a pass, I was expecting one and had been saving up my cigarettes to finance the day. I had them stored in the compartment under the driver's seat of the weapons carrier. The next morning when I checked to see how many cartons I had, I found nothing but an empty compartment. I was absolutely certain no one in our company had stolen them, but immediately suspected German boys from the Hitler Youth who had been hanging around and harassing us in whatever ways they could. On a sunny day, for example, they would get a big mirror and reflect the sun into our eyes. They undoubtedly were prowling our vehicles at night. Nevertheless, my friends in the Company immediately took up a cigarette collection and presented me with even more cartons of cigarettes then I had lost.

There were about twenty-six men from the regiment who would be going, all of whom had seen extensive combat. Two 2½-ton trucks with drivers were assigned to take us. But since Paris was more than 400 miles away over shell-pocked and bomb-cratered roads there would hardly be time to do any more than get there and back. We decided that if everyone chipped in a carton of cigarettes we could bribe the drivers to leave by 9 PM the evening before and return a few hours late. The bribery worked and we were in Paris shortly after sunrise. The first thing we had to do was to convert our cigarettes into French currency. The black marketers surrounded the truck with their offers of 600 francs per carton until after our first refusals. The offers went up to 650 and there were a few takers, but we held out for 700 and soon had a buyer who led us in to a dingy looking cafe (a Parisian cafe is really a saloon). One of the four men from our company said he was not ready to accept 700 as he thought he might get more. We were taken into the back room of the cafe to a desk behind which sat a fat guy smoking a cigar. We started to set the cartons on the desk, when suddenly the other man in our group came rushing in to tell us he had an offer of 750, and his buyer would take all we had. We grabbed the cartons off the desk as the new buyer was escorting our companion into the room. The cigar fell out of the fat guy's mouth as he jumped up and said, "700 is all." Obviously the 750 offer came from another member of the same gang and that unfortunate individual knew he was in deep trouble. I have never seen a man get such a sudden look of fear. He had outbid his own gang member. We all yelled at the fat guy and threatened to tear up the place if he didn't pay up at the rate of 750 for all the cartons we had. His look of rage turned more to one of fear of what we might do and he promptly paid up. Now we were ready to see Paris.

The first thing I wanted to see in Paris was the Cathedral de Notre Dame. When I announced my choice it met with unanimous approval. We soon found a USO information booth and were able to get a small map of downtown Paris and took a subway train to the Cathedral. We had a good look at it, which, in itself, was a thrill for me, but unfortunately we could not go inside as was the case with many places in Paris so soon after the war. The next place on our list was the Champs Elysees and Eiffel Tower. Nearby we found a nice looking restaurant. I don't remember much about the food, but I certainly remember the string quartet that played chamber music all through our lunch. For me this was the most enjoyable experience of the day. Many of the places tourists usually visit in Paris, such as The Louvre, were still closed so soon after the war. We had heard so much about "Pig Alley" (actually Place de Pigalle) that we all wanted to see it. I surmised it was the center of the Parisian underworld, and was a series of cafes (saloons) and brothels. The saloons all contained a number of drunken GI's. They wanted to talk in the hope of getting some sympathy. They had deserted from the infantry and had been living off their association with the Paris underworld. They were mostly involved in going on American military installations, which they could do since they were still in American uniforms, and stealing whatever they could and turning it over to Parisian black-market gangsters. Now that the war was over the allied command was concentrating on stopping the practice and arresting those involved. These men had all committed capital offenses, including desertion, and knew they would be shot when captured, which they thought would be inevitable. They would never see their homes again with allied forces now all over Europe except for the neutral countries, and the borders of these countries were lined with military police. It was virtually impossible for a fugitive deserter to escape. Some may have survived by staying close to where they were, but would find it nearly impossible to earn a living. I doubt if the underworld would help them since they were of no use to them anymore. As far as I know, no one has traced their stories or written about them.

While in Paris we had hoped to see the famous Folles Bergere, but, unfortunately let ourselves get talked into going to the show at the Cafe de Mayol. It featured a French-style slapstick comedy and beautiful undressed girls, but it got a bit boring after a while. We soon left but by that time it was getting too late to do anything but wander the streets before we were to meet the trucks to take us back. Our reception by the citizens was nothing like what it was nine months before when we were so wildly welcomed as liberators. The people we met on the street were not typical French citizens, of course, but mainly street people hoping to take advantage of American GIs. There were countless prostitutes with as many as a dozen of them encountering us in a single block. Some of them were so obviously sick with respiratory diseases they were deathly thin and went into frequent spells of uncontrollable coughing. I'm sure they felt there was no other way they could make a living. It was a very sad sight that left a mental image of the Paris we saw that ranged from the beauties of the Seine River bridges, the Cathedral de Notre Dame, and the string quartet chamber music, to the ugly scenes in "Pig Alley," the barely shielded sidewalk urinals for men, the open sewers which ran under steel gratings in the back rooms of seedier saloons, and the myriads of street-walking prostitutes. That was Paris in its turmoil less than two weeks after the war ended.

We boarded the trucks just after 10 PM after being awake continuously for the previous 40 hours, and now we had at least an eight-hour trip ahead of us. In spite of the fact we were riding on wooden benches in the back of a truck bouncing over badly damaged roads, we all fell asleep almost immediately. We had different drivers from the Army Quartermaster Corps and hoped that they were well caught up on their sleep. The sky was beginning to brighten up early the next morning as it does at that time of the year, and I noticed the truck behind not more than about 50 feet back and swinging rather erratically from one side of the road to the other. I was sitting in the very back on the left side of our truck and could see the driver of the truck behind beginning to slump forward over the wheel. The alternate driver was sitting next to him sound asleep. The truck he was driving would creep up on us each time our driver would slow a bit for a rough spot in the road. I didn't know what good it would do, but I yelled to wake everybody up. If the truck behind crashed into us I would be the first at the scene of the accident and nobody wanted to trade places with me. Our driver finally heard us yelling and started honking his horn and tried to speed up but was hitting a badly damaged part of the road. The truck behind gained on us rapidly and I was about to be badly in need of a miracle. There probably isn't any such thing as mental telepathy but nevertheless, the driver came to just in time to swerve his truck to the left and missed us without an inch to spare. His truck continued into the bushes on the left, and finally came to stop after clearing out a strip of small trees. We were able to get the truck backed out and onto the road. The drivers were informed that if any one of them fell asleep on the rest of the trip, we would promptly execute his death sentence. We arrived in our camp near Bamberg just in time to get in on the morning serving of chow.

Chapter 20

BAMBERG TO THE BEACH

Through the debris where friends lives ceased,
where all creatures suffered man and beast.
We leave behind the scenes of war
and pray such horror shall rule no more.

Capell '03 on withdrawing from the battlefields of Europe

Another enjoyable opportunity came shortly after our Paris trip when an announcement came from Division Headquarters that two famous opera singers would make a special appearance for American troops at Nuremberg Stadium. I knew them very well from radio and movies. One was the famous American singer Grace Moore, and the other Nino Martini, an Italian great. I immediately put in a request to go and was selected. The musical taste of most American GIs, I expected, hit somewhere below the level of opera, but to my surprise there was a big crowd, nearly all in attendance were from the 4th Division. The singers, both of whom had performed frequently at the Metropolitan Opera in New York, gave a beautiful concert. It also gave me a memorable look at Nuremberg Stadium. The huge concrete swastika, under which Hitler gave speeches and where extravagant Nazi rallies were held, was still standing. It was destroyed very soon afterward to prevent it from being used as a neo-Nazi shrine. As far as the GIs appreciation of the concert was concerned, it could not have been more enthusiastic with round after round of applause. The show was sponsored by the USO (United Service Organization), and was the only USO show I had a chance to see in all the time I was overseas. Such Hollywood stars as Bob Hope and Bing Crosby were supposedly in many overseas shows but they played to rear echelon troops only. Of course there was no way they could have or should have brought a show that close to active combat. Nevertheless, the Army could have taken some of us back when a show was nearby, but in my case at least, it never did.

Redfield came to me shortly after I returned to Bamberg with a letter from Division Headquarters. I was astounded to read that I had orders to report to the Division Military Police to which I was being transferred. I immediately went to Captain Glaze to ask him what it was about. He said he had nothing to do with it, and there was nothing he could do about it. He said they had selected me and I should consider it an honor. I told him that now the war was over I wanted to spend my remaining days with some of the men I had been with for so long. Being in the MPs would have been a very good place to be during combat. Having kitchen cooked meals and a tent to sleep in would have been a much more desirable situation during combat, but now that combat was over I was not happy about leaving the company I had been with for so long. This is not to say that a 4th Division MP unit was a safe place, especially when I remember back in Normandy when the anti-personnel bombs fell directly on the truckload of MPs coming up to get our prisoners. The MP unit was encamped at Division Headquarters, which was within shelling range of the Germans, but back a few miles from the actual fighting front most of the time.

Had I not been disappointed at having to leave my old company, I probably would have looked forward to it as a new experience. I also had a friend in the unit with whom I always enjoyed visiting. He had been a professional baseball player before going into the Army and was a very interesting guy. Back in Bamberg, since I had more time to myself, I applied for an Army correspondence course on Meteorology. I completed the course and enjoyed it so much I applied for another on electricity which arrived and was forwarded to me in the MP unit at Ansbach. I was given a shiny new MP helmet, and new clothes. I turned in my old helmet, but not without a final look at the huge dent in the back of it. A big chunk of shrapnel had struck it and sent it spinning off my head one time in Normandy. I wish I still had it as a memento.

My first couple of assignments were guarding American prisoners who had committed a variety of offenses. Then one day I was assigned to stand watch at the gate of Division Headquarters. My friend was on duty there at the time, and I was to relieve him in about 15 minutes. He was facing the gate, as was the standard

procedure, and I was standing with my back to it when a jeep
suddenly drove up. He snapped to attention and saluted. He said,
"TURN AROUND." I did, but was too late. The jeep screeched to
stop and a major shouted, "COME HERE SOLDIER!" My friend
said "I'm sorry, I should have warned you." Suddenly I realized
all the commotion was due to the fact I was wearing a brightly
painted MP helmet and standing by the main gate. I should have
spun around and saluted to show proper respect for an officer.
The major ordered me to take off the helmet and sit on the front
of the jeep with my feet on the front bumper. He had his driver
parade me around the Division Headquarters area before stopping
at the Provost Marshal's office. He had his driver escort me in and
report to the Marshal. The major described my offense and left. I
stood at attention in front of the Marshal while he asked me why
I had not saluted. I told him I had just been transferred from an
infantry regiment and had been in since D-Day, and during all that
time was told not to salute an officer. He asked me how I felt about
being transferred to the MPs; "Do you consider it an honor?" I
told him I hadn't thought of it that way, but I did miss being with
my old company. He thought for a moment, and then said, "If you
don't want to be in the MPs, you don't have to be." He told me to
report to the sergeant at the desk just outside his office. I sincerely
thanked him.

The sergeant told me to sit down and he would prepare papers
for me, and asked where I wanted to go. He agreed that he could
send me back to my old company and asked me what platoon or
section I wanted. He was very considerate and told me to take
my time and think about where I would most want to go. During
combat I had always thought I would find the I and R Platoon the
most challenging, but now that the war was over I preferred the
job as a Message Center driver. I would be out of camp most of the
day seeing a lot of the surrounding countryside, and would be on
my own as long I did not leave the jeep. Furthermore, I liked the
sergeant in charge of the section and he was happy to have me.
When I went back to the MP barracks to get my duffel bag, my
baseball player friend was waiting for me. He said he felt terrible
about what happened and blamed himself for not alerting me as
soon as he saw the major approaching. He realized too late that I
was not accustomed to saluting officers. I told him I would miss
being in the same unit as he was, but I felt I would be happier with

my old company doing a job I liked. Division Headquarters was at Ansbach, which was about 25 miles southwest of Nuremberg. I started walking back but soon was offered a ride most of the way and arrived at Regimental Headquarters. The Message Center Sergeant welcomed me and assigned me a jeep. I was happy to be back and was on permanent dispatch, which meant I could leave the company area with the jeep anytime I wished. However, I was very careful not to abuse the privilege.

It was now the 21st of June and we were slated to head back to the French Coast, and soon after head for Le Havre, where we were to board a troop ship to take us home. The war with Japan was still on and the 4th Division was selected to lead the invasion of the main island. Of course, the whole plan was not revealed to us then, but we had a rough idea. We had recently heard about the point system. We had been issued points for various things such as time in service, time over seas, combat-infantry badge, and wounds acquired in action. Once a man had exceeded a certain number of points he was eligible for discharge from the Army. I had far more points than were needed. Some of the men had even more points than I did and the Message Center chief was one of them. He was soon transferred out of our division. I was asked to take his job, which would have given me an immediate promotion to sergeant. However, I was terribly afraid I might be frozen in the job until replaced and be delayed in getting my discharge from the Army. Therefore, in order to play it absolutely safe I declined the promotion.

There was a great deal of uncertainty about who would go with our Division to the Japan invasion. I gambled that I would not be kept in and hoped I would be right. The Company moved out of the Bamberg area on June 22nd, but four of us were ordered to stay back for a couple of days to police the area. That meant we were to check around for any equipment that might have been left, and to keep the starving citizenry from digging up our garbage holes and spreading disease among themselves. I knew there would be little we could do since there had been four garbage pits in our area and we couldn't keep watch on all of them at the same time. Before we could finish checking all of the holes, the first was already dug up. It was hopeless unless we stationed one-man at each location and shot the people to keep them back, which was unthinkable. It was sickening to see people suffering from hunger like that.

Bridge at city of Bamberg, the line of people along the side are refugees returning to their homes.

To catch up to the Company I drove the four of us in the jeep across southern Germany on a route that took us through Kaiserlautern, Germany and into France to the city of Metz. We arrived there on the afternoon of June 24th and met the Company at the city park where they were scheduled to be. We did not move that evening so Gene Redfield and I spent a couple of hours at a nearby outdoor beer garden. Even though it was in France at that time, it was very German, complete with a German brass band and Bavarian-style costumed waitresses serving beer in steins.

The next stop was Soissons, and then we traveled to the American camp called Old Gold by Ourville, France. This camp is just a few miles from the port of Le Havre. We stayed at Old Gold for about five days before preparing to board the American troop ship *Hermitage*. She was once the Italian luxury liner "Conte de Biacamano." I loaded my belongings in a duffel bag but was not allowed to carry any American weapons. However, we were allowed to keep any foreign ones. I had carried the 38 caliber French pistol ever since I took it from a German soldier shortly after D-Day. I carried it on me all day and slept with it in my hand almost every night since I got it, and now on impulse I turned to my friend Horace Sisk and said, "Here, you take this. Now that I'm through with war I will have no more use for this. I don't ever expect to fire a gun again." Horace thanked me very much, but said I should take it home as a souvenir. I reiterated, "No, I'm giving it to you." He said, "Well, you keep this then." He gave me a very nice little 9-mm Czechoslovakian pistol in an exquisite leather holster. I said, "I suppose you're right. It will be a nice souvenir and I don't have to fire it if I don't want to." I still have it, and it is a good souvenir but I do wish I had kept my original one.

Gene Redfield after the war

A Frenchman we called "Frenchy" had stayed with us ever since he started fighting with us in Normandy. Because we were so short of men, due to the heavy casualties at that time, he was welcomed to fight with us. In exchange he was given an American uniform and supplied with a rifle and fed. Although he was one of a number of Frenchman who fought with us, he was the only one who stayed with us the entire time. He was in line to start walking up the gangplank to board the ship when he was suddenly grabbed by a couple of MPs. He yelled in protest and was almost hysterical as they pulled him away. He had never actually been inducted into the U.S. Army. We all were extremely upset and yelled and booed and some men started to his aid, but we knew it was to no avail.

Chapter 21

HOME TO PARADISE

The battle is done, the peace is won.
No more we hear the Nazi gun.
Now we sing WE'RE HOMEWARD BOUND.
There never was more glorious sound.

Capell '03 aboard troop ship bound for New York

The date was July 2nd, 1945. The July sun was in its glory and there was great joy among us. However we were disappointed and angered that Frenchy had been held back after all his hopes and dreams of the past months. As I boarded the ship I thrilled to the fact that I was going home again and had survived the European war. I knew the war with Japan was something I might yet have to face, but in any case, there would be a furlough at home. Furthermore I didn't expect anything ahead would be as tough as it had been when we attacked the Atlantic Wall.

There were pangs of sadness as I realized my father would not be home when I arrived, but there would be many memories of him, I knew he would have been happy for me that I was coming back alive and healthy. I would see my mother again, as well as my dog Prince. Of course I also had thoughts of the friends I made overseas who were killed and were not coming back with us.

I was so happy to see our sleeping quarters on the ship. It was poles apart from what I experienced on the *Mauritania* coming over. Here we had cots to sleep in with blankets and a pillow. We had three cooked meals per day, and nothing to do except enjoy the cruise. The weather was beautiful and since I loved the sea, it was all a paradise. The trip home was direct because there was no threat of submarines. Anxious as I was to get home, the passage to New

4th Division troops aboard the US troop ship Hermitage heading to New York Harbor

York was almost too soon over. The entry to the New York Harbor was memorable because as soon as we moved into the entrance of the harbor I saw a tugboat towing a barge approaching our port side. Since I was forward standing by the rail on the port side I was one of the first to notice the row of can-can dancers on the barge kicking their legs high in the air. Within seconds men began rushing to the port side of the ship, and with the sudden shift of weight the vessel began taking on a dangerous list.

Suddenly a voice came on the public address microphone and announced, "HALF OF YOU MEN MOVE TO THE RIGHT SIDE OF THE SHIP IMMEDIATELY!" This was followed by another command:

"MOVE RIGHT IMMEDIATELY. MORE DANCING GIRLS ARE APPROACHING ON THE RIGHT SIDE!"

The Hermitage, New York. July 10th, 1945

Some of the men did move toward the right side of the vessel and called out, "THERE THEY ARE!" and sure enough there was another barge load of can-can girls coming up alongside the starboard bow. More men rushed to the starboard side and gradually the vessel ceased its dangerous list. Thus went our chance to go down in history as the first troop ship to be capsized by a barge load of dancing girls.

A female reporter had just come aboard and was interviewing soldiers arriving home. I stood close just to hear the American young woman speaking the language of American English. Except for the few words I overheard from the Red Cross doughnut girls I had not heard an attractive girl speak American English since I left the States more than a year and a half before.

After landing in New York we loaded on trucks to take us briefly to a camp near New York and soon after were on trains headed to our particular parts of the country. I met Harold Cross who was in another company in our regiment and we became friends traveling across the country. He was headed for Portland while I was headed for Seattle, so we were together until he disembarked at Spokane to take another train to Portland. We became lifelong friends.

Fort Lewis was the destination of our train and after checking in and getting an official furlough for 30 days from the time I left New York, I was free to go home. It was a wonderful feeling to walk out of the gate at Fort Lewis and start home. I had no money since I had not drawn Army pay for some time. I went out to the highway and hitchhiked home on a truck. The driver let me off at 8th Avenue and Spokane Street from where I planned to walk home, but when I got out and stood on the streets I was completely disoriented. Some buildings had changed while I was gone and I was lost. I went to a nearby tavern to find out exactly where I was and how to get home. After a few quick questions it all came back to me. Carrying my duffel bag I walked along Spokane Street to the base of the West Seattle hill and walked up to our house. I walked around to the back where through the window I saw my mother and my dog Prince. When I knocked on the door my mother answered it and got a complete surprise. The last she knew of my whereabouts was when I wrote her just before boarding the ship in Le Havre.

Prince's reaction was interesting. He did not seem to fully understand who I was, yet he didn't bark so he knew I was not a stranger. He just stood there looking puzzled. It took him a day or so to fully realize that I had actually come back. After that he got all excited whenever I came home after only a few hours away.

My mother filled me in on all the news she hadn't given me in her letters. I asked her about a girl whom I had met in junior high school and always liked. I thought she was charming and quite pretty and a top student in school. My mother knew where she was working and I went there immediately

Jack Capell before discharge from the Army

and we started dating. She quit her job so we saw each other nearly everyday. The Seattle weather was beautiful and every day we played tennis, swam, sailed and generally enjoyed ourselves. She and I and my mother made a trip to Vancouver B.C. and visited cousins and aunts and uncles, and particularly my cousin Rena Carver, who was like a sister to me. We took our mothers with us to most places we went. Then suddenly the atomic bombs were dropped on Japan and the war ended while I

The author visiting relatives in Vancouver, BC after returning home

was still at home. I reported to Fort Lewis expecting to be released from the Army almost immediately, but instead was put on a troop train heading east to an unknown destination. We wound up at Camp Butner, North Carolina. The wait seemed almost unbearable but I finally got out on October 15th.

Instead of going directly home I decided to visit my relatives in Ontario. Since I was on the east coast I hitchhiked up to Hamilton, Ontario and then to Toronto, where most of my Capell cousins were. I also went to a number of other places in Ontario and Québec and finally back to New York where I rode a bus back to Seattle.

Arriving home in late December, I was in time to start at the University of Washington at a special session for veterans, which started January 2nd. Blake, Moffitt & Towne Paper Co. made special arrangements for me to work there any hours that I was not in class at the University. They did everything they could to help me.

Beth, who was the girl I spent most of my summer leave with, and I both wanted to get married but she wanted marriage immediately whereas I needed quite a bit more time to get readjusted to civilian life. I had problems resulting from the war that I did not realize, and our breakup was the result.

Two and a half years later I met Sylvia, a strikingly beautiful girl, and one that I was certainly glad I waited for. In 1951 we married. She was the love of my life and after fifty-two years of marriage I love her even more. She has been a wonderful wife and given me two fine sons. WHAT MORE COULD I ASK?

Sylvia Capell with sons Tom and John

The end...

Appendix I

EIGHTH INFANTRY COMMAND POSTS (4TH DIVISION)
JUNE 6, 1944 THROUGH JULY 2, 1945

Distances in miles (unless otherwise noted) and true directions are from the CP location. Cities are referenced from city center.

June 1944

6	Blosville, France—3½ SE of Ste. Mere Eglise
7-8	Ste. Mere Eglise , France
9	Fresville, France—2 N of Ste. Mere Eglise
10-19	2 miles SE of Montebourg, France
20	2 miles SE of Anneville, France—11½ E by S from Cherbourg and 3 W from the coast
21-22	2 kilometers W of Saussemesnil, France—9 SE from Cherbourg
23-24	700 meters W of Hau des Blonds, France
25	2 kilometers W of Rufosses, France—5 SE from Cherbourg
26-27	400 yards E of La Glacerie, France—3 S from Cherbourg
28-29	Cherbourg, France
30	Orglandes, France—4 W from Ste. Mere Eglise

July 1944

1-3	Orglandes, France—17 SSE from Cherbourg
4	SE of Orglandes, France
5	5 kilometers W of Carentan, France—7 S from Ste. Mere Eglise
6	Appeville, France—6 S by E from Ste. Mere Eglise
7	Le Bus, France
8	Meautis, France—3 SW from Carentan
9	500 meters S of Les Ormeaux, France

10	2 kilometers NE of Raffoville, France—3½ SW from Carentan
11-17	500 meters SE of Raffoville, France—4½ SW from Carentan
18-20	4 kilometers N of St. Jean-de-Days, France—5 SE from Carentan
21	2 kilometers NE of Le Hommet d'Athrenay, France—5½ N by W from St. Lo
22-23	1 kilometer NE of Le Hommet d'Arthenay, France—5½ N by W from St. Lo
24-25	Vicinity of St. Lo, 1 kilometer N of Amigny, France—4 NW from St. Lo
26-27	SE of La Chappelle-en-Juger, France—4 W of St. Lo
28	2 kilometers SE of Marigny, France—6 WSW of St. Lo
29	2 kilometers SE of Notre Dame-le-Cenilly, France—10 SW of St. Lo
30	Vicinity of La Chasse Doriere—La Vanleria, France—12 SSW of St. Lo

August 1944

1	2 kilometers SE of Percy, France—14 S by W from St. Lo
2	4 kilometers N Villedieu-les-Poeles, France—17 S by W from St. Lo
3	St. Martin le Bouillant , France—11 WSW Vire
4-5	St. Laurent de Cuves, France—10 SW by W Vire or 9 NW Mortain
6-11	Le Mesnil Gilbert, France—5 NW Mortain
12-16	Desertines, France—12 S by E Mortain
17-23	Carrouges, France—13 SSW Argentan
24-25	Courson Monteloup, France—20 SSW of Paris
26	Savigny-sur-Orge, France—11 S or 3 S of Orly (Paris airport)

27 Le Raincy, outskirts of Paris, France—9 E by N of Paris

28-29 Chelles, France—10 E by N of Paris

30 Rozieres (Rosieres), France—30 NE by N of Paris

31-Sept. 1 Brassoir, France—9½ SE of Compiegne

September 1944

1 Brassoir, Pierrefonds-les-Bains, Berneuil, France —9½ SE of Compiegne to 9 ESE Compiegne to 8½ E Compiegne

2-4 Itancort, France—5 SE of St. Quentin

5 Chau Regnault, France—8 N by E Charleville— Mezieres

6 Houdremont, Belgium—12 NE of Charleville— Mezieres

7 Houdremont,(Maissin), Libin, Belgium—(Maissin is 13 N by E from Bouillon, Libin is 15 NNE from Bouillon)

8 Libin—15 NNE of Bouillon

9 Lavaselle—5 WSW Bastogne, Belgium

10 Hemroulle—2 NW Bastogne, Belgium

11 Courtil—18 NNE Bastogne or 21 S by W of Malmedy, Belgium

12 Galhausen—2 S St. Vith or 12 S by E of Malmedy, Belgium

13 Alfersteg—4 ESE St. Vith, Belgium or 14 SE of Malmedy, Belgium

14-15 Radcheid,Germany—1½ N of Bleialf or 16 SE of Malmedy, Belgium or 7 ESE of St. Vith, Belgium

16-Oct. 3 Siegfried Line, Pillbox Schnee Eifel, Germany—19 SE Malmedy, Belgium or 3 NNE of Prum, Germany

October 1944

4-7 Hunningen (Hunnange), Belgium—11 NE of St. Vith, Belgium or 12 E by S of Malmedy, Belgium

8-12 Vicinity of Siegfried Line, Germany—19 SE of Malmedy, Belgium

13-Nov.7   Hunningen (Hunnange), Belgium–11 NE of St. Vith, Belgium or 12 E by S of Malmedy, Belgium

November 1944
8-Dec.11 Hurtgen Forest, Germany—13 ESE from Aachen, Germany (to forest center)

December 1944
12-25   Senningen, Luxembourg—6 ENE from Luxembourg City

26-Jan. 7 Wecker, Luxembourg—14 ENE from Luxembourg City

January 1945
8-16   Betzdorf, Luxembourg—12 ENE from Luxembourg City

17-19   Medernach, Luxembourg—10 W from Echternach, Luxembourg

20-26   East of Eppeldorf, Luxembourg—9 W by N from Echtemach, Luxembourg

27-28   Hoffelt, Luxembourg—12 ENE from Bastogne, Belgium

29-30   Oudler, Belgium—17 S by E from Malmedy, Belgium

31-Feb.1 Lommersweiler, Belgium—15 SSE from Malmedy, Belgium

February 1945
2   Alfersteg, Belgium—14 SE from Malmedy, Belgium

3-4   Amelscheid, Belgium—6½ E by S from St. Vith, Belgium or 15 SE by E from Malmedy, Belgium

5-7   Helenfeld, Germany—7 NE of St. Vith or 10 ESE from Malmedy, Belgium

7- Mar.2   Pillbox Schnee Eifel, Germany—11 E of St. Vith or 19 SE from Malmedy, Belgium

March 1945
3-9   Willwerath, Germany—13 E by S of St. Vith, Belgium or 3 NE from Prum, Germany

10-11	*Honerath, Germany—24 E by N of St. Vith or 21 NE from Prum, Germany
12-13	Weinshein, Germany—14 ESE of St. Vith or 2 ENE from Prum, Germany
14-20	**Gerbervillers, (Gerbeviller), France—7½ S by E of Luneville, France or 21 SE Nancy, France
21-26	Dauendorf, France—7 W of Haguenau, France or 20 N by W from Strasbourg, France
27-29	Bad Durkeim, Germany—15 W of Mannheim, Germany
30	***Erlenbach, Germany—30 SE of Frankfurt, Germany
31	Amorbach & Konigheim, Germany—10 S of Erlanbach, Germany

April 1945

1-2	Reichenberg, Germany—4 S of Wurzburg, Germany
3-5	Ochsenfurt, Germany—10 SSE of Wurzburg, Germany
6-10	Erlach, Germany—7½ SE of Wurzburg, Germany
11-12	Ochsenfurt, Germany—10 SSE of Wurzburg, Germany
13	Marksteft, Germany—4 NE of Ochsenfurt, Germany or 10 SE of Wurzburg, Germany
14	Neuherberg, Germany (Ergersheim Neuherberg)—25 SE from Wurzburg, Germany
15-16	Buchheim, Germany—35 W from Nuremberg, Germany
17-18	Binzwangen, Germany—31 W by S Nuremberg, Germany
19	Weissenkirchberg, Germany

* Limit of Task Force Rhino
** Rest period
***After crossing Rhine River near Worms

20	Breitenau, Germany—4 SE Bad Windsheim, Germany
21	Bergbronn, Germany
22	Stocken, Germany—12 N by E of Aalen, Germany
23	Westhausen, Germany—5 NE of Aalen, Germany or 47 E by N of Stuttgart, Germany
24	Ebnat, Germany—5 NNW of Aalen, Germany or 41 E by N from Stuttgart, Germany
25	****Lauingen, Germany—25 NW of Augsburg, Germany
26	Landensberg, Germany—15 W of Augsburg, Germany
27-29	Grossaitlingen, Germany—11 SW Augsburg, Germany
30	Moorenweiss, Germany—13 S by E Augsburg, Germany or 25 W of Munich, Germany

May 1945

1-7	Gauting, Germany—SW of Munich, Germany
8-15	Burglenfeld, Germany—20 N of Regensburg, Germany
16-30	Bamberg, Germany

June 1945

1-22	Bamberg, Germany
23	Kaiserlautern, Germany
24	Metz, France
25	Soissons, France
26	Camp Old Gold—Ourville, France

July 1945

1	Le Havre, France
2	At sea on U.S.S. HERMITAGE

****Lauingen is where we crossed the Danube River

Appendix 2

Horace Sisk, Inside Man at HQ

Whatever Horace Sisk gave up in physical size, he more than made up in raw courage. He was intelligent and competent, and although physically unsuited for infantry rifle combat, he was ideal as a company clerk. Colonel Van Fleet recognized his value and picked him to be his own regimental clerk. When Colonel James A. Rodwell took over command of the 8th Infantry Regiment after Van Fleet was promoted to general and transferred, he kept Sisk as his clerk. He liked Sisk so much that he kept him by his side much of the time, especially when he went on a reconnaissance mission. In one of these situations Rodwell went to an especially useful observation post set up by our I & R Platoon. They had found a well-concealed promontory overlooking a newly established German position.

Rodwell observed through binoculars the movements of the Germans with Sisk at his side taking notes. He noted a medium-sized truck unloading lumber near a hole being dug by German soldiers. Rodwell concluded a high-ranking German officer was preparing his own private latrine. The lumber was precut and quickly assembled over the hole. Rodwell had Horace help him locate on a military map the precise location of the new German latrine. Rodwell then phoned Cannon Company with the precise coordinates, so at his signal they would lay down a barrage of 105mm shells. Sisk told me the Colonel waited and waited until finally a high-ranking German officer came out carrying a role of tissue to inaugurate the new facility. After the officer had gone inside, and been there for a reasonable length of time, Colonel Rodwell called for the barrage to begin. Sisk told me the first shots were directly on target and the latrine went up in a cloud of smoke, thus ending the career of a proud German officer who made himself a little too conspicuous.

Horace Sisk related this episode to me as he did many of the other activities within the Regimental Headquarters. Whenever I heard a rumor from other men in the company about what was going on with us, I verified it with Horace before believing it. One particular example occurred when I checked out a rumor that spies had infiltrated our Regimental Headquarters. I went to find Horace to get the true story, which occurred shortly after the outbreak of the great German counter attack that led to what is called "The Battle of the Bulge".

An American-made jeep with American markings drove up in front of our Regimental Headquarters and two men wearing American officer's uniforms got out, while the driver remained at the wheel of the jeep. The two officers wore the insignias of a Colonel and a Major. They asked for Colonel McKee, our Regimental Commander at the time. When told he had left for an appointment at Division Headquarters, they became furious and said they were from Corps Headquarters, and that he had made an appointment with them. The said they must have a report from him giving them some specific information and if McKee did not supply it immediately he would be in serious trouble. The assistant Regimental Commander, Lieutenant Colonel Strickland who was in charge while McKee was gone said he knew nothing about it and began phoning Division Headquarters in a frantic effort to locate McKee. However, he was already en route to Regimental Headquarters. This was, of course, long before the advanced technology of efficient small portable radios or radio telephones. To carry a large radio and an operator was usually not considered to be worth the bother.

The visiting "officers" were even more angry when McKee could not be contacted and went to a captain and a lieutenant who were in the Regimental Headquarters at the time and demanded they get the information now. They had to leave immediately and simply could not wait for McKee to get back or for Strickland to get off the phone. The regimental officers had seen the impostors talking to Strickland and therefore assumed he knew them. Since he was busy on the telephone, they assumed they should freely accommodate the visitors and give them the information they wanted. Undoubtedly it included such things as the positioning of our regiments and companies, as well as their strengths. The strangers also probably inquired about where our reconnaissance teams were operating, and what they knew about enemy strength. Strickland, suddenly realized what might be happening and immediately dropped the telephone. The "officers" hurried out, jumped in the jeep and drove away in an unknown direction.

Strickland asked the regimental officers involved exactly what they had said to the strange visitors. Strickland said, "Oh my God!" He knew he had been duped and made a frantic effort to trace where the spies had gone, but it was too late. It was never even determined what route they took to get away, but they carried some valuable information with them. We'll never know how many of our men died as a result of this bit of carelessness by our commanding officers.

In order for this deception to have been carried out as successfully as it was, the Germans must have had spies at our Division Headquarters who knew exactly where McKee was, and when he left and would return. The timing of the spies was so precise it was uncanny. The language they spoke was American and no one suspected a thing from what they said. Equally amazing to me is how they were able to move directly to our Regimental Headquarters and to make their escape without anyone ever suspecting them.

The spies were undoubtedly from a specially trained German unit called The Trojan Horse Battalion commanded by Colonel Otto Skorzeny.

Many of his men had been raised in the United States and then migrated to Germany, and therefore spoke with American dialects. They were trained in popular American culture, and especially in sports events and sports stars etc. A few of them were caught and executed but I'm sure the majority of them were never apprehended. Skorzeny was an SS officer and was a very clever, talented and daring man who was involved in many secret exploits. He was the man who led the rescue of former Italian dictator Benito Mussolini after he had been overthrown and imprisoned.

Horace Sisk continued to feed me information that I could never get elsewhere such as our next objective, success of our previous battle actions, various incidents that occurred in the Regimental Headquarters, and changes in Regimental Command. We remained good friends and although he lived in Illinois we kept in touch by telephone until he died in the 1990's.

Appendix 3

Papa Doc Comes to Visit

Two very familiar names came to visit our company, one of them quite regularly when we were in Normandy, and the other only once. The former was the highly respected Ernie Pyle and the latter the famous author Ernest Hemingway, or Papa Doc as he was known, who had obtained qualification as a war correspondent. He asked to be sent to where the most battle action was. He was told he would find it with the 4th Infantry Division, and therefore should meet with the Division Commander, General Raymond O. Barton. Barton directed him to the 8th Infantry Regiment, commanded by Col. James A. Rodwell. When Hemingway said he wanted to get close enough to "smell the sweat of the Germans," Rodwell responded "I have just the place for you. Go see Capt. Francis Glaze of Headquarters Company."

Rodwell told Glaze what Hemingway wanted and they both agreed that he could best see the action from the new reconnaissance post set up by the I & R Platoon. The wire crew I was in had laid field telephone wire to the outpost the previous night. It could not be successfully done in the daytime because we would have had to move across in plain sight of the Germans to get there.

When Hemingway arrived, he was met by Frank Glaze who explained that if he wished he could be escorted to the lookout during the coming night and could be there for the next morning, and all day long to observe the Germans. However he could not under any circumstances be brought back during the daytime, but would be brought back the following night if he wished. Hemingway agreed to the conditions, but at daylight the next morning the famous author realized he was behind the German lines and was completely surrounded by them. He decided he had enough and called Glaze on the telephone and said he saw all he needed, and was ready to come back immediately.

Glaze said, "We will make arrangements to bring you back after dark tonight."

"But I wanna come back now! We're surrounded by Germans up here and I want out!"

"Not until tonight!"

"Don't you realize who I am?"

"I don't care who you are. I told you what the conditions were, and you will abide by them. I won't risk the lives of my men just because somebody thinks he is more important."

"General Barton will hear about this and you will be court-martialed! You will be carrying a rifle along with the rest of the Privates!"

"We'll be up to get you tonight." and with that, Glaze hung up the telephone.

Hemingway fumed and called again on Glaze's telephone. This time Glaze told someone else to answer and to tell Hemingway that we would pick him up as soon as possible after dark and nothing more need be said. He now knew he had no choice but to wait. After dark a couple of men came up and escorted him back to our Company. He promptly searched out Col. Rodwell. Holding back a laugh, Rodwell suggested he tell his story to General Barton. He got the same amused response from Barton and decided that was the last time he was ever going to do any reporting from the 8th Infantry Regiment.

He made a contact with the 22nd Infantry Regiment of the 4th Division and spent the next month or so with Col. "Buck" Lanham who liked to party as much as Hemingway. I did not see Hemingway again after he left our company.

Ernie Pile was the most loved and most prolific and certainly the best known correspondent at the front lines in Normandy. Unfortunately, as I stated before, he did not survive the war.

Appendix 4

Hollywood Goes to War

Hollywood has on numerous occasions attempted to depict the events of June 6th, 1944 in Normandy. It has failed utterly in all but one movie. The one notable exception was Stephen Spielberg's Saving Private Ryan, which showed the initial attack on Omaha Beach with admirable accuracy. I experienced nearly identical conditions as was depicted in the film when I landed on Utah beach at the same time. Utah Beach was the next one north from Omaha and across the Carentan Channel. Although the landings were much more successful on Utah Beach than on Omaha, the first troops to land faced much the same conditions.

The scenes in the film Saving Private Ryan made me feel as though I were reliving my own experience. No other film has done that. The din, the violence, the utter chaos of battle, and the vivid presence of death and horrible mutilation were accurately depicted. The indescribable sense of fear felt by the attacking troops was well portrayed by Spielberg, and yet the great majority of these men displayed astounding self control in spite of the terror they all felt.

Inaccuracies did occur later in the film, such as when men on combat patrol in enemy territory talked as loud as if they were walking down Main Street. Obviously, the movie director wanted the audience to hear the dialogue. Another was the use of a profane expression that did not come into the language of obscenities until after the time period depicted. I certainly never heard it while living among GIs both in and out of combat for over two and a half years. These inaccuracies are so minor they did not detract.

The opening battle scenes, which were outstanding in an overall superb film, contained a couple of minor points that may be questioned by some. The fact that the captain wore his bright and shiny bars on his helmet as if he were on a training exercise made him more conspicuous as an officer. However, I do not judge this as an inaccuracy because it was a matter of the officer's own choice whether to dull his insignia or not while approaching the enemy. It is also possible that Spielberg deliberately left the insignia conspicuous in order to make his character more identifiable to the movie audience.

Another legitimate criticism which would be noticed by a veteran who landed that day was that the beach in the film was shorter than it was in reality. We landed at low tide in order to avoid beach obstacles, consequently it was a long distance from the low tide line to the head of the Beach. Spielberg may have deliberately sacrificed a little reality to better show the beach action. In my opinion these latter points are not a significant detraction from the film's accuracy.

Usually a film based on the D-Day landings can be judged for accuracy by simply noting the way the soldiers wear their helmets. Without exception no combat infantryman that saw action in Normandy wore his steel helmet with the helmet straps loose and swinging across his face. Movie depictions often show these hanging straps for a reason not known to me, but possibly to show a more macho image. I believe I am typical of my GI comrades when I say that a swinging strap with a clasp or buckle on it would be intolerable if it were wildly swinging across my face.

The GI combat headgear consisted of a helmet liner of hard plastic over which fit the steel helmet itself. Both liner and helmet had chin straps. The liner straps, when not being used, were brought up over the front top of the liner and fastened. The steel helmet was fit over the liner with the chin straps brought up over the top back of the helmet and fastened. Since the steel helmet could be removed so easily it was handy to use as a washbasin. Airborne troops usually did use chin straps with pads under the chin, but not the combat rifleman.

The World War II jeeps were equipped with windshields that could easily be lowered and laid forward and flat over the hood. These were then covered with an olive green canvas cover for the purpose of avoiding reflection off the glass. Certainly all of the jeeps which landed on the morning of D-Day had lowered windshields. Shortly after D-Day, the jeeps were equipped with notched angle irons that extended up from the front bumper. This was for the purpose of protecting the occupants from being decapitated by a wire stretched across a roadway by the Germans.

One criticism that gave me pause appeared in an op-ed type of letter to one of the Seattle newspapers. It criticized the film's use of actors who were considerably older than the young men who landed on D-Day. The point did not occur to me that the men in the film were appreciably older than I remember them. In reality, the actors probably were older than the men I landed with, they just did not appear older to me and I wondered why. On reflection I realize there were two good reasons.

First, the men around me were older than I was. They were mostly in their 20's with a majority in their early 20's. I was just 20 years old and was the youngest in the Company having joined it shortly after it arrived in England. Many of the troops who came in later were undoubtedly much younger on the average being from more recently formed divisions.

Secondly, regardless of whether a man was in his late teens or early 20's he would look older after the months of rigorous training before D-Day. We were anything but clean-shaven when we made the landings, and a few days growth of beard make a man look much older, especially if it was a dark beard like mine. So even if we were younger we didn't look it. I consider the criticism made by the writer to the newspaper as absolutely unjustified. In chapter 4, page 75, there is a picture of the D-Day survivors from A Company shortly after D-Day. They certainly did not look like boys just out of their teens.

Bibliography

Ambrose, Stephen E. *Band of Brothers*. New York, NY: Touchstone, 2001.

Ambrose, Stephen E. *Citizen Soldiers*. New York, NY: Simon & Schuster, 1997.

Ambrose, Stephen E. *D-Day June 6, 1944: The Climactic Battle of World War II*. New York, NY: Simon & Schuster, 1994.

Ambrose, Stephen E. *Pegasus Bridge June 6, 1944*. New York, NY: Touchstone, 1985.

Association Historique et Culturelle de Montebourg. *Le Cacheux, Genevieve et al, Montebourg se Souvient, 6 Juin- 19 Juin 1944*. Conde-Su- Noireau, France: Corlet, 1994.

Babcock, Robert O. *War Stories Utah Beach to Pleiku, 4th Infantry Division*. Baton Rouge, LA: Saint John's Press, 2001.

Bradley, Omar N. *A Soldier's Story*. New York, NY: Henry Holt & Co, 1951.

Chant, Christopher, Eric Grove, David Lyon, & Hugh Lyon. *The Military Hardware of World War II*. New York, NY: The Military Press, 1984.

Church, John. *Military Vehicles of World War II*. New York, NY: Crescent Books, Crown Publishers, Inc., 1982.

Cooper, Mathew. *The German Army 1933-1945*. New York, NY: U.S. Bonanza Books, Distributed by Crown Publishers, 1984.

D-Day at Utah Beach. Coutances, France. May 1982.

D'Este, Carlo. *Decision in Normandy*. New York, NY: P. Dutton, Inc. 1980.

Department of the Army, Historical Divison. *Utah Beach to Cherbourg*. Washington: Government Printing Office, 1947.

Fourth Infantry Division, 8th Infantry Regiment. Baton Rouge, LA: Army and Navy Publishing Co., 1946.

Fussell, Paul. *Wartime, Understanding and Behaviors during Second World War*. New York, NY: Oxford University Press, 1989.

Goolrick, William K. and Ogden Tanner. *The Battle of the Bulge*. Alexandria, VA: Time-Life Books, 1979.

Hitler, Adolf. *My Battle*. Cambridge, MA: The Riverside Press, 1933.

Hogg , Ivan V. *The Encyclopedia of Infantry Weapons of World War II*. Northbrook, IL: Book Value International, Inc., 1981.

Hoyt, Edwin P. *The Invasion Before Normandy*. Briarcliff Manor, NY: Stein and Day, 1985.

Keegan, John. (ed.) *The Rand McNally Encyclopedia of World War II*. Chicago: Rand McNally & Co., 1977.

Keegan, John. (ed.) *The Times Atlas of The Second World War*. Avenel, NJ:Random House, New York and Crescent Books, 1989.

Kemp, Anthony. *D-Day and the Invasion of Normandy*. London, England: Thames and Hudson Ltd., 1994.

Leinbaugh, Harold P. and John D. Campbell. *The Men of Company K*. New York, NY: Bantam Books, 1985.

MacDonald, Charles B. *Battle of the Huertgen Forest*. New York, NY: Lippincott, 1963.

MacDonald, Charles B. *A Time for Trumpets*. New York, NY: William Morrow and Co. Inc., 1985.

Merriam, Robert E. *The Battle of The Bulge*. New York, NY: Ballantine Books Inc., 1972.

Natkiel, Richard. *Atlas of World War II*. New York, NY: Military Press, (Bison Books), 1985.

Neuhausler, Johannes, Dr. *What was it like in the Camp at Dachau?* (16th ed.) Munich, Germany: Published by Manz A.G., 1973.

Neillands, Robin. *The Battle of Normandy*. London, England: Wellington House, 2002.

Neillands, Robin. *The Bomber War-1939-1945*. John Murray Publishers, 2001.

Neillands, Robin. *The Conquest of The Reich: D-Day to VE-Day—A Soldiers' History*. New York, NY: New York University Press, 1995.

Neillands, Robin and Roderick De Normann. *D-Day, 1944: Voices from Normandy*. London, England: Orion House, 1993.

Pictorial History of The Second World War. (Vol. 3) New York, NY: Wm. H. Wise & Co., Inc.,1946.

Pimloh, John. *Battle of the Bulge*. Greenwitch, CT: Bison Books Co., 1983.

Pyle, Ernie T. *Brave Men*. New York: Henry Holt & Co., 1944.

Pyle, Ernie T. *Ernie's War*. New York, NY: Random House, 1986.

Roper, Trevor. *The Last Days of Hitler*. Scranton, PA: Hadden Craftsman, 1947.

Ruge, Friedrich. *Rommel in Normandy*. San Rafael, CA: Presidio Press, 1979.

St. John, Philip A., Dr. *Fourth Infantry "Ivy"Division*. Paducah, KY: Turner Publishing, 1987.

Shirer, William. *Berlin Diary*. US Bonanza Books Distibuted by Crown Publishers, Inc. 1984.

Shirer, William. *The Rise and Fall of the Third Reich*. New York, NY: Simon & Schuster, 1960.

Small, Ken and Mark Rogerson. *The Forgotten Dead*. London, England: Bloomsbury Publishing Ltd., 1989.

Sulzberger, C.L. *The American Heritage, Picture History of World War II*. New York, NY: Crown Publishers Inc., 1966.

Miller, Lee G. *The Story of Ernie Pyle*. New York,NY: US Viking Press. 1950.

Mollo, Andrew. *A Pictoral History of the SS 1923-1945*. New York, NY: US Bonanza Books Co., 1977.

Munro, Ross. *Gauntlet to Overlord*. Canada. The Macmilan Company of Canada. Limited 1945.

Thompson, R.W. *D-Day, Spearhead of Invasion*. New York, NY: Ballantine Books. 1968.

Whiting, Charles. *Siegfreid: The Nazis' Last Stand*. New York, NY: Stein and Day, 1982.

PICTURE CREDITS

Personal Collection:

Pages: 22, 25, 30, 92, 94, 115, 119, 127, 172, 189, 190, 192 top, 192 lower, 194, 204, 208, 209, 220, 221, 226, 227, 228

Courtesy of 4th Divison Association:

Pages: 53, 56, 69, 71, 73, 75, 79, 80, 85, 103, 104, 105, 106, 108, 123, 125, 136, 138, 173, 174, 178, 224, 225

Courtesy of Jon Bridgman, University of Washington:

Pages: 51, 55

Courtesy of Perry Delo:

Pages: 197 lower, 198 left, 198 right, 198 lower, 200, 202 top, 202 lower, 203

Courtesy of Seattle Times, *Seattle, WA.:*

Pages: 111-112

Cairis, Nicholas, Passenger Liners of the World since 1893. *rev. ed. New York: Bonanza Books, 1979, p. 44.*

Page: 33

Sketches by Ron Weil:

Pages: 59, 87, 120, 129, 171, 172 lower, 117, 197 Top

GLOSSARY

TERMS USED IN THE AMERICAN ARMY IN WWII

Ack ack: The fragments from explosive shells fired at aircraft from ground- based guns. The charges are aimed at the aircraft and timed to explode in its proximity.

Army: A country's land warfare force, or a large sub-group of that force.

Artillery: Guns which are larger than those that can be held by hand.

Atlantic Wall: The line of fortifications the Germans built along their western seashores where the there was danger of an Allied attack.

B Rations: food rations supplied to field kitchen units.

BAR (pronounced B.A.R.): A 30-caliber light machine gun. It can be hand held but is usually fired with the barrel supported by a bipod.

Bocage: Structures surrounding small fields built of earth and small stones and covered by vegetation. They are five to seven feet thick at the base, and usually from five to seven feet high. In France they were also known as hedgerows but unlike British hedges which were composed of vegetation only.

Barracks: A building for housing soldiers, usually containing one large room with cots, and a room at one end with sinks, showers, and toilets.

Barrage balloons: Non-rigid inflatable balloons tethered over strategic points to protect against low-flying enemy aircraft.

Bayonet: A knife designed to be mounted on the end of a rifle to be used as a sword or a spear.

Battalion: A unit of soldiers smaller than a Division and a Regiment but larger than a Company. A typical U.S. Division in WWII was divided into Three Regiments and these each contained three Battalions. Each Battalion contained four Rifle Companies, a Headquarters Company, and various support companies.

Beachhead: The land immediately above the high-tide line. The word is also used to refer to the land inland from the beach, which has been captured and is being held by an invading force.

Bolt: The movable part of the firing mechanism of a weapon with a barrel.

Breach: The inner end of the barrel from which the projectile is fired.

Brigade: A body composed of various units from an Army organized for a specific attack or battle.

Bunker: A space protected by thick reinforced concrete walls and roof to shelter against attack.

C Rations: Condensed canned food consisting of breakfast, dinner, and supper units. Each unit also included one can of biscuits, cigarettes, toilet paper, etcetera.

Caliber: The diameter of the inside of a gun barrel measured in decimal parts of an inch or in millimeters.

Carbine: A 30 caliber (measured in hundredths of an inch) long-barreled pistol or small rifle, which is gas operated for semi-automatic firing.

Chaff: see "windows" definition

Company: A body of soldiers, specifically of infantry, commanded by a captain, and consisting of several platoons of men.

Concentration Camp: In this book it refers to German Internment Camps which held persons unfavorable to the Nazis. Prisoners were mostly Jews but also included many political enemies, homosexuals, Gypsies, mentally retarded, some Protestant leaders, and others.

Corps: A large unit of an army made up for a special purpose, comprised of one Division with attached units or most often two or more Divisions with attached units.

CP: Refers to a command post, the location of a headquarters command.

D-Day: Refers to the day a major military attack is begun. Since June 6th, 1944 was the most famous of D-Day's, particularly in modern history, the term usually refers to this particular day.

Death Camp: Camps such as Auschwitz in Poland which were built expressly to exterminate Jews and others unfavorable to the Nazis.

Dog tags: Metal identification tags worn around a soldier's neck giving his name, Army serial number, religion, and blood type.

Division: A major tactical unit of an Army Corps consisting of 14,000 to 15,000 soldiers.

Dragon's Teeth: Tank traps consisting of concrete tetrahedrons, or four-sided pyramids, extending up from the ground to prevent passage of tanks.

DUKW (pronounced "duck"): An amphibious vehicle built on a chassis about the size of one used for a 2½ -ton Army truck.

E-Boat: A German torpedo boat.

E.T.O.: European Theatre of Operations.

Foxhole: A hole dug for shelter from bullets and shell or bomb fragments.

Grenade: An explosive charge, which is usually hurled by hand. With a special fitting it can also be fired from a rifle. The American type is encased in a metal shell, which scatters fragments. Than German type was shaped like a potato masher with the explosive charge on one end and a handle on the other. The handle was used to throw the grenade.

Half-Track: A vehicle with wheels at the front and tractor treads around the rear wheels.

Helmet and Helmet Liner: An American rifleman wore a helmet liner and slipped the steel helmet over it. The helmet liner could be worn alone in which case the chinstrap would be attached under the chin. However, whenever the steel helmet was worn over it, the liner's chinstrap was always brought forward and attached over the short bill of the steel helmet. The chinstrap from the steel helmet was brought back over the back of the helmet and attached. When helmet and liner were both worn by an infantry rifleman, the straps were never brought under the chin because of the danger of an explosion blowing one's head off.

Higgins Boat: An LCPV.

Howitzer: A lightweight short cannon used for firing projectiles at a high angle.

Jeep: Term for a small and light 4-wheel drive vehicle which comes from G.P. which referred to a general purpose vehicle.

I & R: Intelligence and Recognizance Platoon.

K Ration: Consisted of cartons of food, each carton being about the size of a margarine box. One box was designated as breakfast, one as dinner, and one as supper. Breakfast unit included one small can of condensed ham and egg. The dinner unit included a can of cheese and a bar of hard, bitter, slightly-sweetened chocolate. Supper usually contained chopped ham and a bar of condensed fruit. Each unit had biscuits, powdered coffee, and cigarettes, as well as toilet tissue.

L.C.I. (Landing Craft Infantry): Vessels for transporting troops to near an invasion beach where they were then transferred to LCVP's and from these were landed directly on the beach.

L.C.T. (Landing Craft Tank): A landing craft with a bluff bow fitted with a ramp that lowered to unload soldiers and vehicles directly on to a beach.

L.C.V.P. (Landing Craft Vehicles Personnel): Commonly called "Higgins Boats", they were the smallest of the landing craft used to carry personnel and occasionally one or two jeeps. It could carry about forty men standing shoulder to shoulder.

L.S.M. (Landing Ship Medium): A Ship with a bluff bow and larger than a landing craft. It carried men and vehicles and with gates that opened and a ramp that lowered from the bow, in order to land them directly onto a beach or onto a smaller vessel.

L.S.T. (Landing Ship Tank): The largest type of landing vessel. It had two decks with an elevator and was used to carry men and vehicles of all sizes. It had a bluff bow with gates that swung out and a ramp that lowered. It was designed to land its cargo directly on a beach and was used in the latter waves of a beach invasion. After landing their load, some were equipped to be used as hospital ships to receive wounded men brought out on small craft from the beach.

Luftwaffe: The German Air Force.

Mae West: A rubber lifebelt that can be inflated by breaking a capsule of compressed air.

Messerschmitt: One of the manufactures of the more common types of German fighter planes.

M-1 Rifle: A 30-caliber rifle designed by Garand. It is gas operated and automatically resets the bolt to fire the next round.

Mine: An explosive charge encased in a housing with a triggering mechanism to cause explosion upon contact. Used on land or sea.

MP: Military Police responsible for holding and guarding enemy war prisoners as well as American soldiers guilty of felonies or desertion of their duties. Used also for security and policing duties.

Platoon: A team of men within a Company used for special purposes.

Pill Box: A reinforced concrete bunker used as an emplacement for one or more guns. A typical Siegfried line pill box had walls and roof over ten feet thick of reinforced concrete with gun ports in front and a single access port and steel door in back.

POW: Prisoner of War

Regiment: A group of soldiers commanded by a colonel consisting of a number of companies, troops, or batteries.

SHAEF: Supreme Headquarters Allied Expeditionary Force. An acronym which refers to the command of all Allied forces in Europe and North Africa.

Shelter Half: One half of a pup tent, which is a tent large enough to shelter two men lying side by side. Two shelter halves attached make one tent.

Seigfreid Line: The line of defenses along the western frontiers of Germany.

Sentry Post: The location of a soldier or soldiers whose responsibility it is to watch for and report enemy movement and to take initial action against the enemy if required.

Slit Trench: A long narrow trench for use as a latrine.

SS: From the German word Schutstaffel that means "Protection Force". It was Hitler's private Army commanded by Heinrich Himmler. It was the cruelest of the Nazi military groups and used to guard concentration camps. The Waffen SS was its military arm and was highly trained and supplied with the best of German equipment.

Squad: A small team within a platoon, used for special operations.

Tracer Bullets: A stream of bullets, periodically lighted by flare type bullet.

Tree Burst: An explosive shell bursting in a tree and casting its fragments and shrapnel in all directions, particularly downward.

U-Boat: German Submarine

U.S.O.: United Service Organization. An organization to serve servicemen both overseas and abroad, particularly by supplying entertainment.

VE-Day: Refers to the day on which the war ended in Europe and North Africa. "Victory in Europe Day," May 8, 1945.

Volksturm: German troops which were too young, old, sick, or wounded and used in special units not physically qualified to be in the regular German Wehrmacht.

VJ-Day: Refers to the day on which the war ended in Japan. "Victory in Japan Day," August 15, 1945.

Weapons Carrier: A four wheel drive vehicle rated at ¾ tons with at least three times the carrying capacity of a jeep. It was used for carrying weapons, supplies and men.

Wehrmacht: The German armed forces.

Windows: Aluminum backed paper strips, also called "chaff," dumped from bomber planes in large quantities to provide false echoes to enemy radar. Also can be fired from ground based artillery to precede a raid.

WWI: World War 1

WWII: World War 2

Zonder Commandos: Concentration camp inmates selected for special duties and given slightly better treatment than other inmates.

Index

4th Infantry Division and 8th Infantry Regt.
 have not been included in the index
 because they are the subject of the book.